Jack Grapes'

ETHOD
RITING

"I am still relishing class last night, not only to hear people's efforts unfolding so beautifully, but to feel part of a community of writers, the frailty and tenacity of it all, the courage. It is not only provocative but insanely comforting, the relief of stopping there a while, among other strugglers. Something very beautiful is happening in these classes you have created, nothing short of transformative, and the Method works. I am proud and relieved to know you."

Melinda McGraw

"Jack's Method Writing demystified the writing I enjoy with a familiar secret I have used as an actor—process. Starting with finding my voice, my deep voice, all his exercises further train my writing as if it were an instrument to be stretched, disciplined, challenged, focused, and given flight."

Mark Valley

"I attended the SDSU Writers Conference again last weekend. Ran into two people that have used your Method approach and they loved it as much as I have. It was interesting to attend the workshops now after going through the levels of Method Writing. Some of the teachers presented ideas on character or dialogue that were similar to what you teach, but most were tangential. None presented their ideas as cohesively or as completely as you have done. Many of the workshops seemed to be mired in details in the pursuit of product to the exclusion of process. It wasn't like questions of grammar or other points of writing, it was more like they missed the point about the art of it. I felt sort of like a senior in a freshman class. Know what I mean?"

Dan Gribble

"I just returned from the Iowa Summer Writers' Festival. When I am there, I find myself thinking of you a lot and talking about you a lot. I didn't know how lucky I was to be a part of your workshops when I lived in LA. Nothing has come close since, except the Iowa workshops. They draw me back to the times that I worked with you. And I can tell you that the techniques I learned in Method Writing are better than anything else I have experienced. I find myself talking about you because of two things: First, when poets and writers and staff learn that I was part of your workshop for five years, they ask a lot of questions. People are very curious about you and your Method. I think that they hear of it word of mouth and wonder if what they hear is true. You are quite well known throughout the country, but especially here by the Iowa crowd. I also talk about you a lot because your teaching and advice comes through me when I am commenting on other people's work. It is amazing how many talented, published poets and writers don't know many of the basics that you taught us."

David Widup, poet, *Over to You* and *In Country*

Jack Grapes'

METHOD WRITING

The First Four Concepts

**Finding
the Deep Voice**

Writing Like You Talk

The Transformation Line

**The 4 Levels
of Narrative Structure**

**The Magic of
Image-Moment**

**Get Rid of Your Talent,
Discover Your Genius**

PLUS

**The "Dreaded" Association
Exercise**

Method Writing focuses on finding one's inner voice, and developing a style based on its rhythms and tonal dynamics. It is a unique approach to the creative process, based on conceptual techniques drawn from various disciplines: Konstantin Stanislavski's "method" approach to acting; Viola Spolin's use of theater games, and fundamentals inherent to the mastery of athletic skills such as tennis, golf, and baseball. Learning to manipulate the deep voice in order to create dynamic tonal effects brings a piece of writing to life. The emphasis in Method Writing is not on structure, but on the organic impulse and deep voice—the "invisible form" within each piece of writing.

Cover: *Saint Augustine*, Philippe de Champaigne (1650)

St. Augustine's Confessions (397 A.D.) is widely seen as the first Western autobiography ever written, though one could point to Ovid's heartbreaking letters written in exile as the forerunner of a genre that today we call "memoir." One of the most influential literary movements in the 20th century was the rise of a personal poetry that eschewed abstract intellectual themes and references to classical mythology in favor of the simple sorrows of daily life. The so-called establishment poets, believing that poetry should hew to the rigors of academic form, derisively called them "confessional" poets, as if the confessional impulse was outside the sphere of serious literature. Scholarly snobs overlooked how ubiquitous confessional writing had been over the previous two millennia. Between 4th-century St. Augustine and the 20th-century confessional poetry of Robert Lowell, Sylvia Plath, Anne Sexton, and Sharon Olds lie the 12th-century confessions of Peter Abelard's *The History of My Calamaties*, and the 18th-century *Confessions* of Jean Jacques Rousseau. In philosophy, Augustine's *Confessions* influenced not only Medieval and Renaissance philosophy, but 20th-century philosophers such as Edmund Husserl, Martin Heidegger, Hannah Arendt, Ludwig Wittgenstien and Jean Paul Sartre. The tone of Augustine's work is deeply personal, full of inner turmoil as he struggles with his despair over the lustful urges and the wanton life he was living. Augustine ruminates on numerous philosophical and religious issues, but he also touches on writing itself and the workings of memory. He begins to realize that things said simply can achieve the greatest truth, while eloquence for its own sake may lack true substance. In Philippe de Champaigne's painting, Augustine stands at his desk, scrolls and books at his feet. In his right hand he holds a quill; in the left hand, the sacred heart, set afire by the light of "veritas," truth. One could imagine it the other way 'round—that the wounded heart on fire casts the light of truth into the world. From the books to the lower left of the painting, through the hand holding the quill, it's the confessional impulse in writing that can set the heart on fire, casting a light capable of illuminating the world with truth.

11th Edition

Copyright © 2007–2019 Jack Grapes

All rights reserved

ISBN: 978-0-941017-25-1

www.jackgrapes.com
www.methodwriting.com

Cover painting: *Saint Augustin*, Philippe de Champaigne (1650)

Back cover photo of Jack Grapes by A. Karno

Artwork on *Casablanca* pages: Ernie Marjoram

Baloney sandwich artwork: Stephanie Graham

Method Writing logo: Stephanie Graham

Cover and book design: Alan Berman

THE CRAFT OF THE INVISIBLE FORM

The poet or writer must listen hard to the voice. Because the invisible form is not just a reflection of the material; it is an intrusive, enterprising, meddling, subversive, active, intervening form. In order to effectuate. It is the major craft of all writing.

I am delighted by the minor craft. The little craft of adjusting word by word, line by line, detail by detail. Making the piece of writing more presentable is important. But the craft of the invisible is what determines whether the success will be significant.

Sadly, it is just this major craft which is often neglected in writing workshops. I know first hand how much writing workshops can help. But it is crucial that they ask what is going on within the poem or story. Not so much about the meaning or style, but about what kind of motor invisibly powers the particular piece of writing. Or fails to.

—Jack Gilbert

DIVINE DISSATISFACTION

Divine Dissatisfaction

There is a vitality, a life force, a quickening
that is translated through you into action,
and because there is only one of you in all time,
this expression is unique.

And if you block it,
it will never exist through any other medium
and will be lost.
The world will not have it.

It is not our business to determine
  how good it is
  nor how valuable it is
  nor how it compares with other expressions.
It is your business to keep it yours clearly and directly,
to keep the channel open.

You do not even have to believe in yourself
or your work.
You have to keep open and aware
directly to the urges that motivate you.

  Keep the channel open . . . .
  No artist is ever pleased . . . .

There is no satisfaction whatever at any time.
There is only a queer, divine dissatisfaction;
a blessed unrest that keeps us marching
and makes us more alive than the others.

—Martha Graham to Agnes deMille

Contents

The Craft of the Invisible Form 5
Divine Dissatisfaction 6

Chapter 1
It Was a Dark and Stormy Night 9

Chapter 2
Mortal Stakes 13

Chapter 3
The Craft of the Invisible Form 21
Introduction to the Method 26

Chapter 4
Concept #1: Writing Like You Talk / Finding Your Voice 31

Chapter 5
Concept #2: The Transformation Line 47

Chapter 6
Concept #3: Image-Moment 73
Frequently Asked Questions 134
"My Story Is Boring" 140

Chapter 7
Concept #4: The Dreaded Association Exercise 145

Chapter 8
Method Writing Redux 153

Chapter 9
Going with the Flow VS
The Triangle Offense 161

Chapter 10
Making a Chapbook 173

Bon Voyage
Patient Insistency 179

Appendix
Note on "Stream of Consciousness" 183
The Art of Genius: Eight Ways to Think Like Einstein 196
On Michael Michalko's "The Art of Genius" 199
First Person vs. Third Person 201
Counseling Artists: The Twelve Challenges of an Artist 205
An Overview of the Eight Levels of Method Writing 210

Biography 213

⌗

Chapter 1

IT WAS A DARK AND STORMY NIGHT

I became a writer because I fell in love with words, not because I had something to say or stories to tell. To this day, when I open a book to that first page, I feel as if I'm waiting to be swept away by the writer's words.

It doesn't matter where you are, the words can take you somewhere else. You could be listening to the rain pound the shutters of your New England cottage in the dead of winter, and the words can take you to the Sahara desert, the sun beating down on your back, your mouth parched, your throat dry. You could be eating figs on the sprawling lawn of a Manchester estate, and the words can take you to a damp cell, your face enclosed in an iron mask. You could be sitting first class on a transatlantic flight from New York to Paris, and the words can take you on a journey you never planned.

> Midway through this journey of our life,
> I found myself lost in a dark wood,
> for I had wandered from the straight and true way.[1]

Later, when your friends say, "How was the flight?" you can smile and say, "It was hell."

The words evoke sensations you thought you'd never feel again—what it's like to be young, for instance, startled by the world's variety.

> Once upon a time and a very good time it was there was a moocow coming
> down along the road and this moocow that was down along the road met a
> nicens little boy named baby tuckoo . . .[2]

You could be propped in bed, nibbling a cucumber sandwich, and the words will take you to the beaches of Normandy amid the tumult of war.

> Nobody could sleep. When morning came, assault craft would be lowered
> and a first wave of troops would ride through the surf and charge ashore on
> the beach at Anopopei. All over the ship, all through the convoy, there was a
> knowledge that in a few hours some of them were going to be dead.[3]

Say, for a moment, life makes sense. Say you like it that way. Still, the words lead you to a world in which nothing is sure and all that is solid melts into air.

---

[1] Dante, *The Inferno*

[2] James Joyce, *Portrait of the Artist as a Young Man*

[3] Norman Mailer, *The Naked and the Dead*

Mother died today. Or, maybe, yesterday. I can't be sure.[4]

It doesn't matter that the rent is due, that the roses need pruning.

> It was a queer, sultry summer, the summer they electrocuted the Rosenbergs, and I didn't know what I was doing in New York. I'm stupid about executions. The idea of being electrocuted makes me sick, and that's all there was to read about in the papers—goggle-eyed headlines staring up at me on every street corner and at the fusty, peanut-smelling mouth of every subway. It had nothing to do with me, but I couldn't help wondering what it would be like, being burned alive all along your nerves.[5]

Your life comes into focus, the edges less blurry.

> It happened that green and crazy summer when Frankie was twelve years old. This was the summer when for a long time she had not been a member. She belonged to no club and was a member of nothing in the world.[6]

Someone is speaking directly to you, his mouth at your ear. *Call me Ishmael.*[7] Not to a roomful of people; it's just you and the writer. *Marley was dead; dead as a doornail.*[8] You can almost smell his breath. *I am ill; I am full of spleen and repellent.*[9] Perhaps you want to turn away, but this is what you wanted. To be held by a truth that you couldn't imagine before. *Lolita, light of my life, fire of my loins. My sin, my soul. Lo-lee-ta.*[10] You want to know things, personal things, that aren't usually talked about. *My wound is geography. It is also my anchorage, my port of call.*[11]

And sometimes, the words can change your life.

I was six years old. No, I was five. I had learned to read before I was five. I was crouched on the floor of the living room and it was raining. It was night. I could feel the rug beneath my knees, soft and a little scratchy. I was small, crouched on the floor, and everything was high above me. The chairs, the mantelpiece, the lamps on the end tables, the doilies on the arms of the armchairs. The book was blue. It was called *My Tree House.* It was open to the first page, and there was a picture of a purple cow. Under the picture was a short, four-line poem. My mother stood in the doorway, the phone to her ear, her face red and contorted, her voice hysterical. She slammed the phone down. "Your father is drunk," she said, "and he's coming home to chop

---

[4] Albert Camus, *The Stranger*

[5] Sylvia Plath, *The Bell Jar*

[6] Carson McCullers, *The Member of the Wedding*

[7] Herman Melville, *Moby Dick*

[8] Charles Dickens, *A Christmas Carol*

[9] Fyodor Dostoyevsky, *Notes from Underground*

[10] Vladimir Nabokov, *Lolita*

[11] Pat Conroy, *The Prince of Tides*

our heads off!" She harumphed a few times, put her hands on her hips, a battleship ready to head out to open sea. "We're going to *ma-Ma's* house." Then she hurried upstairs to get our things. I looked back at the purple cow, at the poem printed beneath it.

> I never saw a purple cow,
> I never hope to see one.
> But I can tell you anyhow,
> I'd rather see than be one.[12]

Was there really such a thing as a purple cow? All the cows I'd seen were brown, or black with white spots. But maybe there *were* purple cows. If there were, where would they be? Maybe my dad would take me to the zoo or a farm, and we could see one, I thought. Why wouldn't a person want to see a purple cow? I was crouched there on the floor, and I imagined for a moment that I was a purple cow, and that no one wanted to see me. Maybe because I'd done something bad. Probably because I was purple. I looked back at the picture of the cow. All that purple on the page was pretty, I thought. Then I read the poem again. *But I can tell you anyhow, I'd rather see than be one.* It was nice the way the words rhymed, but especially the rhyme inside the line, *see than be. I'd rather see than be.* I whispered the words to myself. *I'd rather see than be.* I thought about the words. It was better to *see* a purple cow than to actually *be* a purple cow. Without realizing it, I was confronting the existential difference between being and perceiving. To *see* the purple cow, or *be* the purple cow. There was a difference, it seemed; a big difference. Whoever wrote that poem, they were making an important choice; if both options were distasteful, which choice would they rather make? *Being* a purple cow must be really bad. You just didn't want to be a purple cow. It was bad enough *seeing* one, but it was worse to actually *be* one. If you had to make a choice, you'd choose to *see* rather than *be* one. And then, to top it all off, there was the way the whole line rhymed with the other line. The rhyme inside and the rhyme at the end. I read the poem aloud and something sizzled in my brain: one minute the universe was large, incomprehensible; the next minute, it all was reduced to those four lines, the mystery of existence in a grain of sand, that "temporary stay against confusion" that Robert Frost said was the essence of poetry.

> I never saw a purple cow,
> I never hope to see one.
> But I can tell you anyhow,
> I'd rather see than be one.

My father was going to come home and chop our heads off, but I was thinking about the purple cow and what the words meant and how they rhymed.

"Here's your suitcase," my mother said, "you can carry it." My suitcase was really a duffle bag. She handed it to me and grabbed my arm and yanked me up. "Let's go outside and wait for the taxi." We stood on the porch until the taxi came. It was still raining, a dark and stormy night. I'd read that in a book somewhere. A dark and stormy night. It felt good to say the words to myself. *It was a dark and stormy night.* We were on the porch, but every so often a gust of wind

---

[12]Anonymous

blew some water onto the porch and my legs got wet. It was scary, but I liked it. The street was dark but occasionally a bolt of lightning would light everything up and you could see Mr. Seenac's house across the street, you could see the muddy water swirling down the gutter. Then it would get dark again, and a few seconds later a rumble of thunder seemed to shake the branches of the trees. When the next bolt of lightning came, sure enough, there in the street were branches from the trees. I wanted a closer look. I took a few steps toward the edge of the porch and waited for the next gust of wind. "Don't stand in the rain!" my mother said and yanked me back. She was talking and crying, but I wasn't listening. I was thinking about the purple cow, about the poem. How the words were things you could play with. I decided then that this was something I wanted to do. I wanted to write down words on a piece of paper and make up stories and poems. Maybe I wouldn't have to make anything up. Maybe I could write about things that really happened. True stories. Maybe there'd be a boy somewhere who'd want to read them, who'd want to be someplace else.

A yellow cab pulled up in front of the house. The driver got out and ran around to open the door for us. He was all hunched over and getting wet. He wore a yellow cab driver's hat. We ran down the steps and got in the cab. I stepped in some muddy grass and heard the squish. Before he closed the door, another gust of wind blew the rain into the back seat. It was scary and exciting. My mother gave the driver the address of my grandmother's house. She lived in Metarie. A long drive. The driver pulled down the handle on the meter and the numbers started rolling as he drove. The bigger the number, the more we'd have to pay. My mother had stopped being hysterical. She was rearranging the suitcases. When we turned the corner onto Ferret Street and headed up Napoleon Avenue, I leaned over and said to the cab driver, "My father's coming home and he's going to chop all our heads off." Then I went back to thinking about the purple cow. I was thinking that I was going to be a writer someday, I was going to write about the purple cow and the dark and stormy night.

Chapter 2

MORTAL STAKES

I don't remember the first words I ever read or wrote. What I do remember is the nervous feeling I had sitting in the backyard with a blank piece of paper when I was eleven years old. I began to write a story. Not for school, just for myself. I was sick with the flu and my mother made me stay home. She fixed me up with tea and toast and I took it with me out to the back yard because I could throw the tea into the bushes without her seeing me. I hated tea. Tea is what you drank when you were sick. I watered the camellias with it, then took little bites out of the toast and began to write a story. I printed the letters neatly so they would look like the words in a book. When I was finished, I gave it a title: "The Living Corpse." That was because, in an effort to get me to read, my father had brought home a few mystery stories. Some of the titles had the word "corpse" in them, which really grabbed my attention, so I figured it would grab other readers' attentions too. I sat in the sun and read the story to myself, and enjoyed the freedom I had from school, enjoyed the feeling of the creative process. This is the life, I said to myself, I'm going to be a writer.

To this day, when I sit down to write, I have the same nervous feeling facing the blank page that I had when I was eleven. My book-cluttered study has replaced the sunny garden, but the feeling is the same. What will come of this, I wonder, what will I write about? And I never really know until I'm finished. It's not unlike the feeling an actor has in the wings, waiting to make an entrance. The fear of failure, the anticipation of success. All that might come from this moment. What if you make a fool of yourself? What if something unexpected happens: something terrible, something great, something ridiculous, something marvelous? Then what? And if it's great, will you be able to pull it off again?

Terrifying Beginnings and the Beginnings of Terror

Many years ago I was in a production of *Romeo and Juliet*, playing the part of the Friar. It was one of those productions done "in the round," in which exits and entrances were made from all four corners of the stage, as well as from the aisles. Before the opening tableau in which everyone appeared on stage after a blackout, I was standing in the dark, waiting to make my entrance alongside the actor playing Mercutio. His experience was obvious. He brought Mercutio to the stage with flair and confidence. I respected his command of the stage, and most of all, I respected his process, so that standing next to him in the dark, I never spoke, never dared break his concentration or preparation.

One night, he turned to me and said, "Does this feeling ever go away?"

"What feeling?"

"You know," he whispered, patting his stomach, shuffling his feet. "This nervousness."

Ah, I thought. He feels it too. The same anticipation and dread. It wasn't just me. A part of me would just as soon run back to the dressing room. Another part can't wait to hit the boards and get on with the play. What to do then with this feeling? Some directors and acting coaches might suggest relaxation exercises, but most will tell you to value it and bring it with you into the part; it's often the key to the emotion you'll need. Trust it. Let it be. Give up the idea that you need to feel fine before you can go on. Go on anyway, dread in tow. Be a beginner. Trust the moment. As Hamlet says, "There is a special providence in the fall of a sparrow. If it be now, 'tis not to come; if it be not to come, it will be now; if it be not now, yet it will come. The readiness is all."

Picasso worked throughout his life to become a beginner. He once said, "When I was a child I could paint like a master, and I've spent the rest of my life trying to paint again like a child." Putting oneself in such a state, of not knowing where one will end up, can be both an exalted and uncomfortable experience, or even terrifying. The great German poet Rainer Maria Rilke addresses this concept of beginning anew in "The First Elegy," from *The Duino Elegies*, which he wrote over a period of ten years, beginning in January 1912. The line in German, *des Schrecklichen Anfang*, can be rendered as either "the beginnings of terror" or as "the terrifying beginnings." I tend to favor the former translation, rendered so beautifully by Stephen Spender: "For Beauty's nothing but the beginning of terror we're still just able to bear, and why we adore it so, is because it serenely disdains to destroy us."

Allowing oneself to receive, to be open to what comes without trying to impress, without trying to be "good," can be terrifying, but taking such risks needn't destroy us. I think of Rilke often when I sit down to write because he, like so many of us who prefer "having written" to the act of facing the unsettling vastness of the blank page, seemed to know that one must find a process, rather than an idea, from which to generate poetry or prose. Or anything else that springs from the mind. A block of wood that becomes a horse. A sign in a store window that becomes a play. A nervous breakdown that becomes a symphony. The creative process is mysterious, but if we fail to trust its very nature—that it is a *process*, not a prescription for *product*—we make the mistake of relying on talent, rather than on the accidents of our genius.

Talent. How I longed when I was young to have my parents and teachers grant me the attribute of talent. Handing in a story or a drawing, all I needed was a pat on the head and the declaration, "How talented you are!" I went looking for those crumbs of praise. It was the Holy Grail, for without the gift of talent, all would be lost. And like so many kids who could draw or write stories or play music, I was proud of my ability to dash off a story while others labored to achieve similar results. I couldn't have known at the time that such facility comes with a price. In time, I watched as others achieved—through focus and hard work—something beyond my own efforts. I saw them take chances. I saw them achieve greatness through the accidents of process, the accidents of genius. I saw how they flung themselves into the void, risking failure. I noticed how some avoided risk, relying instead on innate talent, which was capable only of making them good. That's what I settled for, the good. To be good every time.

Talent vs. The Accidents of Genius

During my first year of graduate school, I was doing a play with another actor. The play was written by Luigi Pirandello, who also wrote *Six Characters in Search of an Author*. It was a two-character play, so it was just me and Gerald Dumont, whom we called Monty. I was the better actor and I knew it. I often imagined how after opening night I would be the star of the show. Rehearsals proceeded without incident, except that Monty was all over the place, trying this, trying that. Sometimes his interpretation of a scene was outrageous, other times confusing. The director seemed patient with him, though, and allowed him free reign. I, on the other hand, was a model student, doing everything right. Subconsciously, I suppose, I was showing the director how good an actor I was while Monty continued to fall on his face. Sometimes, when he wasn't looking, I'd shake my head like a tolerant parent. Poor Monty, I thought, he's really going to stink up the joint. Once in a while, something Monty did worked. He stood on a table to deliver a speech about death. He crawled around the floor and barked like a dog while delivering a speech about love. Often, the director would say, "Interesting approach, Monty, but it doesn't work here." Monty was undaunted. After all, what did he have to lose? He didn't even think of himself as an actor, he was really in the directing program, so he had nothing to prove. He was having a good time. Every so often, something he did intrigued the director and he kept it in. All right, I thought, so he'll have a few moments. But I'll still be the one who shines at the end. The rehearsals dragged on and slowly the play came together, and eventually Monty's moments began to string themselves together, scene after scene, into something quite brilliant. A few days before opening night, I stood at the back of the theater and watched Monty do one of his monologues, wheeling himself around on a desk chair. It was a mad scene, the character coming apart at the seams, and Monty's arms flailed about, his heels digging into the floor, swivelling around and around from one end of the stage to the other. His character's breakdown, as he played like a child in that chair—well, the effect was electrifying and strangely moving. And me? I was competent. I was good. Not much had changed from the first few rehearsals. I was good at the beginning and I was good at the end. But not Monty. In the beginning, he was awful. By the end, he was brilliant. I stood in the wings and realized that it was too late for me to explore aspects of my character that I had barely touched. I had wasted my opportunity to take creative risks, to fall on my face, and now it was too late. When we opened, the play was a success. I was good but Monty was the star. Most painful for me was the well-intended praise of my friends and colleagues, when I knew that they knew I had fallen short. I could see it in their eyes when they came backstage after the show. They shook my hand and said, "Good. Really good." When Monty came over, it wasn't handshakes they gave him, but backslaps. It was he who had manifested his genius. I had avoided looking foolish and realized that nothing great comes from playing it safe. I had to learn to circumvent my talent and allow the accidents of genius to emerge.

Easier said than done. Talent colludes with the part of us that wants to look good rather than risk failure, with the part of us that is afraid we really aren't any good at all. Failure might prove that fear true. But greatness comes after having failed again and again, when all is lost, and you throw yourself into the unknown. This is what Rilke meant when he talked about terrifying beginnings, the beginnings of terror. The blank page. The act of writing without knowing where you're going, or even if you have what it takes to get there.

And then one day I opened a fortune cookie. "Talent does what it can," it said, "genius does what it must." A universal truth, known by Zen masters as well as the workers in the factory making the fortune cookies. Genius does what it must. When we are adrift in the middle of the ocean of the creative process, we do what we must to survive. It's not the mind with its reliance on talent that we call upon, but the body, in which the desperate act of genius saves us. Athletes know this too, when out of desperation their bodies surpass anything they could have done coming only from talent. That's what the movie *Rocky* was about. As an athlete in school, I saw it happen time and again. Sometimes, I'd risk everything and fail. Sometimes, I'd win. It applies to sports, to writing, to acting, to art. That's what Picasso meant when he said he spent his life trying to paint again like a child. It's what Samuel Beckett meant when he said: "No matter. Try again. Fail again. Fail better." But what prevents us from taking such risks, from avoiding failure at all costs? Talent. It has a hold on us. If we are ever to relinquish our dependence on it and open ourselves to the possibilities of genius, we need a process, a method, "a craft," to quote Jack Gilbert, "of the invisible form." Inspiration will not do it. Great artists do not depend upon inspiration. Inspiration, if it comes, comes once in a blue moon. Artists and actors and athletes show up, day after day, and do the work. And they have a craft, a tool box of techniques. Not a prescription for the finished product, but a way of working in the dynamic of process, a willingness to fail and an openness to the discoveries of genius.

You Do Not Have to Be Good

I am often confused while writing. Where am I heading? Yet, a scene, a story or poem that doesn't know where it's going often ends up seeming as if its arc were inevitable. A discovery was made in the act of writing. Writers often say they write to discover what it is they want to say. Picasso once said, *Si l'on sait exactement ce que l'on va faire, à quoi bon le faire.* "If I know exactly what I am going to do, what's the point of doing it." I think that the joy—no, the high—that comes from making something out of nothing, is seeing what comes from a liberated impulse: a phrase, an image, a sentence. True artists risk failure at every turn, unafraid of the unknown; they dive into it headfirst, trusting they will encounter there the magic that comes from ancient depths.

Over the last forty years I've taught creative writing in dozens of schools throughout California as an artist-in-residence. In most schools, students are taught to brainstorm before beginning to write. Sounds like a good idea at first. But what are we really teaching these young people about the creative process? We're teaching them not to trust it. To be afraid of it. To avoid heading into the dark woods of process without a map and a compass. The creative process is often about getting lost; it means to fly by the seat of your pants. If you know exactly what you're going to do ahead of time, what is there to discover in the doing of it?

Good writing is re-writing anyway, but that comes later. I'm talking first drafts, here, where we follow associations to who-knows-where, where accidents and whims lead to revelations of character and story. There'll be time for editing later. Somerset Maugham said, "Only a mediocre writer is always at his best." What exactly does that mean? Was he saying that great writers aren't trying their best? No, what he's saying is that great writers aren't always aiming for greatness; they're focused on the "way" of getting there. They're not worried about mistakes, they're not coddling their talent. They throw caution to the winds. They take wrong turns, they head down dark alleys, throw themselves off cliffs, cut power on the boat and head straight for the whirlpool. They know that the good is often the enemy of the best. They do not collude with their talent, which keeps to the center line of the highway of good. If they're going to discover the accidents of genius, they have to be willing to risk being bad, to let process take them into the tangent of miracles. Process is about the first draft, the whoosh of take-off. Later, one can shape and re-arrange and flesh out. Not while writing, but later, over coffee and Krispy Kremes at the donut shop or in bed with the dog at your feet.

It's possible that Mary Oliver in her poem "Wild Geese" knew where it would end up before writing, "You do not have to be good," but I doubt it. My instinct tells me she was having a bad day. Perhaps, even, a terrible day in which she was struggling to unburden herself of the guilt or dread that had settled upon her shoulders like an ancient yoke. Then (and this is still my fantasy, remember), some geese flew overhead, and without knowing where such a thought came from or where it might lead, she wrote,

> You do not have to be good.
> You do not have to walk on your knees
> for a hundred miles through the desert, repenting.
> You only have to let the soft animal of your body love what it loves.
> Tell me about despair, yours, and I will tell you mine.

Somehow, her psyche, or her fingers on the keyboard, or the gods forgotten by most of us for centuries and now embodied by those glorious geese, led her to this:

> Meanwhile the world goes on.
> Meanwhile the sun and the clear pebbles of the rain
> are moving across the landscapes,
> over the prairies and the deep trees,
> the mountains and the rivers.
> Meanwhile the wild geese, high in the clean blue air,
> are heading home again.
> Whoever you are, no matter how lonely,
> the world offers itself to your imagination,
> calls to you like the wild geese, harsh and exciting—
> over and over announcing your place
> in the family of things.

She couldn't have planned it, where she ended up. There is no map for that destination. Only a state of mind that allows you to risk getting lost. Most of the time, you will get nowhere. But you can increase your chances of getting somewhere. Like a baseball player at batting practice who knows his job is to get the mechanics down. His focus is on that. Not where the ball goes, but on his swing. And then being in the moment as the ball comes toward him. A writer writes in order to practice writing, the way a ball player practices his swing. The same idea is expressed in this saying about golf: the difference between the best amateur golfer in the world and the worst professional is that the professional takes a thousand more practice swings a day. It is the attention to the mechanics of process and the willingness to risk failure that leads to discovery, for the writer certainly, but also for the reader, who is always looking to be changed by words.

Keep Your Eye on the Ball

Process is a vague idea, like telling someone to "write from the heart," or "just let it flow." Commendable thoughts, but even the act of meditation requires focus that is refined over time. Practiced. Actors working from Stanislavski's method practice specific exercises, which are points of focus. The ball player's not trying to hit a home run, he's keeping his eye on the ball, finding the groove by concentrating on one thing at a time through the entire arc of the swing. So, too, can we break down the process of writing. The habit of process is not intellectual, it is a knowledge acquired by the body. For a writer, a thousand practice swings a day means three or four pages a day in a journal, practicing the mechanics of voice, making the voice deeper and truer. From these specific exercises, the first four concepts of Method Writing, you will discover your voice and learn to deepen it in order to affect the reader. The Image-Moment technique and the Dreaded Association exercise will make your writing vivid and convey the emotional content to the reader. This is not writing in a journal to make you feel better, this is not morning pages in which you "go with the flow." (See chapter 9 on "Going with the Flow vs the Triangle Offense.") The first four concepts of Method Writing are specific techniques that you must practice, because being in process does not mean you go with the flow. There's a focus. Just as you must focus on one thing in order to clear the mind when meditating, you must focus on the exercises in this book, not on the subject or theme of what you've decided beforehand you want to write. There is no subject, there is no theme, there is no idea. You're going to plug into a method that will allow the accidents of your genius to emerge, and in the process of practicing the techniques of process, you will improve and deepen your writing in ways you never thought possible. Method Writing works, if *you* work *it*.

Mortal Stakes

Why learn technique and craft, why edit, why change a paragraph that I love in order to make the writing clear to another person? Because I don't write only for myself, I want my work to go out into the world, to get published or produced, to find an audience. To be heard. To be seen. Perhaps this goes back to childhood—those who create do so because at some point in childhood they were not seen, or heard. Sometimes, they were cajoled into invisibility, battered into silence. August Strindberg, whose plays influenced writers as diverse as Samuel Beckett, Eugene O'Neill, and Sean O'Casey, survived a childhood marked by misfortune and affliction, and as recounted in his autobiography *The Son of a Servant* (1886), it was nothing short of calamitous. Writing of himself in the third person, he describes the misery of his childhood.

> Hungry and afraid, afraid of the dark, of spankings, of upsetting everybody. Afraid of falling and hurting himself, afraid of being in the way. Afraid of being hit by his brothers, slapped by the maids, scolded by his grandmother, caned by his father and birched by his mother . . . he could do nothing without doing wrong, utter no word without disturbing somebody. Finally, the safest thing was simply not to move. His highest virtue was to sit in a chair and be quiet. It had effectively been dinned into him that he had no right to exist.

Nevertheless, through his art, Strindberg triumphed. Whatever the origins of the creative impulse, art is a way of saying we were here, we mattered. Somewhere among those cave paintings of bison and antelope, there's a palm print. The artist put his hand against the cave wall, took a mouthful of ink, and sprayed around his hand. It's not a picture of a hand, it's the unmarked space of a hand seemingly appearing out of the stone wall of the cave. A declaration, an announcement: "I was here." I've always been moved by that handprint. Thousands of years ago that human being inside that cave lit only by fire wanted to share something with me. We are here: we want to be seen. We are speaking: we want to be heard. Of course, first and foremost, I write for myself. But I have a goal that goes beyond that. Playing without a goal in mind is what children do; they quit when the play is no longer fun. The artist, like a child, is driven to play, to make something. But the artist combines the work ethic of the adult with the playfulness of the child. Having a goal in mind, then putting that goal aside to "play" is what an artist does. Finally, it's not enough to speak, to be heard, to be seen. We want to make something, something that will stand apart from ourselves, something like that handprint, something that will live beyond us.

It's a paradox: know what you want to achieve, then forget about it and focus on the process. This act of letting go, of committing to the creative act, is what builds character as an artist. As Robert Frost wrote:

> My object in living is to unite
> My avocation and my vocation
> As my two eyes make one in sight.
> Only where love and need are one,
> And the work is play for mortal stakes,
> Is the deed ever really done
> For Heaven and the future's sakes.

To commit to the creative process, to let go of the desire for product, when what we want is product . . . . well, that takes character. It comes down to refusing to succumb to your fear of failing. And that's what I take Frost's poem to mean.

> When we are in process as children, the work is play.
> When we are in process as adults, the work is play
> . . . . for mortal stakes.

❖

Chapter 3

THE CRAFT OF THE INVISIBLE FORM

When I was a kid, my father often took me with him when he played golf. I didn't get to walk the links with him; instead, the club pro was paid to teach me how to swing the club. I can't remember how old I was before he let me actually hit a ball, but I learned the basic mechanics of the swing long before it became attached to an end result—hitting the ball onto the fairway. All I did was swing the club, there was no ball to hit. If he had let me hit the ball, I would have focused on where the ball went, and not the swing—the process, the *Tao*, the way. By focusing only on the mechanics of the swing, it was all about process. My body learned it, so I wouldn't have to think about it anymore. When I finally got to hit the ball, I was amazed at how far it went and how straight. No hooks, no slices. Straight and true down the fairway. I noticed this with other sports, too. I played quarterback in high school, gained weight, and was switched to fullback. I swam competitively in high school. My father, who boxed during the depression to make a buck, took me to the local gym on Saturdays to watch the fighters. He had me get into the ring once or twice with the old pro. Everything I learned in sports came down to the same thing: mechanics. How you hold the club, how you swing the bat, how you follow through on your backhand, how you plant your feet and turn your body *before* you throw the punch. I didn't know it at the time, but I was learning the essence of process—the way you wear your hat, the way you sip your tea.

In college I had a double major—history and English—but I was gradually drawn to the theater department and appeared in numerous plays. I did my graduate work in theatre, and was exposed to the Stanislavski system, or Method Acting as it has become known. My teacher was Arthur Wagner, who laid out a detailed program over the course of three years in which we worked through the concepts, exercises, and points of focus detailed in Stanislavski's three books, *An Actor Prepares, Building a Character*, and *Creating a Role*. What struck me at the time was that it was a process, a way of working through a scene, moment to moment, beat by beat, much the same as one worked through the mechanics of a sport. Having been an athlete throughout high-school and college, I found the techniques of Method Acting no different from the techniques I learned when swimming competitively, playing football and basketball, and especially in sports such as tennis and golf. I spent hours in the pool practicing my kick, or the turn; I spent hours mastering the grip in tennis and golf, hours hitting the ball focusing on the basic stroke and footwork. In a game, it all seemed to "flow," but such flow was an illusion, created by the seemingly instantaneous connecting of all the dots. When I began to study acting, the concepts I learned and the sense of flow achieved in performance were no different from what I experienced playing football or tennis.

In acting workshops, we spent the first year learning the basic concepts from Stanislavski's first book, *The Actor Prepares*: the "inner technique" whereby the actor learns to harness his or her sensations, emotions, intentions, and ultimately the creative imagination in order to create the characters and situations of the drama. It stressed inner truth while building a character, not form and technique. Stanislavski provided various exercises for accessing authentic emotion: the magic "if," tempo-rhythm, emotional memory, etc. He also set out a hierarchy of elements to clarify a character's intentions: activity, action, objective, and super-objective. Those elements could be strung across the arc of the play like beads on a string, and together they formed the "through-line" of the character's motivating force. I learned to work from within to create a character, and to resist shortcuts to a preconceived result. Contrary to popular belief, it was not a simple matter of *becoming* the "character," nor was it a question of creating a biographical background for the character. Of course, one had to do that, but Stanislavski's method is a dynamic construct that informs the process of performance, it is not simply a matter of research. Actors have always thought about character and even delved into their motivations and physical behavior. Method acting went beyond that. It gave the actor a *process*—a way of working in the moment, a dynamic approach to accessing the deep truth of a scene and bringing it to life. It's what you did in the flow of the scene—whether in rehearsal or performance—that brought out the unexpected moments, the flashes of brilliance. Without such concepts, the actor was liable to fall back into pre-conceived notions, the playing of an "attitude."

We spent the next year working through Stanislavski's second book, *Building a Character*, which showed in detail how the actor's body and voice could be trained for more physically demanding roles. Where the first book stressed inner truth—a kind of sacred dictum that the actor never do anything he doesn't first feel—the second book turned that concept on its head. It was all about techniques the actor learns in order to use his body as an instrument: language, tempo, rhythm, gesture, costume, mannerisms, etc. The first book emphasized "feeling" first; now Stanislavski was saying that an action or gesture could trigger the desired feeling. You're in a scene in the kitchen where you're angry at your husband. The playwright doesn't specify the activity, just the dialogue. So if your character is making bread, and you pound the dough as you say your lines, you might feel the anger rise out of you as you smash the dough. Try this: scrunch up your face as if you were about to cry. The act of doing that often brings up the emotion, as if the body remembers the feeling from the physical gesture. The first book was translated into English in 1936, and influenced a generation of American actors who worked from within, who seemed to eschew theatrical affects. They were introspective and moody, actors like Montgomery Clift and Marlon Brando. Method Acting came to be referred to as the "itch and scratch" school of acting. Stanislavski's second book didn't appear in English until 1948, and seemed to contradict what the Russian master had stressed in the first book. But Stanislavski had a larger vision of the actor's art than just scratching an itch. At the core of the second book lay Stanislavski's concept of "the truth of physical actions." The truth doesn't always have to come from the psychology of the character, it can come from physical action.

Much of what is contained in the first two concepts of Method Writing—"Writing Like You Talk," and "Massaging the Transformation Line"—parallels the theories in Stanislavski's first book, but those concepts have been modified to fit the act of writing, not acting. They also parallel the type of work one does in sports—learning to find the natural body rhythm and flow before one takes on the specific techniques. The concept of "Image-Moment" parallels Stanislavski's second book. Where the Transformation Line is all about coming from within, the technique of creating an "Image-Moment" approaches the story from the outside, creating a cinematic effect to convey the story's emotional drama. It doesn't *tell* the story, it *shows* it.

When I later worked in Second City in New Orleans, I learned the principles of improvisation as set forth by Viola Spolin in her book *Improvisation for the Theatre*. I studied with her son, Paul Sills, who founded Second City and went on to create *Story Theatre*. What seemed freewheeling and chaotic on stage was actually based on techniques that made improvisation a vehicle for drama, as well as for comedy. The theatre games Spolin came up with have been used by improv groups ever since. Spolin used theatre games as a way to distract the actor from consciously shaping the scene. But actors must have a focus that distracts them from doing what they might do when left to their own devices: conjuring funny or profound things to say, trying to "shape" the scene based on an idea. Spolin calls this "playwrighting." What she means is that the actor's mind is outside the scene shaping it as it goes, rather than being inside the experience of the improv, letting unexpected accidents create and shape the story. When actors "playwright," what they end up with can be pedestrian, because it comes from talent, rather than the accidents of genius (see Appendix article "The Art of Genius," p. 196, and the note that follows on p. 199). But when actors follow the rules of the game, they learn to respond to the moment, to the object of the game, and by doing so, unexpected situations arise that are far more imaginative than anything the actors could come up with by planning it out beforehand. Games, or exercises such as "transformation of object," "supplication," "whisper—shout," "who started the motion," "silent tension," "wandering speech," "throwing light," "lone wolf," "gibberish," "creating a where," "outrageous assumption," "who's knocking," and "hidden conflict," are simply ways of getting to something unexpected. The concept underlying all theatre games is the point of focus, or POF, which is also a Stanislavski term. If the actor is focusing on the object of the game, she cannot focus on the plot or story. Spolin's ultimate goal, remember, was not to create material for comedy acts, but to create theatre. Most of us think of improvisation as ad-libbing by quick-witted actors like Jonathan Winters, Robin Williams, Eddie Murphy, Dave Chappell. But that's the opposite of what Spolin was trying to achieve. When the actors have to play the game, to focus on the demands of the exercise, they are forced to stay in the moment, and in so doing, the plot or story develops in ways that go beyond anyone's expectations. Accidents of genius often trump the skills of talent. As the quote I found in a fortune cookie said: "Talent does what it can, genius does what it must."

This idea lies at the heart of all the concepts in Method Writing. The writer focuses on the exercise, and out comes unexpected revelations of character, story, and plot. This is the secret of process. Every art has a method, and all the methods boil down to the same thing: the specifics of process, the craft of the invisible form.

Most books on writing focus on form and structure: story, character, point of view, setting, dialogue, etc. But how does the writer approach the blank page? What's the invisible motor that powers the writing? It's voice, of course. Voice is the invisible motor. Voice and how it's used to create *tonal dynamics*. Everybody tells stories, but not everyone is a Storyteller, a master of the art of capturing an audience, of holding a reader in thrall. Great writers have an intuitive understanding of tonal dynamics. When we read their novels, we think it's the story or their literary style that makes them great. It's not. It's the vision of the world their voice creates. It begins with a tone or rhythm in the writer's head, a kind of music.

Call me Ishmael.[1]

It was the best of times, it was the worst of times . . . .[2]

For a long time I used to go to bed early.[3]

You don't know about me, without you have read a book by the name of "The Adventures of Tom Sawyer," but that ain't no matter.[4]

I was born in 1927, the only child of middle-class parents, both English, and themselves born in the grotesquely elongated shadow, which they never rose sufficiently above history to leave, of that monstrous dwarf Queen Victoria.[5]

To begin my life with the beginning of my life, I record that I was born (as I have been informed and believe) on a Friday, at twelve o'clock at night. It was remarked that the clock began to strike, and I began to cry, simultaneously.[6]

If you really want to hear about it, the first thing you'll probably want to know is where I was born, and what my lousy childhood was like, and how my parents were occupied and all before they had me, and all that David Copperfield kind of crap, but I don't feel like going into it, if you want to know the truth.[7]

But how do you find your voice? Imagine Tiger Woods telling a student, "Don't hook the ball, just aim for the middle of the fairway." Aim? You don't "aim" in golf. You adjust the mechanics of your swing: the grip, when to break the wrists, when to move the body into the downswing before bringing down the arms, and remember to keep your eye on the ball. Aim? That's the last thing you do in golf. You don't try to hit the ball onto the green: product. You swing the club correctly: Process.

Another story that illustrates the point. A director was having trouble communicating his wishes to an actor. Each time they shot the scene, the director shook his head in frustration. It wasn't what he wanted. He approached the actor and patiently gave him another direction, another motivation, another way to think about the scene. Nothing seemed to work. After the tenth take, the director pulled him aside, put his arm around his shoulder, hemmed and hawed a bit, then finally blurted out, "Act . . . . better." Well, there are techniques that help one access inner truth, that ground the scene in reality, but you can't just "act better." There's no crying in baseball, no aiming in golf, no acting in acting. Telling a writer to find his voice is the

---

[1] Herman Melville, *Moby Dick*

[2] Charles Dickens, *A Tale of Two Cities*

[3] Marcel Proust, *Remembrance of Things Past*

[4] Mark Twain, *The Adventures of Huckleberry Finn*

[5] John Fowles, *The Magus*

[6] Charles Dickens, *David Copperfield*

[7] J. D. Salinger, *The Catcher in the Rye*

equivalent of telling an actor to "act better." Everyone talks about the importance of "voice," but finding that voice requires a method.

In the beginning, we're less schooled and more natural. As we begin to investigate the great writers, we subconsciously imitate their "style" in the belief that we'll develop our own, as if style were the goal, as if style and voice were the same thing. You don't often hear the word "voice" in college classrooms when talking about writers, you hear the word "style." Hemingway's style, Faulkner's style, Toni Morrison's style. Is there a way to evolve a "style" and still retain one's "voice"? That question for me was more than academic. I was falling into the same trap myself.

After my third book of poetry was published, I realized that my work was becoming mannered, academic and lifeless. Well-written, but stale. Stylish, but devoid of personality. I wasn't sure what to do about it. I didn't want to give up writing well, but I knew that mine was not the book one would reach for at 2 A.M., unable to sleep, looking for the consolation of an authentic voice, like those found in the work of poets such as Yeats, Frost, Rilke, Pablo Neruda, Frank O'Hara, Aimé Cesaire, Anne Sexton, Amiri Baraka, Elizabeth Bishop. I knew I had to throw out the technique I'd learned and start over. But I didn't want to. I was proud of what I knew about structure and form, my ability to craft a sentence. I was proud of my technique, lifeless though it was. But those writers I loved, with their enviable prose, also had unmistakable voices. I could sense the person, the humanity, the mind beneath the dazzling craft: Virginia Woolf, William Faulkner, Eudora Welty, James Baldwin, Thomas Wolf, Carson McCullers, Saul Bellow—their style was impressive, but it was the voice that held my attention, chapter after chapter, the voice that left me feeling changed by the experience of reading.

For a year I kept a journal. I stopped writing poems and stories because I didn't want to be tempted to craft a product, to go for results. I was like a scientist conducting an experiment. How does one connect to an authentic voice when writing is an artificial construct, no different from acting on stage? How can a writer access that deep voice, the way an actor has to be believable? I caught myself again and again reaching for the old tricks. I would stop, reassure myself that I was on to something, and go on, in search of an authentic voice I wasn't even sure I possessed. After a year of writing this way, I stumbled upon tools, one of which I call "the transformation line," which extends the voice through tonal shifts. One can learn to write sentences as simple as Hemingway's, as passionate as Toni Morrison's, as complex as Henry James's, and still retain one's essential voice. By breaking things down to the fundamental elements, one can find that deep voice and learn to use it authentically.

Method Writing is not a book that covers the traditional elements of writing: structure, story, character, plot, point of view—there are plenty of books that do that. It is also not a rehashing of what some think of as method writing, by writing from one's feelings or researching one's characters. Those are static approaches, not dynamic experiences. *Method Writing* is an approach to the creative process—the process, the dynamic flow of energy that runs like an electrical current through the act of writing. But the genius of Stanislavski's method was that it gave the actor specific points of focus—similar to Spolin's theatre games—points of focus that cathected bursts of creative insight and action. The goal in Method Writing is the same, but we are using different techniques, concepts, points of focus. These concepts help writers to find their own voice by showing them *how* to do it. The exercises are arranged in a specific order, each one illuminating a basic concept of the method. When put together, the exercises constitute an overall approach to writing, whatever the form: poem, story, memoir, play, screenplay. The method provides a structure, a process, rather than a formula for product. A step-by-step approach to mastering the craft of the invisible form.

INTRODUCTION TO THE METHOD

Writing from the Deep Voice:
The First Four Concepts

This first level course I call The First Four Concepts. Writing from the Deep Voice forms the core of the method. Those of you who have studied acting will recognize the homage I am paying to a disciple of Stanislavski, Richard Boleslavsky, who wrote a wonderful little book on method acting called *The First Six Lessons*. So in a nod of appreciation, I call this first level course in *Method Writing,* The First Four Concepts. By the time you finish working on them your voice will be deeper, your writing more vivid and compelling. Even though your focus will be on process, the material you produce will form the basis for a larger project.

The work takes place in a journal, though this is not a "journal writing" course. The techniques learned in the course of writing in a journal apply to any kind of writing. You will not be working toward a product, you'll be practicing the mechanics of process. It's an old zen maxim that you get what you want by letting it go. Being in process means giving up the *desire* for product. Wait. Let me clarify that. Your *commitment* to process allows you to forego—for the time being—your attempt to produce a polished work and allows you to fall on your face, to attempt anything your imagination permits. When I look at the work habits of great artists and writers, I find one habit common to them all—their desire for product takes a back seat to the risk-taking that comes from being in process. They are willing to fail. This willingness is at the core of their daily discipline. I'm not asking you to give up your desire for product; as a matter of fact, I'm asking you to re-affirm that desire. And if the desire is great enough, your commitment to the work will be that much greater, and thus, your commitment to the process.

What about form and structure as it pertains to poetry or prose?

I've often heard the cliché that poetry is more concentrated than prose and requires a different kind of writing. Untrue and misleading. Except for the fact that some poems are dense as far as language is concerned, I could show you paragraphs in novels that are more concentrated than poems. In the film *The Perfect Storm*, George Clooney's character has a short speech that could be set down as a poem, word for word, the only difference being you'd break the speech into lines of varying lengths, so it would *look like a poem*. That speech becomes the closing voice-over of the film because of its emotional intensity, clarity of visual detail, and personal revelation. It's the kind of writing you'd do in a journal, yet, that speech becomes the message of the film. It's about the love of the sea, passion for one's work, and the willingness to risk everything for something true. By the end of the film, we know the story wasn't about a man catching fish, it was about the exaltation of following one's bliss.

A passage in your journal in which you are working on one of the exercises in this book might become a poem, part of a novel, a piece of dialogue, even a monologue in a play or screenplay. Writing is writing. The only difference between poetry and prose is the way it looks on the page.

 THERE IS NO DIFFERENCE BETWEEN THE WRITING ONE DOES

IN A POEM, A NOVEL, A PLAY, OR A SCREENPLAY.

Writing is writing.

 Good writing is good writing.

Bad writing is bad writing.

Method Writing:

Level One

The First Four Concepts

Chapter 4

CONCEPT #1:

WRITING LIKE YOU TALK /
FINDING YOUR VOICE

Like Konstantin Stanislavski's concept of method acting, which uses internal processes to create a believable and deeply felt human spirit, Method Writing is a series of concepts that lead to an authentic voice.

In his essay, "The Craft of the Invisible," poet Jack Gilbert writes:

> The poet or writer must listen hard to the voice. Because the invisible form is not just a reflection of the material; it is an intrusive, enterprising, meddling, subversive, active, intervening form. In order to effectuate. It is the major craft of all writing.
>
> I am delighted by the minor craft. The little craft of adjusting word by word, line by line, detail by detail. Making the piece of writing more presentable is important. But the craft of the invisible is what determines whether the success will be significant.
>
> Sadly, it is just this major craft which is often neglected in writing workshops. I know first hand how much writing workshops can help. But it is crucial that they ask what is going on within the poem or piece of prose. Not so much about the meaning or style, but about what kind of motor invisibly powers the particular piece of writing. Or fails to.

Whatever form it takes, writing must ring true. Overwrought writing is like bad acting, in which the actor indicates a feeling through dramatic gesture, chewing the scenery. So what makes a piece of writing compelling? The natural rhythms of speech, even when couched in a literary style.

We will begin with the journal as the place to develop a believable voice. What we write is not as important as *how* we write. Writers write. So write. Write in a journal at least a few pages a day. By making a habit of that, you establish a rhythm. It's no longer about inspiration. You're writing to stay in shape, like an athlete. Don't try to be good. Or interesting. Hemingway wrote two pages a day. John Cheever put on a suit and tie every morning and went down to his basement to write. Adele Rogers St. John put on a panama hat as she typed her stories, imagining herself on a romantic island in the South Pacific. Whatever it takes to get you to write, do it. If you write two pages a day, at the end of the year you'll have written 700 pages. *War and Peace*. Success as a writer depends upon one's ability to write, regardless of quality, regardless of inspiration. Pitchers pitch no-hitters when they don't feel like pitching. Waiting for inspiration, for an idea or concept, makes it impossible to discover something unexpected. Trying to write something good may prevent you from writing something great. As the old saying goes, "The good is the enemy of the best." What counts is the discipline of using a true, simple voice to direct the flow of the lines, and developing a habit of writing.

How to approach the journal

Maybe it's a plain spiral notebook, maybe it's one of those fancy leather-bound books. Maybe it's on the computer. Whatever it is, your journal is your lab, just as Einstein's pen was his. After writing your entry for the day, you may see a poem embedded in it, or the beginnings of a short story or essay; you might realize that what you've written is a section of a novel or a play or screenplay that's been at the back of your mind. It's not that you consciously strove for that result when you began. You began merely as another workout in *process*, but what you ended up with was *product*. These products are small gifts, magical accidents, but not what you're aiming for directly. Most of the time, much of what you write will come to nothing. Who cares? You're practicing your swing, not trying to hit a home run. There's no brainstorming, no aiming. You're working out, building muscle, and finding a habit of "writing," not a habit of "producing."

When writing in the journal, there should be no subject, no theme or idea that impels you. Do not sit and think first of what to write about. The goal is to WRITE LIKE YOU TALK. No literary sentences meant to show off your talent:

> As the defiant day broke, gray and dull, I looked out toward the stark mountains as they leaned against the horizon like drunken elephants and contemplated my next move.

This is not how you talk. This is not how anyone talks. If an actor acted the way that writer wrote, the audience would storm the exits before the end of act one. No eloquent descriptive passages. No words or phrases that wouldn't actually come out of your mouth in normal conversation. This first concept, writing like you talk, lies at the core of your work as a writer, and it is essential that you know the difference between writing from natural speech, and writing in a literary style. Most students—especially those who have developed a "style"—are often unaware of the difference. Their writing style has become an ingrained affectation acquired over years of writing, just like the actor who hams it up when the camera's rolling. Good actors do not "play" the emotion; they let the emotional truth come naturally. They don't "act" it. So it is with "voice," with writing like you talk. Don't push for literary effects, unnecessary adjectives and adverbs, fancy phrases and metaphors, or any syntactical phrases that might constitute a literary style. Sometimes the difference can be subtle, but you can develop an ear for the difference. After you've written a journal entry, go over it and inspect each sentence. "If I were actually saying this sentence," you might say to yourself, "would I say it this way?" Learn to love the truth of your voice, not the showy effects of writing.

Writing like you talk requires restraint, especially when you get to set pieces, the siren call of lush description and fancy images. Good acting is most often a question of restraint. Our training as actors teaches us how *not* to act. As Hamlet tells his actors, speak the speech trippingly on the tongue, but do not make too many gestures, do not to saw the air too much with your hands, "for in the very torrent, tempest, and (as I may say) whirlwind of your passion, you must acquire and beget a temperance that may give it smoothness."

Anton Chekhov gave similar advice to the young Maxim Gorky when he sent him this polite admonishment:

> Your nature descriptions are artistic; you are a true landscape painter. However, your frequent comparisons to humans (anthropomorphism)—the sea breathes, the sky looks on, the steppe basks in the sun, nature whispers, speaks, weeps, and so on—these kinds of personifications make your descriptions somewhat monotonous, a touch saccharine, vague; in descriptions of nature, vibrancy and expressivity are best produced by simple techniques, for example: using simple phrases such as "the sun set," "it got dark," "it started to rain," and so on.

Many writers have spent time and effort learning to write fancy, to write in a literary way. Writing like one talks seems easy. You can imagine the actor, after being admonished by a director to keep it simple, saying, "I didn't spend all that time learning to act just to do . . . . nothing! Where's the fun if I can't saw the air with my hands!" Likewise, the writer might say: "I didn't read all those classics just so I could write 'the sun set,' and 'it got dark.' Where's the fun in that?" Well, the fact is, all great writers have a true and distinctive voice, and it is your job to find your own, which begins with being able to write simply, like you talk.

Do not write "you" journal entries

You are going to forget this, so make a note of this and tape it above your writing desk—NO "YOU" JOURNAL ENTRIES. Many times you will address your journal entry to someone in particular. I call these "you" journal entries. We've all read poems that use that device, addressing the poet's mother or father or friend or lover. But avoid that device and write in the first person. (See appendix note on first person vs third person.) For the purpose of these exercises do not address a particular person in your journal entries. "Dad, we were never close, but when *you* came home that summer, I know *you* tried but *you* were unable to connect because *you* were so into *your*self." Talk instead "about" your dad. "My Dad and I were never close, but when he came home that summer, wearing the red-plaid hunting shirt he always wore, we stood on the front porch and talked for an hour. I think he tried to connect, but gave up and talked on and on about himself, the way he always does." Notice the details that give a more vivid picture of the father. We tend to leave that kind of information out when writing in "second person" because there's no reason to tell the person we're talking to what they were wearing, or other details of that nature. Addressing someone directly seems more intimate, but it's actually less so. It excludes the reader and leaves out important information. Speak to the reader, to the world, not to Uncle Fred or your father or your lover or your spouse. **Do not write "you" journal entries. You're not paying attention: no "you" entries!**

Open to a blank page and begin writing like you talk. (Some people call this kind of writing "stream of consciousness," going from one random thought to another. See appendix note on stream of consciousness.) Begin with the moment. Where are you, what are you thinking, what are you feeling, what do you see, what's going on in your life at that moment?`

> I'm sitting at the kitchen table with a cup of coffee. This is the best time for me to write, because in an hour I have to pick up the kids. It's always like that around here, rush rush rush. I guess if I'm going to get any writing done, I'll

have to get up an hour earlier when everyone is sleeping. When I was 16, that's what I did. I took my journal—well, actually, it was a loose-leaf binder—out into the yard and wrote for hours. Well, it seemed like hours. It was probably more like 30 minutes. But I felt like a writer. I imagined that *that's* what writers did, they sat in some quiet room, or in their back yard, and wrote for hours, writing a story or a poem or something. No chores, no homework, no nothing. It was all so romantic. Maybe that's why I wanted to be a writer. It seemed like a good way to get out of doing real work.

Just in case you've forgotten it, allow me to say it a third time: NO "YOU" JOURNAL ENTRIES.

"Is this what Method Writing is about, writing simple but pedestrian sentences?"

Of course not. Is that what baseball is about, swinging the bat a thousand times? Of course not. But it's essential to begin by finding one's own voice, and from that a "style" will develop. Good actors can sense the degree to which they are acting. They know how to rev up the intensity or tone it down. Like an athlete who can gauge how far or how hard to throw a ball, writers control the tone and depth of the writing. They know the difference between a speech-based voice and a more ornate style. You have to know the difference and be able to control it. The following is a well-written sentence, but it is not the way people speak.

"Standing in the doorway, I could tell that someone had broken into the house."

A perfectly fine sentence. We see sentences like that all the time in stories and novels. It's good basic writing. No fancy adjectives, no adverbs, no ornate phrases, no straining for effect. But it's not how we talk. Its syntax and structure conform to a literary construct, not to everyday speech. That sentence begins with a participial phrase. When speaking, no one begins a sentence with a participial phrase, except maybe William Buckley or Gore Vidal. Beginning a sentence with a participial phrase is one of the most common constructs in literature. There's nothing wrong with it. But it's not how we structure a sentence when we speak. Usually, we say something like, "When I stood in the doorway, I could tell someone had broken into the house." Or, "I was standing in the doorway, and could tell that someone had broken into the house." But you wouldn't begin a sentence with a participial phrase. No one would. It's not how we speak. Once you learn to see the difference, you'll have control of when and when not to do it.

"How do you know how I talk? Maybe writing eloquently is how I talk."

I'm talking about how language is structured when *anyone* talks. It's the way our brains are hard-wired. If we're writing a shopping list or a note to a friend, we tend to write in the syntax of speech. When we write in what we imagine to be a literary construct, we tend toward the artificial, the literary. It's the same with acting. We're all quite natural when going about our daily lives, but put us on stage and we tend to "act." Using heightened language isn't wrong, but a writer must know how to differentiate between a literary sentence and a spoken one. Spencer

Tracy used to say that the secret of acting was to "hit your mark, look people in the eye, and tell the truth." (It was James Cagney who said, "Learn your lines and don't bump into the furniture.")

There are other literary effects we use when writing that are rarely used when speaking. Adverbs, for instance. When speaking, we run down the stairs, we tip-toe into a room, we tuck the children into bed, and we yell at our spouse. But give us a quill pen, some candlelight, a portrait of Shakespeare on the desk, and suddenly we're writing how we *quickly* ran down the stairs, *softly* tip-toed into the room, *gently* tucked our kids into bed, and *angrily* yelled at our spouse. For writers trying too hard to cook a writerly stew, adverbs are the first spice they reach for. One day in class a writer read a journal entry that had seven adverbs, all of them unnecessary. "If I had $5 for every adverb used in this class," I said, "I'd be able to retire." Someone suggested we get a cookie jar and start a party fund: "Adverbs cost $5," she said. So I gave everyone an option whenever they used an adverb. If it was indispensable to the action described in the sentence, they'd put $5 into the cookie jar. If it wasn't worth the money, they'd cut it. So far, the cookie jar remains empty. No one has found an adverb worth $5. The verb ends up being stronger with the adverb gone; the sentence sounds cleaner and is more efficient.

The same is true—though to a lesser extent—for adjectives. More spice. Now we gently tip-toe into the dimly lit, cozy room and gently tuck our rosy-cheeked kids into the large, soft bed as the full moon begins its mournful climb into the starry sky. When we talk, we're economical with language, but worked-up into a literary lather, we scatter adjectives like Johnny Adjectiveseed.

When someone reads a journal entry aloud, filled with adjective and adverbs, I ask the writer to close the journal and tell me about the experience. When he does, he leaves out all the adverbs, and most of the adjectives. In almost every instance, the way he tells it will be better and more vivid than the way he wrote it. Often, in our attempt to sound like a writer, we construct sentences that are not as well-written as sentences that arise out of natural speech.

Many of us have been taught to search for the "right" word or the imaginative metaphor, and we end up embellishing sentences with verbiage and awkward syntax. We are thinking in a literary way, not writing from the mouth. Each "well-crafted" sentence follows another until, soon, there is no modulation of voice or tone, no sense of a real person telling a story. Eventually, your reader will lose interest and your story will die on the vine.

Mannered writing requires an unnatural effort. That's why so many people have trouble keeping a journal on a regular basis. It becomes exhausting. The writer avoids the tyranny of the blank page. Like the amateur poet, he waits for a bolt of inspiration. But that's a dead end. The Latin root of inspiration is *spiro*, to breathe, to draw breath. Not a burst of energy, but an even flow, in and out. So: Be a real person, not a "writer." Write something every day. Breathe. Write like you talk.

It doesn't matter what the journal entry is about. It might be therapeutic—an ongoing process of discovery that one finds healing, if not revelatory. But it is not therapy, it is not the discovery of the self in psychological terms; rather, it is the discovery of the sound of your own voice, which lives in the language of speech.

That voice becomes the foundation for all the variations found in good writing. What develops is a characteristic tone, a "style" that individualizes the work, separates it from everyone else's, even later, when the piece is more stylized.

When you write in your journal, remember that story is irrelevant at this stage. Don't be seduced by your desire to write something interesting. Don't try to entertain the reader. Focus instead on the voice, one sentence at a time.

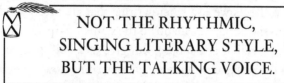

NOT THE RHYTHMIC, SINGING LITERARY STYLE, BUT THE TALKING VOICE.

Stanislavski said of method acting, "It is only when one's inner and outer life is flowing naturally in the work of art that the deeper source of one's subconscious opens, and we are able to create the life of a human spirit in a beautiful, artistic form." He revolutionized the art of acting by training actors to come from an emotional truth. Before that, actors often mimicked emotional truth; their actions did not arise out of inner necessity. Likewise, many writers use "well-written" phrases that mimic preconceived notions of "good writing." Your goal as a writer is the same as that of an actor: to be believable.

In 1908, Ezra Pound wrote that all English-speaking poets except Yeats were on the wrong track. He believed that the poets of his day were writing in a "poetic" style far removed from natural speech. A century earlier, William Wordsworth in his "Preface" to the second edition of his *Lyrical Ballads* (1800), called on poets to use "a selection of language really used by men." Throughout his preface he repeated the edict in various ways: "The language of poetry should be a selection of the language really spoken," "to adopt the very language of men," and "to bring the language of my poems near to the language of men." A century after Wordsworth, Pound wrote to Harriet Monroe, editor of the newly founded magazine *Poetry,* and made this famous pronouncement:

> Poetry must be as well written as prose. Its language must be a fine language, departing in no way from speech save by heightened intensity (i.e., simplicity). There must be no book words, no periphrases, no inversions. It must be as simple as De Maupassant's best prose, and as hard as Stendhal's.... Objectivity and again objectivity, and expression: no hind-side-beforeness, no straddled adjectives, no Tennysonianess of speech; nothing—nothing that you couldn't, in the stress of some circumstance, in the stress of some emotion, actually say. Every literaryism, every book word, fritters away a scrap of the reader's patience, a scrap of his sense of your sincerity.

Once every century or so, when literary style has become too mannered, failing to keep up with the natural rhythms of speech, a writer or a group of writers issues a call for change. Then, over time, that new "modern" style becomes the paradigm of the time, and succeeding generations of writers mimic it, while speech continues to naturally evolve. This happened to Latin over the course of the Middle Ages, where written Latin adhered to classical forms and spoken Latin evolved to become such languages as French, Spanish, Italian, and Romanian. Then another pronouncement occurs, and writers once again discover natural speech. Dante called for such a change when he urged the literati of his day to write in the vernacular—to reach them, he wrote a book on the subject (*On the Use of the Vulgar Tongue*) in Latin—then proceeded to write his great *Commedia* in Italian, the so-called "vulgar tongue." This was a revolutionary act at the time. Latin was the language of literature. Italian was the everyday speech of the common man, yet Dante used the vernacular to write his great poem, believing that for writing to be timeless, it has to come from speech. Shakespeare was looked down upon by those "university wits" whose plays are no longer read and rarely produced: Richard Greene, Thomas Nash, John Webster, Cyril Tourneur, Thomas Kidd, etc. Shakespeare wrote in the language of his day, the way people talked. Whitman took to the streets and brought the voice of the populace to his breathless style. Go back two thousand years to the poetry of Catullus—the language of speech. In his anthology of American poetry titled *The Voice that is Great Within Us*, Hayden Carruth says of Robert Frost: "Frost's poetic practice was based on what he called 'sentence sounds,' the natural tones and rhythms of speech cast loosely against standard poetic forms. Conventional as it may seem today, it was a new departure in its time, making Frost a distinctly modern poet."

It's not unusual for writers to use the term "voice" when talking about writing. Paul Mariani talks about how stultified his writing was, how his "squibs and haiku and images never became poems, the breath of poems, until I realized that poems were voice, were telling sentences." He wanted his readers to realize, once they'd gotten through his syntax and metaphors and line breaks, that, "yes, that's a living language, that sounds like someone talking, that sounds like a real person, an American speaking at the beginning of the second millennium."

That's what Stanislavski wanted for his actors. He wanted the actor (playing Hamlet, for instance) to seem like a real person. The operative word here is "seem." No one in the audience thinks they're seeing a real person named Hamlet. We know it's an actor. But the actor's job is to *seem* like a real person, so that we can "suspend disbelief." When the actor becomes mannered or artificial, we become aware of our disbelief, and lose our connection to what's occurring on stage or screen.

> One cannot always create subconsciously and with inspiration. No such genius exists in the world. Therefore, our art teaches us first of all to create consciously and rightly, because that will best prepare the way for the blossoming of the subconscious, which is inspiration. The more you have of conscious creative moments in your role, the more chance you will have of a flow of inspiration.
>
> If you take all these internal processes, and adapt them to the spiritual and physical life of the person you are representing, we call that living the part.... The artist's job is not to present merely the external life of his character. He must fit his own human qualities to the life of this other person, and pour into it all of his own soul. The fundamental aim of our art is the creation of this inner life of a human spirit, and its expression in an artistic form.
>
> —Konstantin Stanislavski, *The Actor Prepares*

Each piece of writing is an experience shared by writer and reader, an act of discovery.

I look at a poem as a performance. I look on the poet as a person of prowess, just like an athlete. He's a performer. Every poem is like that: some sort of achievement in performance.

Another thing to say is that every thought poetical or otherwise, every thought is a feat of association; having what's in front of you bring up something in your mind that you almost didn't know you knew. Putting this and that together. That click.

No surprise for the writer, no surprise for the reader.

This thing of performance and prowess and feats of association—that's where it all lies.

—Robert Frost, *Paris Interviews*

Think of the downhill racer, skiing between poles. From a distance he appears to be "going with the flow," yet he's making choices at every turn that require focus, agility, strength, vision, and patience. When beginning a journal entry, you are poised for a downhill race. The piece carries you along and you have to be ready to take this turn, that turn, follow this association, that image. At the same time, you hold on to one central focus: *Write like you talk.* Don't lose sight of that. And don't fixate on a theme or subject. Allow yourself to follow an impulse, to let an image or a feeling take you away from where you thought you were going.

The Creative Encounter

The concept of encounter also enables us to make clearer the important distinction between talent and creativity. Talent may well have its neurological correlates and can be studied as "given" to a person. A man or woman may have talent whether he or she uses it or not; talent can probably be measured in the person as such. But creativity can be seen only in the act. If we were purists, we would not speak of a "creative person," but only of a creative act. Sometimes, as in the case of Picasso, we have great talent and at the same time great encounter and, as a result, great creativity. Sometimes we have great talent and truncated creativity, as many people felt in the case of F. Scott Fitzgerald. Sometimes we have a highly creative person who seems not to have much talent. It was said of the novelist Thomas Wolfe, who was one of the highly creative figures of the American scene, that he was a "genius without talent." But he was so creative because he threw himself so completely into his material and the challenge of saying it—he was great because of the intensity of his encounter.

—Rollo May, *The Courage to Create*

Talent is your biggest obstacle.

—Jack Grapes

Talent comes with a curse. It blinds us to the real work of creativity. We get by with talent, and then when the going gets tough, talent alone will not produce the work of art trying to emerge. One must practice the fundamentals of one's craft over and over, until they become part of the body's truth. The product of the encounter between talent and process is an accident of the gods. It can't be reproduced at will, like something on an assembly line. What you can do is humbly enter into the creative encounter one more time, and another time, and yet again, committing to the process, and if you're lucky, you'll have an accident that comes not from your talent, but from your genius.

> Talent does what it can. Genius does what it must.
>
> —Fortune Cookie

Talent can take you only so far. Greatness is within all of us, but talent may prevent you from stumbling upon the accidents of your genius. The process is a way to subvert your talent, and you must do it with focus, one step at a time, with the humility of the tortoise.

> The good is the enemy of the best.
>
> —Old Romanian Proverb

Work through the four concepts in this book like a yogi, methodically building flexibility and strength, muscle by muscle. Each concept strengthens a different muscle until, eventually, a way of working will emerge that will broaden your approach to writing.

> Process requires patience and risk, and the capacity to work. Our poems and stories are not finished pieces so much as attempts to focus on the process and performance of the work: performance as it relates to the responsibility to speak with a true and clear voice, and process as it relates to the unfinished task of growing throughout one's life, and not the finished perfection of the other.
>
> —Hector of Bulgaria

> I believe the secret in writing is that poetry or fiction never exceeds the reach of the writer's courage. The best writing comes from the place where terror hides, the edge of our worst stuff. And I know you can fake that courage when you don't think of yourself as courageous—because I have done it. And that is not a bad thing, to fake it until you can make it. I know that until I started pushing on my own fears, telling the stories that were hardest for me, writing about exactly the things I was most afraid of and unsure about, I wasn't writing worth a damn.
>
> —Dorothy Allison, from *Poets & Writers Magazine*

So let's take it one step at a time. **Write at least two pages a day**. Don't make it significant. Just fill up two pages a day, minimum. You can write more than two pages, but don't burn yourself out. I've seen students start out by writing 30–40 pages a day. They last a week. Be realistic. You have miles to go before you sleep, and miles to go before you sleep.

It doesn't have to be good, any more than one's breathing has to be good. The goal is to write in your natural voice. Your speaking voice. Unplanned. In the moment.

It's like going to the gym and doing a minimum cardiovascular workout. There are some who actually enjoy working out, but most of us enjoy it more when it's over. Same for the writing. Writers don't always enjoy writing; they enjoy having written.

Method Writing doesn't mean your voice will be limited to the rhythms and inflections of natural speech. After all, whether acting or writing, you want to be able to achieve grand effects. It's not enough to play Willie Loman or Hedda Gabler, you also want to play Macbeth or Medea, or that royal poet, Richard II. Hemingway, yes, but why not Proust or Faulkner or Virginia Woolf, too. As we say to the acting student, first play yourself, then you can play Hannibal Lector or Lady Macbeth. First deepen your own voice, then you can write like Toni Morrison or Arundhati Roy. In the second level of Method Writing, we work on the Four Voices, which gives your writing the tonal dynamics found in writers like Gabriel García Marquez, Kazuo Ishiguro, Marilynne Robinson, Cormack McCarthy, and Elizabeth Bishop, to mention just a few. Writers like these are stylists who elevate their language and diction.

> In the long unfurling of his life, from tight-wound kid hustler in a wool suit riding the train out of Cheyenne to geriatric limper in this spooled-out year, Mero had kicked down thoughts of the place where he began, a so-called ranch on strange ground at the south hinge of the Big Horns.
> —Annie Proulx, "The Half-Skinned Steer"

This is not writing like one talks. It's lush. Writing like you talk isn't better than writing in a lush, poetic style, nor is lush, poetic writing better than writing like one talks. I'm saying you want to know the difference, and be able to do both. But even highly stylized writing is grounded in the diction of speech. One *must* start there. Here's the opening of *The God of Small Things* by Arundhati Roy. This is a style that many try to imitate before developing their own, authentic voice.

> May in Ayemenem is a hot, brooding month. The days are long and humid. The river shrinks and black crows gorge on bright mangoes in still, dustgreen trees. Red bananas ripen. Jackfruits burst. Dissolute bluebottles hum vacuously in the fruity air. Then they stun themselves against clear windowpanes and die, fatly baffled in the sun. The nights are clear, but suffused with sloth and sullen expectation....
> It was raining when Rahel came back to Ayemenem. Slanting silver ropes slammed into loose earth, plowing it up like gunfire. The old house on the hill wore its steep, gabled roof pulled over its ears like a low hat. The walls, streaked with moss, had grown soft, and bulged a little with dampness that seeped up from the ground. The wild, overgrown garden was full of the whisper and scurry of small lives. In the undergrowth a rat snake rubbed itself against a glistening stone. Hopeful yellow bullfrogs cruised the scummy pond for mates. A drenched mongoose flashed across the leaf-strewn driveway.

Here's another example of a writer using elevated language, yet one can hear the everyday speech that underlies it:

> She stood with her black face some six inches from the moist window-pane and wondered when on earth would it ever stop raining. She heard rain droning upon the roof, and high up in the wet sky her eyes followed the silent rush of a bright shaft of yellow that swung from the airplane beacon in far-off Memphis. Momentarily she could see it cutting through the rainy dark; it would hover a second like a gleaming sword above her head, then vanish.
> —Richard Wright, "Bright Morning Star"

In the next example, the author uses a poetic style that, if broken into lines, could easily be taken as a poem.

Ralph Kabnis, propped in his bed, tries to read. To read himself to sleep. An oil lamp on a chair near his elbow burns unsteadily. The cabin room is spaced fantastically about it. Whitewashed hearth and chimney, black with sooty saw teeth. Ceiling, patterned by the fringed globe of the lamp. The walls, unpainted, are seasoned a rosin yellow. And cracks between the boards are black. These cracks are the lips the night winds use for whispering. Night winds in Georgia are vagrant poets, whispering.

—Jean Toomer, *Cane*

In contrast to the poetic voice, here are several beginnings to novels or stories rendered in a natural, speaking voice.

They were supposed to stay at the beach a week, but neither of them had the heart for it and they decided to come back early. Macon drove. Sarah sat next to him, leaning her head against the side of the window.

—Anne Tyler, *The Accidental Tourist*

We are on the front porch at Frank Martin's drying-out facility. Like the rest of us at Frank Martin's, J.P. is first and foremost a drunk. But he's also a chimney sweep. It's his first time here, and he's scared. I've been here once before. What's to say? I'm back. J.P.'s real name is Joe Penny, but he says I should call him J.P. He's about thirty years old. Younger than I am. Not much younger, but a little.

—Raymond Carver, "Where I'm Calling From"

Sth, I know that woman. She used to live with a flock of birds on Lenox Avenue. Know her husband, too. He fell for an eighteen-year-old girl with one of those deepdown, spooky loves that made him so sad and happy he shot her just to keep the feeling going. When the woman, her name is Violet, went to the funeral to see the girl and to cut her dead face they threw her to the floor and out of the church. She ran then, through all that snow, and when she got back to her apartment she took the birds from their cages and set them out the windows to freeze or fly, including the parrot that said, "I love you."

—Toni Morrison, *Jazz*

Notice how the author writes sentences just as they might come out of a person's mouth. Not: "The woman whose name is Violet," but "when the woman, her name is Violet . . . ." Were you to write that sentence in school, your teacher would probably correct it. It may not be a *well-written* sentence, but it's a *truly* written sentence.

These examples show the range of effects between simple speech and a dense literary style. Find your voice, learn to deepen it, and proceed from there. But no matter what style you eventually land on, you must first locate your own speech patterns, your own rhythms.

It was Sunday. Chance was in the garden. He moved slowly, dragging the green hose from one path to the next, carefully watching the flow of the water. Very gently he let the stream touch every plant, every flower, every branch of the garden. Plants were like people; they needed care to live, to survive their diseases, and to die peacefully.

—Jerzy Kosinski, *Being There*

After the Second World War, the great Irish writer Samuel Beckett began writing in French because it made it easier for him to write without style. The Irish are partciularly known for their poetic word play, and their influence on Western literature goes back to the Middle Ages. Beckett knew that the influence of those Irish dramatists, poets, and prose writers was more than a question of learning—it was in the very culture of Irish speech. To list all the great Irish writers would take pages, but a sampling that had an influence on his writing would include W. B. Yeats, James Joyce, Liam O'Flaherty, Elizabeth Bowen, Sean O'Casey, Alice Milligan, Martin MacDonagh, and Emily Lawless. When Beckett said he wanted to write without style, he meant without affectation and cultural baggage; most of all, he wanted to subvert the influence of James Joyce, who dominated the literary scene in which Beckett came of age as a writer. For a time, Beckett worked as Joyce's secretary, just as Ezra Pound had assisted Yeats when he was a young man. In order to break from such influence, Beckett felt that the discipline of writing in a second language would allow him to produce a radically spare style, an economy of expression which characterized his greatest works:: in drama—*Waiting for Godot, Endgame*, and *Krapp's Last Tape*; in prose—the extraordinary post-war trilogy *Molloy, Malone Dies*, and *The Unnamable*. (Beckett won the Nobel Prize in 1969; Yeats was awarded the Nobel in 1923; Ezra Pound was nominated in 1950 but failed to win; James Joyce was never nominated.)

A writer using stylized sentences may distance the reader unless one hears, beneath the surface, a voice grounded in natural speech. Such a voice can rise to other registers, but we must *believe* it can level off again and become natural; that it is a voice familiar with the human condition. Even if the voice is literary, spokenness must form its backbone. And to convey that, one must first master the spoken voice. Once your voice is grounded in the rhythms of natural speech, the emotion you wish to evoke will be felt by the reader no matter what style you write in.

Throughout this course, I don't care what you write about. You can write about not being able to write. You can write about not liking the pen you're using. You can write about your underwear being too tight and those awful headaches. It doesn't matter how you start, and it doesn't matter how the piece develops. The more you try to make it "good," the more likely it is you will sabotage the "creative encounter." The more you try to make it "good," the more you will find yourself relying on your talent, and the less chance you will have of your genius accidentally emerging.

The poet Richard Jones shared with me a zen koan that I keep pinned above my computer:

> *You find out who you are by acting naturally.*

The sentence contains its own contradiction, but in my zen heart I understand it. Writing naturally is a conscious act, a performance that seems to eschew performance. That's the trick.

Autobiographia Literaria

When I was a child
I played by myself in a
corner of the schoolyard
all alone.

I hated dolls and I
hated games, animals were
not friendly and birds
flew away.

If anyone was looking
for me I hid behind a
tree and cried out "I am
an orphan."
And here I am, the
center of all beauty!
Writing these poems!
Imagine!

—Frank O'Hara (1926–1966)

Sometimes the voice is sure and strong. Sometimes it's small, wounded, fragile. The words you write may even shock you with their truth. The French poet Paul Aluard said that God gives the poet a first line, and after that it's up to the poet.—Rilke's terrifying beginnings. Entire novels have been built on the impulse of a first line. One day I was thinking about my sister, the one who would have been my older sister had she not died in childbirth. The line "my sister dies" hung in the air like a balloon that would neither float away nor settle on the ground. My sister dies. I knew that if I thought about it, the poem would go away, crumble into plot or story. So I kept the line at bay until I could get home. I wrote the line down and could feel where it was in my body. It was deep, but more than that, it was constricted. Like the child in Frank O'Hara's poem above, I was alone, suspended, afraid to show myself. I could feel my breath, tucked away in my chest: thus, the short sentences, the short lines. It was as if I were speaking through a hole in a wall to the reader to come and find me.

A Deed of Light

My sister dies.
I am not born yet.
She barely strikes soul
and goes.
My Uncle Jack dies.
I am not born yet.
It is right
to give me his name.
Among other things
it means
something smaller
than the usual of its
kind;
a small stuffed puppet
set up to be pelted
for sport.
For years they call me
Jackie.

My father sneers.
What kind of name is that!
Uncle Charles dies.
Everyone in the kitchen
stands and cries.
A year later
on the kitchen floor
Uncle Lou dies
vomiting on the newspaper
under his head.
I bring him more newspaper.
My socks flap at the toes.
My name is Jack:
a small national flag
flown by a ship.
The next year
we move to the new house.
This time of brick.
Martin Shapiro dies.
My mother drags me to the wake.
In the open coffin
his nose can be seen
all the way from the back
of the chapel.
Applejack, jacknife,
jack-o-lantern.
Aunt Adela dies
all summer in the back bedroom.
Withers on the sheets of cancer.
Jackie, she says,
show me the movies.
My mother prances
with grief around the grave.
Sarah Bernhardt.
A year later, of cancer too,
she gets it down.
Hisses bitch at the nurse
the last two days.
When I leave for Europe
I forget to tell my father goodbye.
In Italy, the phone rings.
Come home, it says,
you're the man in the family
now.
Jacksnipe, jackstraw,
jack-in-the-box.
From tides to bushes
on Sundays,

each of us digs holes
in the backyard.
This growing further apart.
Karl who is my brother.
Louis who is my brother.
Charlaine who is my sister.
Jacksmelt, jackshaft,
jackpot.
I am Daniele's Uncle Jack.
I am Benjamin's Uncle Jack.
I am Ari's Uncle Jack.
My arms become trees
solitary with the base pale face
of a green kitchen door,
jewels for teeth to kill my father,
see me, see you,
see who dies on Tuesday.

No more of graves and names.
On the dead I spit on the dead of the dead.
The Jack deads and the Charles deads
and the mother deads and the father deads.
My name beats the bush
that sends up flocks of birds.
This lantern cut to look
like a human face.
The name looks out of my eyes.
The meaning looks out of my name.
Jack is a deed of light.

Chapter 5

CONCEPT #2:

THE TRANSFORMATION LINE

In the movie *The Karate Kid*, Mr. Miagi teaches his student how to perform a basic move by having him wax a car. "Wax on, wax off," Mr. Miagi tells him, "wax on, wax off." The kid's frustrated. He wants to learn karate, not wax a car. But Mr. Miagi is insistent. "Wax on," he says, "wax off. And don't forget to breathe. Breathing very important." Even the audience is unsure where this will lead. But those who understand the concept of process know what is being taught here. A thousand practice swings. The body learns in a way the mind cannot. By repeating the task as if it were a Zen koan, the kid learns his first basic block.

In an acting class, your first exercise might be to walk into a room and perform a simple action—pack a suitcase, look for a pair of glasses, hide a wad of money. The goal is to get the feel of doing something without "acting." At the end of the scene, the phone might ring. Your task would be to answer it, say "Bernie's not here, he went to Jamaica," and hang up. Then leave the room. If there were moments in the scene where you seemed to be "indicating" to the audience what you were thinking or feeling by exaggerating a gesture or facial expression, you would keep working at it. Your task is to learn to convey subtext (feelings, thoughts) through actions that are real and true. No "acting." Just complete the task—wax on, wax off.

Likewise, a writer strives to be believable. For at least a week now, you've been writing a few pages a day in your journal, trying to write like you talk. Before moving on to this week's assignment, it's important to evaluate what you've written so far.

The first question to ask is, "Do I believe it? Does the writing seem natural, the way people speak?" If there's a phrase or sentence that doesn't seem natural, underline it. This doesn't mean it's badly written. The question is, was it written in the syntax of speech, or in the syntax of "writing"? Read the piece aloud and try to be objective. Be picky, even. Examine each adjective, each adverb. Would you have used that adjective if you were just talking? Most adverbs end in "ly": quickly, slowly, tenderly, softly, gingerly, etc. For every adverb you decide to keep, send me $5. Is that adverb really worth $5? If not, cut it. My advice is to cut all your adverbs. I've never met an adverb that was absolutely necessary. Let me re-phrase that. I've never met an adverb that was necessary. Cut 'em all. Save your money.

As you read your work aloud, ask yourself: Does the sentence sound spoken or literary? Is there a part of it that sounds overwrought, a phrase or word perhaps? Some of us use words that others do not. Notice how the word was used in the context of the sentence, the structure and syntax, or "prosody," as it's called. It's not always a question of the word itself, but how it fits into the sentence. That's how you can tell if you're writing like you talk. It's not always a question of one's vocabulary, but the way we string phrases together. It's a visceral experience. You've heard someone trying to sell you something over the phone, and you can tell when they're reading from something printed, when they've memorized a salespitch. You can tell they're not just talking.

When my younger brother was in college, his friend was selling encyclopedias. He asked me if he could practice his salespitch on me. Now the last thing I could afford at the time was a set of encyclopedias, but I let him practice on me. We sat in the living room and he brought out his kit and began his spiel. At one point, I interrupted him to ask a question, and suddenly he was talking naturally, though making the same points. When he departed from his pitch, he was alive and interesting. Then he'd go back to the memorized text and it was lifeless, well-written but dead. (If you're wondering, by the way, the answer is yes, I bought a set of encyclopedias. They sit on a shelf in my son's room like the Velveteen Rabbit, discarded but expectant. When he needs to look something up, he uses the internet.)

I've also experienced this disconnection between the written and spoken word when listening to a speech. A graduation ceremony, perhaps, with Dean Flugelmeister at the podium. He reads the speech, looks up occasionally and makes eye contact, just as we're taught to do in Oral Interp. 101, but by the second paragraph, your mind is wandering. It's because there's a vitality to our sentences when we speak that's missing from the written speech. We live in a post-literate society. Over the centuries, we've developed a way of writing that has probably become wired into our brains. We learn it in school and from reading other writers. Subconsciously, when writing something important, we adopt a literary tone. You're liable to assume that many of your "literary" flourishes are actually the way you speak, but they're not. It's going to take some objective evaluation on your part to see the difference. Don't take your writing for granted: sometimes you'll be writing like you talk, but there will be times when you'll slip into a well-worn, stylized phrase and not even realize it, unless you're really on guard and can hear the difference. Learning to distinguish between speech-based writing and literary style will make you a better writer.

I've gotten into the habit of noticing these differences when I should be listening to what is being said. It really bugs my wife. She can see by the look in my eyes that I'm listening to syntax rather than content. Her toes nudging my ankle under the table are the signal: *come back, come back*. The other day I switched stations on the radio as I was driving and came to a commentator in the middle of making his point. There was something about the syntax that sounded written. I thought to myself, he's reading from a book or news article. When he finished, he said, "That was from Conrad Flugelmeister's book, *The History of Graduation Speeches and the Students Who Love Them*." Ah-ha, I said to myself. The radio commentator was skilled enough to make it sound like he was speaking off the cuff, but the syntax tipped me off. I gave myself a well-deserved pat on the back.

When I was a young writer, I unofficially apprenticed myself to writers I loved. I immersed myself, and when I wrote I tried to imitate them, allowing their influence to affect my writing. I ingested them, their tonality and phrasing, their use of language, and when I was done I imagined myself absorbing their craft and making it my own, their influence settling into my cells. I spent months with each writer: Faulkner, Hemingway, Eudora Welty, Virginia Woolf, F. Scott Fitzgerald, Thomas Wolfe, Carson McCullers, Henry James (*The Ambassadors*), Saul Bellow (*Augie March*). What, I asked myself, was Dashiell Hammett doing with that sentence? Wilkie Collins? Proust? Mann? Malcolm Lowry (*Under the Volcano*). Salinger. Chandler. Elizabeth Bowen. Ralph Ellison. Wyndham Lewis. James Joyce (the moooo cow). Each had a unique voice beneath the "style." You can copy a Picasso, but not his voice, the way his hand moves the brush across the canvas. You can imitate the mannerisms of Brando, but not his deep truth. You can imitate a writer, but you're just imitating mannerisms. Your work will be like Frankenstein's monster, a style assembled from the effects of other writers. Understanding what other writers do is essential, but eventually you have to find your own voice. As Doctor Praetorius says in *The Bride of Frankenstein*, "Shall we put in the heart now?" It starts with this simple exercise: Write like you talk. Of the first four concepts, this is the most important.

A sentence is like a bridge. There's the engineering of it, the way the struts and supports prevent the bridge from collapsing, and then there's the architecture, the way it looks, the modern lines or the baroque flourishes. No matter how pretty the architecture, the bridge had better be well engineered or I won't drive across it.

"The big green car sped quickly down the long narrow street."

This is not a spoken sentence—no one piles up adjectives and adverbs like that when speaking. Remember, I'm not *giving* you $5 for every adjective or adverb, I'm *fining* you $5 for every unnecessary adjective and adverb.

So examine the syntax and prosody of your sentences. Underline the ones that seem "written," not spoken. Develop your ear. Once you have a sense of your own voice, move on to the second concept of Method Writing: getting your voice to go deeper by massaging the Transformation Line.

☞ The Transformation Line:
Using the Head Voice, the Reporting Voice, and the Deep Voice

What is a transformation line? It's a term I made up. Not the transition line, but the transformation line. Put quite simply, a transformation line is **any sentence that has the word "I" in it.**

✍"I like ice-cream."
✍"Sometimes, I like to think I'm pretty."
✍"I had no idea what he was talking about."
✍"When it rains, I stay inside."
✍"When my brother walked into the front door, I was hiding the birthday cake."
✍"I pushed away the table and stood by the door."
✍"I'm always afraid something bad will happen."
✍"It's hard for me to trust people." (The "me" in this sentence is equivalent to "I" since the sentence could read: "I have a hard time trusting people." But the sentence "My dad never trusted me" cannot be transposed to an "I" sentence, since the sentence is not about you, it's about your father.)
✍"Sometimes, when I listen to Jack talk, I get a headache."

In each sentence, I've underlined the core of the transformation line. It's the core that provides the basis for the massage. Some of the lines, of course, are more potent than others. "I like ice-cream" does not have the same resonance as "I'm always afraid something bad will happen." We could say that **a transformation line is a personal statement that has the word "I" in it, and involves a self-discovery**. In the poem "Birches," Robert Frost writes: "So was I once myself a swinger of birches," then realizes something about himself. In the next line, he makes an even deeper discovery. "And so I dream of going back to be." A personal statement (or transformation line) reveals something to the writer—it's an epiphany, of sorts. Such statements deepen the tone by guiding the writer to a deeper place.

Which brings us to the three voices, or more accurately, the three places from which the voice comes.

1) **The Reporting Voice** is simple narration or exposition. The writer is not connected to a deep emotional state, but recounts information in a matter-of-fact way. When a section of your journal entry does that without emotional resonance, make a note in the margin: "the reporting voice."

2) **The Head Voice** is analytical, a working out of some problem or situation. "If this was that, then I wouldn't have known, but she thought this and I figured that, and that was then and this is now, so there." The head voice may *seem* to be emotionally connected because it's talking about feelings, but that's the point. It's talking *about* a feeling, not coming *from* the feeling. It's removed from the experience even as it talks about it. There is nothing wrong with either the reporting voice or the head voice; I just want you to know the difference.

3) **The Deep Voice** comes from the gut. It's meditative, introspective, charged with feeling. There's a sense that the writer is reliving some deep emotion. When writing about a sad or painful experience, the deep voice might come naturally. But even happy times, because they are fleeting, are often reflected upon with poignancy. That's the deep voice. It's the intimate voice you use when talking to a friend late at night, trying to find words to describe an ineffable experience.

The deep voice has degrees. There's the deep voice, the deeper voice, the really deep voice, and the I'm-about-to-have-a-breakdown voice. What counts is that the voice goes beyond mere reporting. Some parts of what you write will be deeper than other parts. It's important that you learn to recognize a transformation line, and just as important that you learn to separate the core of the transformation line from the rest of the sentence. Our second concept involves the core transformation line and learning to go deeper with it, or as I call it, learning to massage it.

"Massaging" the Transformation Line

Some transformation lines take us deeper into a story when we massage them. "When my brother walked in, I was hiding the birthday cake" is a sentence about a simple action, but the core phrase is "I was hiding." If you take that phrase out of context, it's the deepest of all the transformation lines mentioned above because it reveals a truth about the self that has nothing to do with the birthday cake. Follow the core transformation line: "I was hiding." Massaging it means to follow the truth revealed there. Remember, it's no longer about a birthday cake, it's about hiding. I might ask myself, "Why would I be hiding?" And begin the massage by writing, "I don't want anyone to see me." That's the second transformation line that follows the massage. And so on. Each succeeding transformation line is a deepening of the original one, almost as if you were a detective working backwards to arrive at the truth. The object of massaging the transformation line is to go deeper. How deep is up to you.

"What is the story of my life? What is the truth of who I am?"

Of all the concepts in this book, massaging a transformation line is the hardest. The tendency will be to focus on the birthday cake part of the sentence. But you must erase it from your mind when you begin the masssage. Here's a little trick that will help you. Before you begin your massage, think of the transformation line as the answer to the question, "What is the story of my life? What is the truth of who I am." The transformation line is "I was hiding." Not "I was hiding the birthday cake." So get rid of the birthday cake, and sit with that line, "I was hiding." It's the answer to the question "What is the story of my life; what is the truth of who I am." I'm a person who hides. I'm not someone hiding a birthday cake. If you go off into that direction, you will end up writing about the birthday cake, and there will be no discovery. But if you massage the fact that the story of your life is about hiding, if you massage the fact that the truth of who you are is that you are hiding, then the discovery at the end of the massage will create a moment of truth that will startle both you and the reader.

> When my brother walked in, **I was hiding** the birthday cake. I'm always hiding something. **I don't want anyone to see me.** Not the real me. **I'm afraid no one will like me.** The real me is a blur. I've learned to fake it, but I know the truth about myself. The real me is lazy, stupid, incompetent, confused. The real me is . . . The real me is ugly. **I'm ugly.** I'm the reason my father drinks. I'm the reason my mother sleeps till noon. I never want to go to school. I just want to stay under the covers. **I'm lazy.** I'm the lazy boy. The stupid boy. The ugly boy. Not just ugly, but a bad person. **I'm a bad person. I'm a bad boy.**

It starts from the reporting voice—"When my brother came in I was hiding the birthday cake." But once I started to massage the core transformation line of that sentence, I was no longer talking about hiding a birthday cake; it wasn't about *what* I was hiding, it was about *hiding*. It was the answer to the question, "What is the truth of my life?" Answer: I was hiding. But there's a deeper truth below that. The deeper truth was that I didn't want to be seen because—to massage deeper—I was afraid that if people really saw me, they'd reject me. And deeper: Because I was ugly. No, go deeper: Because I was a bad person. Deeper: Because I was a bad boy.

We all hide parts of ourselves, so that realization didn't plummet into the deep voice, but it was the first step of the massage, and eventually I got to a truth that was deep enough to stop me in my tracks—"I'm a bad boy." As I wrote those words, I could feel my gut churning. After years of self-actualization, all the layers of confidence and self-possession and there I was, still haunted by the sense that deep down, I'm a bad boy. What struck me was not the bad part, but the bad *boy* part. I was still a boy. A child. A scared child locked in the closet because I had done something bad. I was in the deep voice. I could feel it. Like the actor who has said a line a hundred times in a particular scene and then, one night, the impact of the words sink in. The actor feels it as she's never felt it before.

Horizontal vs. Vertical Massage

One minute you could be writing about your brother and his birthday cake, the next about a childhood pain so deep it's in your bone marrow. It's not the whole journal entry, but it takes

51

the writer somewhere unexpected; it takes the writing from the reporting voice to the deep voice. Be careful not to confuse the object of the sentence (the birthday cake) with the meaning of the transformation line. The birthday cake itself won't take you deeper. You'll just list all the things you're hiding. "I'm hiding the birthday cake, I'm hiding my feelings," etc. I call this horizontal massage. You're not going deeper, you're merely making a list. Nothing wrong with that; lists can be interesting in a piece grounded by the deep voice. But in a vertical massage, each new sentence is a deeper transformation line. You're peeling back the layers of the onion, getting to the core.

The list that results from horizontal massage:

I was hiding the birthday cake. I was hiding my feelings. I was hiding my love. I was hiding my fear. I was hiding my . . . (fill in the blanks).

Massage it vertically and we get something different:

> I was hiding.
> I don't want people to see me.
> I'm afraid people won't like me.
> I'm ugly.
> I'm a bad person.
> I'm a bad boy.

Had I massaged the transformation line horizontally, I would have discovered a series of truths, I might have gone deeper, but not as deep. I felt exposed writing those words. I wanted to get into bed and turn the TV on. Maybe watch an episode of *The Office* or *Seinfeld*, where smart people humiliate themselves and I can feel superior. But such characters are written by people who have made contact with their own humiliation. That's the deep voice. That's a willingness to follow a feeling to its core. You can make a poem out of it later, or a sitcom. But people will be drawn to it because of its truth.

The Birthday Cake

Most transformation lines have what I call "a birthday cake." The *what* part of the sentence. "I never take my time when I do my homework." The core part of that transformation line is "I never take," and the birthday cake part of that sentence is "my time when I do my homework." If I get into the birthday cake part of the sentence, it won't take me as deep as the core transformation line. If I massage "I never take," it's about my not taking, not feeling like I deserve anything. So don't get distracted by the cake. It's interesting, but it won't take you deep. You can always come back to the cake, later, when you're re-writing. But for now, get into the habit of following the core of the transformation line, rather than the story you were telling. It's easy to get distracted by the story and miss the best transformation lines. Writing in your journal is a workout in process, so for now the exercise is more important than the story. As you write, it's inevitable that some story will emerge. The transformation line is like an off-ramp on the freeway. You're driving in a certain direction, toward Bakersfield, say, but remember you're looking for the transformation line exit, so don't miss it because you're focused on getting to Bakersfield. The transformation line will always take you somewhere unexpected. Say you're writing about tying a suitcase to the top of your car. "I'm trying to hold on to the rope, but it slips out of my hands," you write. You're not in the deep voice, you're reporting a story of your road trip. But the transformation line has nothing to do with the car or the suitcase or the rope. It has nothing to do with the road trip. If you follow the transformation line, it's going to take you to a deeper place, an emotion you weren't expecting. "I'm trying to hold on." That's the core of your transformation line. You're trying to hold on. Forget the rope. What's the truth of your life? "I'm trying to hold on." Massage that transformation line vertically, and you'll be off on a road trip to the heart of your truth. You'll be in the deep voice, and so will your reader, alongside you. What to do once the reader is hooked is the subject of the next chapter, but for now, I want you to get the hang of writing like you talk; learn to spot juicy transformation lines and learn to massage them to reach the deep voice.

A "Two-Fer"—Two Transformation Lines for the Price of One

Before writing further in your journal, review what you have already written, go back and underline all your transformation lines. Any sentence that has "I" in it is, by definition, a transformation line. The deepest, juiciest, most potent transformation lines will *not* be about feelings. That's why I want you to get into the habit of spotting them. The best ones seem innocuous. You're hiding a birthday cake, holding on to a rope. But the core of the transformation line reveals something about character: hiding, for instance, or never taking, or holding on.

A woman in one of my classes read a journal entry about shopping for antiques in Pasadena. "I'm always on the lookout for a bargain," she wrote. Then she proceeded to write about how she liked shopping and about the old chest she found, took home, refinished, and put in her bedroom. It wasn't deep writing, just a narrative told in the reporting voice. She was so intent on her story that she passed up the transformation line, which would have taken her somewhere deeper. She was always on the lookout for a bargain. No self-revelation there, no big discovery. But once you make note of the fact that it's a transformation line, you're more likely to massage it. And how do we know it's a transformation line? Because it has the word "I" in it. It's an easy one to pass up—she's wasn't talking about her feelings. But there were actually two transformation lines in that sentence—a "two-fer" 'cause you get two for the price of one.

Once you get rid of the birthday cake, which in this case is " . . . for a bargain," you're left with "I'm always on the lookout." What's the story of your life? I'm always on the lookout. When she went back and massaged it, she went deeper than she thought she'd ever be comfortable going. She was always on the lookout, she wrote, never at ease. She was guarded, afraid of being hurt, never at ease with herself. Mistrustful, suspicious, fearful. Always on the lookout. By the time she had massaged the line to the deep voice, she retrieved a story of a mother who was always anxious, a father who would lose his temper at the drop of a spoon. Had she not massaged the transformation line, she'd never have discovered that truth in her writing. But when you are aware of the potential of a transformation line, when you get rid of the "birthday cake" and massage the core of the sentence, you will find yourself going into the undiscovered country of your deep voice.

Now what about the second transformation line? The one inside the first? In the sentence "I'm always on the lookout for a bargain," we cut "for a bargain," because it's the birthday cake part of the sentence. But what about "the lookout." Maybe that's a birthday cake too. If we cut it, we get "I'm always on." When she massaged that, the piece went in a totally different direction. She wrote about the persona she showed to the world, how she never let anyone know who she really was. She was always "on," like a nightclub comic. Once again, the piece became compelling because everyone could relate to it. She was always on, wearing a mask, putting on a show, hiding her deepest self.

From Caboose to Locomotive

Note how we got to the second transformation line, the one inside the first. Imagine a train with several cars trailing behind the locomotive. The locomotive is the engine, the core transformation line, and the cars are all the words in the rest of the sentence. You start by disconnecting the cars, one by one, working backwards from the caboose until you get to the core transformation line. So with the sentence—"I'm always on the lookout for a bargain."—we disconnect "for a bargain," and we're left with "I'm always on the lookout." But we can also disconnect "the lookout." Now we've got, "I'm always on." Good transformation line, worth massaging. What if we disconnect "on." Now we've got, "I'm always." Might be worth massaging as well. Or maybe it's too vague. Maybe there's not enough there for your psyche to dig into. Sometimes, you can cut too much. The more you practice massaging transformation lines, the more you develop a knack for isolating the core of the transformation line, of finding that engine that will take you deep into territory you might never have discovered.

The Other Side of the Same Coin

Notice the chart on page 57. I've broken down various sentences under component parts. The first sentence is easy—*I was hiding the birthday cake*—the first part is the transformation line *I was hiding*, and the second part is the birthday cake; in this case, literally, the birthday cake. When you go down the chart, you'll see the sentence, *I'm still sitting on the dock of the bay*. There are three parts to that sentence, and one of the parts is a two-fer. So you could massage that sentence as having a transformation line, *I'm still*, (the story of my life is that I am still, I remain, I hold back, I am solitary, etc.), or one could massage it as *I'm still sitting* (I haven't moved, I hold my place, etc.). In either case, the phrase *on the dock of the bay* is your birthday cake and should be ignored. The last few examples on the chart give you a sense of how to contextualize a transformation line in terms of "the other side of the same coin." When you say, *I always keep*, the implication is *I never give*. But seeing the transformation line in terms of "the other side of the *same* coin" can be tricky. We're not going for the opposite. Remember, it's the *same* coin, so both statements are compatible. *I always keep* is compatible with *I never give*. It's the other side of the SAME coin, so it's not the opposite, but the SAME idea expressed from the other end. Same house, but there's the front door and the back door.

> Front door: "I always keep."
> Back door: (therefore) "I never give."

Same coin, same house, same idea. It might be helpful to link those two statments with a "therefore." *I always keep*, therefore, *I never give*. If you go to the opposite, you'd get *I always keep* therefore *I never keep*. Nope, that doesn't work. Remember, when thinking of both possibilities, both sides of the SAME coin, inserting "therefore" between them will help you see whether or not the two statements mean the same thing.

I hold on to the rope as I descend the side of the mountain.

First, let's get rid of the birthday cake—"to the rope as I descend the side of the mountain." Now we're left with the core transformation line, "I hold on." Before I start to massage that, I say to myself, "What is the story of my life, what is the truth of who I am?" Answer: "I hold on." But what about the other side of the SAME coin. Let's imagine a "therefore."

I hold on, therefore, I never let go.

Aha! Another transformation line, another way to think about the implication of that massage. "I never let go." I could massage it in the direction of "holding on," but I could also massage it in the direction of "never letting go." Both possibilities are provocative, both will take me to a deeper truth. Not all transformation lines offer the possibility of both sides of the SAME coin, but when they do, it's a good idea to have a sense of that, since it will suggest different ways of massaging it.

Let's try another sentence: "I hope it won't rain tomorrow." The birthday cake is "it won't rain tomorrow." We cut away the caboose and as many cars as we can until we get to the locomotive: "I hope." So far so good. Now, what's the other side of the same coin? It's not "I don't hope." That would be the opposite. We're saying the same thing from a different perspective, the other side of the coin, but the SAME coin, the SAME idea. If one hopes all the time, they're not taking action, they're not getting involved. So the other side of the same coin would be "I don't act. I stand back. I wait. I don't get involved. I'm someone who hopes, but not someone who takes action." These are not opposite ideas, they are just two different ways of thinking about the same. "I hope, therefore, I don't take action." Each one will work as a transformation line. When it comes to massaging those transformation lines, you can follow the idea of hoping, or you can follow the idea of waiting, of standing back, of not getting involved. Either approach will lead to discoveries through the deep voice.

Verbs with Double Meanings

Occasionally you'll bump into a verb that has two different meanings. It's not a two-fer. It's a case of the word containing different ideas. "I miss the time I spent in high school." Okay, let's get rid of the birthday cake and all the rest of it, and we're left with "I miss." One idea of missing implies lacking, being without, longing for something. But missing can also refer to being off target, failing to hit the mark, falling short, etc. When you massage it, be aware of the possibilities, and choose the one that seems most compelling. What about the sentence "I used to work at the restaurant on the corner." Once we get rid of the restaurant on the corner (the service was bad anyway), we're left with a two-fer: "I used to work" and "I used." There's no double meaning with "I used to work." But "I used" presents two different meanings. "I used" can refer to abusing substances. It can also refer to taking advantage of others. You can be a user in that you take drugs or alcohol to alter your state of mind, or you can be a user in the sense that you take advantage of others, manipulate situations, etc. You can massage that any way you'd like, it's up to you. It's possible that both options are compelling. Pick one, or try to massage both.

What about, "I left the water running"? Transformation line: I left. But left is a verb with two possible meanings: the verb can be transitive, or intransitive. As an intransitive verb, it means you moved away, you took off, you skipped out, etc. There is no direct object. But as a transitive verb, there's an object. You left something behind, you abandoned something, you failed to bring something with you, you took nothing. In English we use the same word for either meaning, but in French, for instance, there are two different words: *partir* means to skip out, to walk away, etc., but *laisser* means to leave something behind, to leave the book on the table, to leave the clothes in the laundromat, to leave your wallet in the car. So pay attention to those tricky verbs in English that can mean two different things. I miss, I leave, I used, etc.

When you come upon a provocative transformation line, it's as if you've come to an intersection where you can turn left, turn right, or continue straight ahead. You've got several options. Same with transformation lines. Become aware of the possibilities—is it a two-fer, a verb with two meanings, is there another side to the SAME coin, will I massage it horizontally or vertically? Over time, you will develop a knack for choosing the most provocative massage, knowing which will take you deeper. When I think of writing a journal entry with every third sentence a transformation line, I imagine I'm a downhill racer who has to zig and zag around one pole after another as I speed down the snow-covered mountain. The more you do it, the better you'll get. Practice, practice, practice.

Rocket Science, Brain Surgery, and the Whole Enchilada

I realize that this is beginning to feel like rocket science or brain surgery. Why can't we just write whatever pops into our heads and go with the flow? Well, you certainly can do that. There are thousands of people who do that every day. They open their journals and write away, expressing thoughts and feelings, telling their stories. But Method Writing is about becoming a better writer, a more effective writer, creating memorable prose and poetry by touching the reader with well-developed scenes and vivid images, using the deep voice to create a tone that captures the reader's interest. Clever plots and interesting stories won't do that. It all comes down to the writing, and good writing comes down to the authentic voice of the narrator. If your approach is scattershot and lacks craft, you'll be just another writer scribbling in your journal or tapping away on your laptop in some cozy coffeeshop, hoping the muse of greatness will descend upon you. Trust me, it doesn't work that way. The muse of greatness lies within you, but unless you're willing to learn your craft, your writing will remain lifeless. The concepts considered here are not rocket science or brain surgery, but do require diligence and patience, and a willingness to master your craft through practice and a focus on process. At the table in the corner, someone is writing whatever pops into his mind. You, on the other hand, are also writing whatever pops into your mind, but your focus is on the writing itself—writing like you talk while taking notice of each transformation line; like the downhill racer, you take the ones that suggest the deepest massage. This is process with a focus, an informed craft and set of techniques that guide you through the creative flow.

Let's talk about one last idea when massaging a transformation line. I know, you've got a headache already. So take two aspirin and come back to this page in the morning. Then we'll discuss "The Whole Enchilada."

The Whole Enchilada

Okay, you're back. Hope you had a good night's sleep, or maybe you just got yourself another cup of coffee. Either way, I hope you're refreshed and ready to go on to the last tweak of massaging a transformation line. Let's say you've parsed your transformation line, cut the birthday cake, detached the caboose and the remaining cars so all that's left is the locomotive; you've considered the "two-fers" and the horizontal massage vs the vertical massage; you've even flipped the coin and looked at both sides. And after you've done all that, the whole sentence as you originally wrote it seems too compelling to break apart. The whole sentence says it all. When you come to that realization, I say just forget it and massage the whole sentence, birthday cake and all. Go for the whole enchilada.

"I blew off my life."

"I'm too jaded to love."

"I'd never realized before how alone I've felt all my life."

These sentences are too compelling to break into smaller sections. The sum is greater than their parts. You've got to massage the whole enchilada.

Now take a look at this chart, examples of transformation lines and birthday cakes, including "two-fers.":

Transformation Lines	Two-Fers	Birthday Cakes
I was hiding		the birthday cake.
I can't believe		the keys were under the table.
I never let go		of the rope in my hand.
I'm still	sitting	on the dock of the bay.
I'm always on	the lookout	for a bargain.
I'm not allowed	to take	the car on Sundays.
I quit	hoping	for rain.
I always keep	wondering	if it'll rain.
[other side of the same coin: I never give]		
I never take		my time.
[other side of the same coin: (therefore) I always give]		
I always wait		for the bus.
[other side of the same coin: (therefore) I never act, never participate]		
I wonder		if it'll rain on Sunday.
[other side of the same coin: I wonder, (therefore) I never act, never participate]		

Go back over the entries you wrote this past week and identify where the voice was coming from—head, reporting, or deep/deeper/deepest—and underline the transformation lines. Then double underline the core part of the transformation lines. Don't go back and massage them yet. For now, learn to spot a good transformation line as soon as you write it. In the next exercise, you'll follow it into unexpected directions.

☞ Further instructions will be found under the big rock by the waterfall.

Massaging the Transformation Line

"So you wanna be a writer"

At this point you may be wondering when we're gonna get to the dramatic stuff, the *sturm* and *drang* that wins Oscars. A few years after making *Frankenstein*, James Whale directed a fictionalized yarn about the British actor David Garrick, titled *The Great Garrick*. It starred Brian Aherne as Garrick and Olivia de Havilland as Germaine Dupont, the Countess de la Corbe, fleeing a marriage arranged by her father. Also in the cast were Edward Everett Horton, Lionell Atwill, Marie Wilson, and Lana Turner in a bit part as Mademoiselle Auber. In the story, Garrick is visiting France to work with the members of the *Comédie Française*. Hearing that Garrick intends to instruct them in correct acting technique, the outraged members of the troupe decide to perpetuate a hoax. Their plan is to deflate the great actor's ego by frightening him so thoroughly that he returns humiliated to England without ever setting foot in the *Comédie Française*. Before Garrick arrives from London, he stops at an inn on the outskirts of Paris. The French actors are already there, pretending to be servants. The director of the French troupe plays the innkeeper, while the rest take parts as maids, bellhops, waiters and janitors. At night, they try to frighten the actor with a series of spooky shenanigans: rattling chains, headless sleepwalkers, gunshots in the courtyard, and blood-curdling screams at the midnight hour. Their goal is to force Garrick to admit how skilled they were at playing their parts. In one running gag, Luis Alberni plays a high-strung Don Knotts-type whose job it is to sleepwalk like a madman through Garrick's room, carrying the proverbial candle. Each time he enters to begin his mad scene, he's stopped by the others who inform him that Garrick is elsewhere, wooing Olivia de Havilland, or walking in the garden, or getting a glass of milk from the kitchen. The actor is chomping at the bit, dying to play his mad scene. Finally, toward the end of the film, he's just about to go into his act when he's stopped yet again. With his hair wildly disheveled and his eyes wide with frustration, he yells, "If I don't ... get ... to go crazy, ... I'm going to go . . . . CRAZY!" Of course, in the end, Garrick teaches them a lesson or two, showing them how they gave themselves away, either by overacting, or with gestures and body language that belied their station in life. The guy playing the porter should have been more stoop-shouldered from carrying heavy baggage; the janitor's hands were as smooth as a barrister's; the inn-keeper's accent wasn't regional enough; the maid folded sheets incorrectly. Such attention to detail is what made Garrick a great actor, his ability to spot the difference between behavior that's stereotyped and behavior that's authentic to character.

"Well," you might say at this point, quill poised in your outstretched hand as the candlelight flickers on the walls of your darkened room, "what's the point of being a writer if you don't get to ... WRITE!" I'm not consigning you to bland, everyday speech forever, But first you must learn not to write well, but to write truly.

The Transformation Line as a Tool to Deepen the Voice

The deep voice is usually the hardest of the three voices to reach and sustain. The transformation line will get you there without sweating bullets or blood. When writing in your journal, the objective is to move the voice a notch deeper. You might begin with the reporting voice, then use the transformation line to take a step downward. Maybe not all the way to the gut, but a little deeper. And from there, using another transformation line, massaging it, you can get the voice down to the chest or the diaphragm, and with another transformation line, down to the gut. The transformation line is the ladder that takes you into the deep voice.

Feel the place you're coming from. Have a sense of it in your body. Is it in your throat? Your chest? Now take a breath. As you exhale, feel where your voice is in your body. Now take another breath and, as you exhale, see if you can go one notch lower. Locate yourself again. Feel where you are. Exhale. As you exhale, go deeper. Now, breathe again and this time, as you exhale, let the exhalation include a written sentence, writing (without thinking) as you exhale. The sentence that comes out does not have to be connected to what you wrote before. It *can* be, but doesn't have to be. Your breath can lead you more deeply into the body. You can do three or four such transformation lines, until you've gotten the voice to go quite deep.

Now, follow the transformation line for awhile. Take a few sentences to explore it, as if it's a path off the main trail leading you deeper into the woods of your subconscious. All well and good. But what happens if you begin writing in your journal and after a few paragraphs, you still haven't written a transformation line? You're willing and able to massage one, but nothing's come up. You might, to quote one of my former acting teachers, try faking it. Just write a bunch of sentences with "I" in them. One of them is bound to be juicy enough to massage. "But shouldn't all transformation lines come naturally? After all, this is method writing. Like Stanislavski's method acting, aren't we supposed to be coming from our truth?" Yes, of course, but it's also okay to fake it until you connect with something real.

That same acting teacher often told the class to trust that all the emotions we needed would come as long as we didn't force them. I asked once during a rehearsal, "What happens, come opening night, if I'm still not able to get the emotion in the scene?" Without hesitation, he said with a laugh, "Then you'd better act up a storm." Stanislavski called this "the truth of physical actions," where the physicality of an action—throwing a book, kneading dough, punching a pillow, contorting the face or tightening a muscle—brings on the emotion. In his first book he moved from emotion to action, but in his second book, he admitted that going from action to emotion could also work.

Laurence Olivier once told a story of working with Dustin Hoffman in *Marathon Man*. Hoffman was going through arduous preparation for a difficult scene with Olivier, but couldn't get the emotional pitch he wanted. He tried all kinds of exercises that had become basic tools for method actors. Finally, after another take that didn't go as intended, Olivier, sitting calmly in his chair, said to Hoffman in that dry, British drawl, "Have you tried .... ACK ... TING?"

Stanislavski realized that while a timid man might knock timidly on a door, the actor playing the part might feel timid merely by knocking timidly on the door. Sometimes the action feeds the emotion. It's okay to fake the massage. Eventually, the transformation lines will come naturally. Remember the Zen koan Richard Jones shared with me? "You find out who you are by acting naturally." How can one "act" naturally? That's the point of the koan. Ultimately, it's all the same, doing and feeling, each feeding the other.

The purpose of this second concept is to practice moving the voice from the *Head Voice* or the *Reporting Voice* to the *Deep Voice*. And the mechanism that does it is the Transformation Line. Don't focus on the subject matter or the quality of what you write. Whether or not you get a "good" journal entry is beside the point of the exercise. What I care about is your workout in the process.

WRITE LIKE YOU TALK.
PAY ATTENTION TO TRANSFORMATION LINES.
WHEN YOU GET A JUICY ONE,
FOLLOW IT, MASSAGE IT.

Practice Practice Practice

We already know how to get to Carnegie Hall. And we know what Tiger Woods did to win the Masters. Athletes and musicians practice, practice, practice; actors rehearse, rehearse, rehearse. When doing a scene in which the lines and the blocking have all been memorized, how do you keep a performance alive, night after night, or take after take? Actors are trained to move through a scene "moment to moment." In other words, don't play the third act while you're in the middle of the first one. To be in the moment, the actor must be "available" to the unexpected. Great actors feel an impulse, then act on that impulse. They practice doing that. A thousand practice swings a day. Ninety-nine percent of performance is the ability to repeat words and actions, not unlike a musician who repeats a series of notes. And yet, within this framework of repetition lies a crucial ability to remain open to impulse. This availability to impulse is not something you can merely turn on. It needs to be practiced. The mind doesn't follow impulses. The body does. The body reacts without thinking. As Hamlet says, "The readiness is all."

If your focus is always on the story you've already formulated, you will be hesitant to follow an impulse, an off-the-wall digression. You might say that these exercises are digressions. You can't know for sure that the exercise will work. But if you stop to think about it, the impulse is lost. Writing in your journal is about practicing the exercise, and the exercise is designed to distract you from the product/subject/idea/result. The exercise moves you into process, the tao of the moment. You can never perfect meditation, you can only practice it. So: Write like you talk. See your transformation lines. Massage the good ones. Let the massage take you somewhere unexpected.

Debunking the Myth of the 10,000-Hours Rule: What It Actually Takes to Reach Genius-Level Excellence:

How top-down attention, feedback loops, and daydreaming play into the science of success

The question of what it takes to excel—to reach genius-level acumen at a chosen endeavor—has occupied psychologists for decades and philosophers for centuries. Groundbreaking research has pointed to "grit" as a better predictor of success than IQ (see page 162), while psychologists have admonished against the dangers of slipping into autopilot in the quest for skill improvement. In recent years, one of the most persistent pop-psychology claims has been the myth of the "10,000-hour rule"—the idea that this is the amount of time one must invest in practice in order to reach meaningful success in any field. But in *Focus: The Hidden Driver of Excellence,* celebrated psychologist and journalist Daniel Goleman, best-known for his influential 1995 book *Emotional Intelligence,* debunks the 10,000-hour mythology to reveal the more complex truth beneath the popular rule of thumb:

The "10,000-hour rule"—that this level of practice holds the secret to great success in any field—has become sacrosanct gospel, echoed on websites and recited as litany in high-performance workshops. The problem: it's only half true. If you are a duffer at golf, say, and make the same mistakes every time you try a certain swing or putt, 10,000 hours of practicing that error will not improve your game. You'll still be a duffer, albeit an older one.

No less an expert than Anders Ericsson, the Florida State University psychologist whose research on expertise spawned the 10,000-hour rule, and was the basis for Malcolm Gladwell's book *Outliers,* said, "You don't get benefits from mechanical repetition, but by adjusting your execution over and over to get closer to your goal" (see page 162).

"You have to tweak the system by pushing," he adds, "allowing for more errors at first as you increase your limits."

The secret to continued improvement, it turns out, isn't the amount of time invested but the *quality* of that time. It sounds simple and obvious enough, and yet so much of both our formal education and the informal ways in which we go about pursuing success in skill-based fields is built around the premise of sheer time investment. Instead, the factor Ericsson and other psychologists have identified as the main predictor of success is *deliberate focused practice*—persistent training to which you give your full concentration rather than just your time—and where this persistent practice is often guided by a skilled expert, coach, or mentor. It's a qualitative difference in how you pay attention, not a quantitative measure of clocking in the hours. Goleman writes:

> Hours and hours of practice are necessary for great performance, but not sufficient. How experts in any domain pay attention while practicing makes a crucial difference. For instance, in his much-cited study of violinists—the one that showed the top tier had practiced more than 10,000 hours—Ericsson found the experts did so with full concentration on improving a particular aspect of their performance that a master teacher identified.

Goleman identifies a second necessary element: a feedback loop that allows you to spot errors as they occur and correct them, much like ballet dancers use mirrors during practice. He writes:

> Ideally that feedback comes from someone with an expert eye and so every world-class sports champion has a coach. If you practice without such feedback, you don't get to the top ranks. The feedback matters and the concentration does, too—not just the hours.

Additionally, the optimal kind of attention requires top-down focus. While daydreaming may have its creative benefits, in the context of deliberate practice it only dilutes the efficiency of the process. Goleman writes:

> Daydreaming defeats practice; those of us who browse TV while working out will never reach the top ranks. Paying full attention seems to boost the mind's

processing speed, strengthen synaptic connections, and expand or create neural networks for what we are practicing. At least at first. But as you master how to execute the new routine, repeated practice transfers control of that skill from the top-down system for intentional focus to bottom-up circuits that eventually make its execution effortless. At that point you don't need to think about it—you can do the routine well enough on automatic.

But this is where the amateurs and the experts diverge—too much automation, and you hit the "OK plateau," ceasing to grow and stalling at proficiency level. If you're going for genius, you need to continually shift away from autopilot and back into active, corrective attention:

> Amateurs are content at some point to let their efforts become bottom-up operations. After about fifty hours of training—whether in skiing or driving—people get to that 'good-enough' performance level, where they can go through the motions more or less effortlessly. They no longer feel the need for concentrated practice, but are content to coast on what they've learned. No matter how much more they practice in this bottom-up mode, their improvement will be negligible.

The experts, in contrast, keep paying attention top-down, intentionally counteracting the brain's urge to automatize routines. They concentrate actively on those moves they have yet to perfect, on correcting what's not working in their game, and on refining their mental models of how to play the game, or focusing on the particulars of feedback from a seasoned coach. Those at the top never stop learning: if at any point they start coasting and stop such smart practice, too much of their game becomes bottom-up and their skills plateau.

But even with the question of quality resolved, there's still that of quantity: Just how much "deliberate practice" is enough? Focused attention, like willpower, is like a muscle and gets fatigued with exertion:

Ericsson finds world-class champions—whether weight-lifters, pianists, or a dog-sled team—tend to limit arduous practice to about four hours a day. Rest and restoring physical and mental energy get built into the training regimen. They seek to push themselves and their bodies to the max, but not so much that their focus gets diminished in the practice session. Optimal practice maintains optimal concentration.

The Accidents of Genius

Don't allow your talent to limit you. Allow for the accidents of genius. (See Appendix article "The Art of Genius," p. 196 and the note that follows it on p. 199.) How many times have you seen a play in which an object falls to the floor by accident, and the actors ignore it because it's not central to the scene and they didn't rehearse picking it up? They go on talking, saying their lines as rehearsed, but the audience remains focused on that object. You're waiting for someone to pick it up, or at least notice it. In shooting a scene in a film, the actor's tendency would be to stop the scene and start over. There's a scene in *Midnight Cowboy* when Dustin Hoffman as the creepy con man Ratso Rizzo walks down the street with his new friend Joe Buck, played by Jon Voight. The filmmakers had no permit to take over an entire New York City block, so director John Schlesinger rigged up a hidden camera in a van and radio-miked the actors. It was finally going well after numerous takes when a cab ran a red light and almost hit Hoffman and Voight as they were crossing the street. Hoffman—still in character as Rizzo—banged on the hood of the cab and yelled, "We're walking here!" Schlesinger wisely kept the take and it has become one of cinema's indelible moments. Later, in an interview in the *Los Angeles Times*, Hoffman commented, "That was me reacting very angrily, partly out of fear because we almost got hit but also because he was ruining the take . . . I really wanted to say, 'We're shooting here! And you're ruining it!'" But Hoffman stayed in character and followed the impulse, coming up with one of the signature lines of that movie.

Sometimes the impulse is a small action that reveals something profound about the character. It isn't rehearsed but the actor is "available" to the moment, so when the moment comes, he reacts without thinking. During the filming of *On the Waterfront*, Marlon Brando and Eva Maria Saint were shooting a scene on a playground, near a swing set. As they were walking, Saint accidentally dropped one of her gloves. Most actors would have ignored it and gone on with the scene. Or picked it up and handed it back. But what Brando did was truly unexpected. He picked it up, continuing the dialogue, and some impulse took over. He fondled the glove, played with it, then in a gesture completely incongruous for the boxer he was portraying, he put the glove on his own hand and sat on the swing. All this went on while they were saying their lines. The boxer sits on a swing wearing a woman's dainty white glove. It was shocking and poignant, so revealing of this character's inner life, of the tenderness buried there. And it was typical of Brando to have done something like that. Whatever had been rehearsed, he was available to the impulse of the moment.

It's something you practice, being available to an impulse. The pull of what was planned is very strong. The same is true for writing, when an idea has formed in your mind and you write to flesh it out. Thus, if you're writing about a road trip, it takes a certain "availability" to take the detour of your transformation line. I call this "taking the Slauson Cutoff." (Johnny Carson had a running joke about taking the Slauson Cutoff, and I've used that expression in my classes for over 30 years. Some years ago, during a tribute to Johnny Carson, David Letterman happened to make a joke, referring to the Slauson Cutoff. The next day, one of my students asked me if Letterman had ever taken my class.)

So you're driving up the San Diego Freeway, going north toward Bakersfield, and you see the Transformation Line (the Slauson Cutoff). Take it. Forget Bakersfield. See where the transformation line takes you. Maybe you'll get lost. Instead of pulling over to use your GPS or call a friend, keep going, one massage after another. The more you write, the further away from Bakersfield you get. Only now, you're paying attention to where you are. You look at the houses, at the trees lining the street, at the buildings. One has a broken window. It scares you for some reason. You don't know why. You keep driving (writing). You see a car on someone's front lawn. The tires are flat. Then you remember something. A broken window, the one in the back door of the house you lived in as a child. You're getting further and further away from Bakersfield, you're not even on the Slauson Cut-off any longer, but on a dirt road leading you into the past. Your mother broke the window when your father wouldn't talk to her. He sat at the kitchen table eating his dinner and refused to look at her. As if she weren't even talking. You watched her grow agitated, then she started breaking things. You went down the hall to your room. You didn't cry. You felt flat. Emptied of air. Now that you think of it, you felt that way even after you left home. In college, in the dorm when your roommate was laughing with friends—they were your friends, too—you noticed that flat feeling. As if you weren't really there, with them, but back home, in that kitchen. The air's gone out of you. Where's the air? The sky is beautiful, punctuated by clouds, but the air's missing. There's never enough air.

When you take the Slauson Cutoff—that is, when you follow the transformation line—you're not aiming for product, you're in the creative process. So: write like you talk, pay attention to the possibilities of the Transformation Line, and be available to impulses (those accidents of your genius!). Once you're done with the massage and where it takes you, you can always find your way back to the freeway, back to the road that leads to Bakersfield.

Tonal Dynamics

In the poem "Birches" by Robert Frost, the poet's use of tonal dynamics is dazzling. Sometimes he's simply reporting; other times he has the inflection of a comedian. Sometimes he's down in the deep voice, and sometimes his language is elevated and literary. When he catches himself being self-important (using poetic effects), he switches to a conversational tone, as if to say, "Well, as I was saying before I got carried away, I really like potato salad." To shift tones from the reporting voice to the deep voice, from spoken diction to a literary style, is what I call tonal dynamics. It is the mark of a writer who can hold the reader's attention, not with *what* he's saying, but with *how* he's saying it. Frost's use of natural idiom and everyday diction set him apart from most of the poets of his day, and along with Ezra Pound and William Carlos Williams, he changed our notion of what a poem could be. Hayden Carruth's excellent anthology of 20th century poetry, *The Voice That Is Great Within Us*, leads off with the work of Robert Frost, and says this about him in the biographical note:

> Born in 1875, his first poem was published in 1894; but during the next twenty years his work was consistently rejected by American editors. Finally, discouraged but still determined, Frost went to England in 1912, and there won the support of influential poets and critics, including Ezra Pound. His first two books, *A Boy's Will* and *North of Boston* were published in London. In 1915 he returned to America. Thereafter his success was unquestioned: he won many honors, including four Pulitzer Prizes for poetry, and became not only the most popular serious poet in the country, but one of the most generally respected among fellow writers. Frost's poetic practice was based on what he called "sentence sounds," the natural tones and rhythms of speech cast loosely against standard poetic forms. *Conventional as it may seem today* [my italics], it was a new departure in its time, making Frost a distinctly modern poet.

The opening lines of "Birches" have a poetic flair, but if you pay attention to the diction, you'll see how the tonal dynamics of everyday speech carry the writer's passionate intent.

> When I see birches bend from left to right
> across the lines of straighter darker trees,
> I like to think some boy's been swinging them.
> But swinging doesn't bend them down to stay.
> Ice storms do that.

Anyone reading those lines would notice their lyricism, their poetic effects, but what is significant is Frost's use of "natural tones and rhythms of speech." What is significant is not the poetic phrases, but the structure of the sentences themselves. There's an aliveness to the speaker's voice, and we're hooked, not by the lyricism, but by the tonal dynamics. The speaker continues, at first with an introspective tone, then he gets carried away again, so much so that Frost realizes the need to break the tension with another tonal change.

> Often you must have seen them
> Loaded with ice a sunny winter morning
> After a rain. They click upon themselves
> As the breeze rises, and turn many-colored
> As the stir cracks and crazes their enamel.
> Soon the sun's warmth makes them shed crystal shells
> Shattering and avalanching on the snow-crust—

Reaching a fever-pitch of poetic diction, Frost switches tone once more and snaps off a sentence much like a comic saying, "There were so many broken bottles all over the floor you'd think my brother won the lottery!"

> Such heaps of broken glass to sweep away
> You'd think the inner dome of heaven had fallen.

Then the voice drops and becomes poetic again. So poetic, in fact, that he's in danger of losing the reader, so he returns to a casual, off-hand diction.

> They are dragged to the withered bracken by the load,
> And they seem not to break; though once they are bowed
> So low for long, they never right themselves:
> You may see their trunks arching in the woods
> Years afterwards, trailing their leaves on the ground
> Like girls on hands and knees that throw their hair
> *Before them over their heads to dry in the sun.*　　　　　*[now comes the tonal shift]*
>
> But I was going to say when Truth broke in
> *With all her matter-of-fact about the ice-storm*　　　*[then back down to a*
> I should prefer to have some boy bend them　　　　　　*transformation line]*
> As he went out and in to fetch the cows—
> Some boy too far from town to learn baseball,
> Whose only play was what he found himself,
> Summer or winter, and could play alone.

The poem continues with a story of the boy who subdues his father's trees, climbing as high as he can, making the trees bend as he gets closer to the top, until the treetop becomes a springboard, and he jumps "outward, feet first, with a swish, kicking his way down through the air to the ground." Here is where the poem deepens as the speaker recognizes how personal—and important—the story really is.

> *So was I once myself a swinger of birches.*　　　*[big transformation line,*
> And so I dream of going back to be.　　　　　　　*Frost is massaging from one*
> It's when I'm weary of considerations,　　　　　*transformation line to the next]*

And life is too much like a pathless wood
Where your face burns and tickles with the cobwebs
Broken across it, and one eye is weeping
From a twig's having lashed across it open.

[now the last series of transformation lines brings
the poem to its metaphysical conclusion]

I'd like to get away from earth awhile
And then come back to it and begin over.
May no fate willfully misunderstand me
And half grant what I wish and snatch me away
Not to return. Earth's the right place for love:
I don't know where it's likely to go better.
I'd like to go by climbing a birch tree,
And climb black branches up a snow-white trunk
Toward heaven, till the tree could bear no more,
But dipped its top and set me down again.
That would be good both going and coming back.
One could do worse than be a swinger of birches.

[the voice goes back up, as if
to say, "whoops, knock on
wood, I wasn't complaining."]
[Then the last few
transformation lines]

Frost's poem is an example of how the rhythms of speech give a piece of writing power and immediacy. The deep voice and transformation lines make the poem intimate and revelatory. It doesn't matter whether it's in the form of a poem or in prose. When we write with the flow of speech, with the inflections and tonal dynamics that come naturally when we're open to impulse, the sentences jump off the page. When Hayden Carruth wrote that Frost's ability to use natural spoken tones cast against standard poetic forms made him a distinctly modern poet, he should have added that this ability was characteristic of all great writers, from the Greeks to the Romans, from Dante to Shakespeare, from Proust to Hemingway. Many writers strive to write well-written sentences; often they strain to be interesting, not realizing that it's the deep voice that hooks the reader, not the clever sentence. These kinds of tonal shifts are integral to what the Greeks and Romans called rhetoric and dialectic. When Plato listed them as prime components of good writing and speaking, it set the standard for oratory throughout the Middle Ages, the Renaissance, and into modern times. In every age there's a tendency to forget these principles; writing becomes stultified. Then along comes a writer—like Shakespeare, say—who writes in the natural speech of his time. It sounds easy, but it's not, because so many of us are scared that our experience, our own voice, is not enough to hold people's attention, so we fancy it up, thinking, "that'll show 'em I've got something to say and the skill to say it," but the rhythms of speech and authenticity of voice are what compel the reader.

When you work in your journals this week, you may be tempted to emulate the poetic effects of Frost's poem. Don't. It's important to stay with the exercise: Write like you talk and use the transformation line to get the voice deeper. Frost didn't massage the transformation line as much as I want you to, because he wasn't doing an exercise. "Birches" has an intensity of emotion and image that you may not get in a simple journal entry, but you're doing an exercise, not writing a poem or story. To try to create a finished piece now may lead to "overacting," rather than mastery of this essential process. Eventually, going deep will become so natural you won't have to use the transformation line. You'll simply go there, instinctively. But for now, just do the exercise. You'll thank me in the morning.

> Every day we slaughter our finest impulses. That is why we get a heartache when we read those lines written by the hand of a master and recognize them as our own, as the tender shoots which we stifled because we lacked the faith to believe in our own powers, our own criterion of truth and beauty. Everyone, when they get quiet, when they become desperately honest with themselves, is capable of uttering profound truths. We all derive from the same source. There is no mystery about the origin of things. We are all part of creation, all kings, all poets, all musicians; we have only to open up, only to discover what is already there.
>
> —Henry Miller

I struggle with the process every time I write. It would be so much easier if I knew what I was going to write about. Even in a longer piece, such as a novel or a play, one gets lost in the dark. What will happen next? What are these characters going to do? It takes energy to write from the deep voice, to massage those transformation lines, energy I don't always have. Those images from movies of the writer hitting the typewriter keys, plumes of smoke rising from his cigarette—those images show a writer in deep thought, trying to squeeze something out of his brain. Well, that to me is child's play compared to the act of trying to dig something out of your soul. Why does it wait for me to come calling? Can't it come looking for me for a change? I was asked to contribute a piece of writing for a project celebrating the opening of the Los Angeles Museum of Contemporary Art, or MOCA. A dozen other Los Angeles artists had also been asked to contribute: a painter, a photographer, a graphic artist, etc. I had a six-month deadline, and procrastinated day after day. Finally, on the Friday it was due, I got a call from one of the designers of the book.

"How's it coming?" he asked.

"Great," I said. I hadn't written one sentence.

"Well," he said, "we're going to San Francisco for the weekend. Can you drop it by our offices on Monday?"

"Oh, terrific," I said, "that'll give me a chance to do some last-minute polishing."

Polishing? More like dynamiting granite. I'd written nothing. What was I going to write? I couldn't think. To top it off, I hadn't even been to the museum yet. I had no idea what it looked like, what it felt like to walk around in its galleries. So I went there Sunday afternoon, and came home and started to write. I still had no idea what I was going to say, so I started with the moment and tried not to think of a result. What eventually came up was a memory of one of the formative experiences of my life. It didn't come up until I was in the middle of the piece; then, as if by chance, it popped into my head. One of those lucky accidents. And it came out of the transformation line and the deep voice.

Sunday Morning

Sunday morning. Spring. I wake to the sun lifting one leg over the top of the Ticor Building on Wilshire Boulevard. The new leaves on the tree outside my bedroom window are tinged with sunlight. If only I were a photographer or painter I'd freeze this moment and crawl into it.

Sunday morning. I have to get up but my body wants to drown right here in the bed. Spring ambles up the street waving its arms. A matinee today. I have to be at the theater by two. Yesterday, I find out from my agent that I didn't get the part I was counting on.

> *Eat this, they say.*
> *It's good for you.*
> *You've eaten it before.*
> *The next one will be sweet.*

I eat and concentrate on the window, on the tree, on the sun beginning to beat its chest as it comes over the top of the tallest building.

I drive down Beverly Boulevard, take the curve where it changes into 1st Street, turn on Grand and park right across from the museum. It's just after ten, hardly any cars on the street. MOCA doesn't open till eleven. The sun has followed me all the way, reflecting off the Security Pacific Bank Building, glass and steel going all the way up.

I get off on this urban sleekness, especially the unfinished building across the street, another skeleton of steel and concrete. Someone should stick a sign on it, make it part of MOCA, part of the Permanent Collection, and leave it just as it is, unfinished. No clear line where the museum ends and the rest of the city begins. One easy flow, stretching all the way back into our homes, into the very center of our lives.

I walk past the California Plaza sign, running my hand along the chrome and glass, then head downstairs for a cup of coffee and cinnamon roll at the "Il Panino." There's a girl two tables over, in the sun. We both drink our coffee in silence, checking our watches, writing something down in our journals.

She's an art student from Santa Barbara come to see the Jasper Johns. She asks what am I here to see. "Oh," I say, "the art. Just the art. I don't care. Just something."

> *I AM FIVE YEARS OLD.*
> *I don't understand anything.*
> *Hot and humid days;*
> *nights, dark and mysterious.*
> *They take me to school.*

I stare at the blackboard.
The kid from around the corner beats me up at recess.
Some nights my father doesn't come home.
My mother shrieks on the telephone.
My pet turtle dries up in the sun.
My uncle dies on the floor in the empty kitchen.
Who is the world?
Why is the moon where the sun is?
If the street goes nowhere, why is it in my bed?
What is the rain that rains just rain,
and why does it rain crows, or bats, or baseball gloves?
How is the pencil writing my name,
and why is my name the name for the thing that fixes tires,
the name for the flag on the pirate ship,
the name for the clown crushed in the box?
Outside, the kids continue to jump rope on the sidewalk,
singing, "A my name is Alice,"
seeing everything, but knowing nothing.

I AM SIX.
The class takes a bus with Miss Cook
to the Delgado Museum on Elysian Fields Avenue.
We're going to see Vincent Van Gogh.
Later, when I tell my mother,
who was born in Antwerp,
she says to say it like this,
Vincent Van Gough,
and she coughs as she says it.
Van Gough! Van Gough!
But Miss Cook says Van Go.
We are marched single-file from one room to another,
walking past each painting that hangs just above our heads.

I look up at the painting.
I can't believe what I am seeing.
Everything mysterious and horrible about the world vanishes.
He paints like I paint!
Trees outlined in black.
All those wavy lines, all those colors.
And he piles the paint on.
He's wasting all that paint,
just like I did before they told me not to waste all the paint.
He sees everything I see.
The moon is where the sun is.
The street that goes nowhere is in his bed.

It's not just raining rain,
it's raining crows and bats.
He sees the blood, he see the faces.
Everything so bright it's on fire.
Everything so dark it swallows me up.
The man cuts his ear off.
The man leans against the table so sad.
The man dies on the floor of the empty kitchen.
I stop in front of the painting with crows above a cornfield.
The world I see is real.
I bring my hand up and touch the dried paint.
It's real!
Mounds of paint, swirls of paint, rivers of paint!
But it's not paint.
It's real.
It's the world.

"Don't touch the painting!" Miss Cook yells.
She pulls my hand away.
She yanks my arm into the center of the room.
"Never ever touch a painting!"
She shoves me into a seat in the back of the bus.
It doesn't matter.
The world is real.
I fold my hands in my lap.
I know what I will do.
I will write about the real world.

11 o'clock. The girl heads off toward the Jasper Johns. I walk into the J. Paul Getty Trust Gallery and find the Geary cardboard chairs and cardboard houses. "Can I sit in them?" I ask the guard. "They can be sat in," he says, "but you can't sit in them."

"Oh," I say, and walk into the room with the huge pavilion shaped like a fish. I walk into the belly of the fish. The wood inside is so beautiful.

"Don't touch the wood, please," says the guard.

I wander over to the Nauman video. A clown is being tortured on simultaneous video screens. "Clown Torture," it's called. Later, in the Permanent Collection, I bump into the girl from Santa Barbara. In the center of the room, a metal sculpture of a man moves his motorized mouth

up

and

down.

A silent
                    YAK

                         YAK

                                             YAK

This, I understand. I stand as close to it as I can. The guard watches me suspiciously.

Over in the North Gallery there's an empty spot in one corner. Something was there, but it's been   removed. I make a sign for myself and hang it around my neck. I stand in the corner of the Permanent Collection, North Gallery, as still as I can, one arm out in the gesture of an actor about to speak.

> *Eat this.*
> *You've eaten it before.*
> *The next one will be sweet.*
> *The street that goes nowhere is in your bed.*
> *You know nothing,*
> *but you can see everything.*

A woman and her little girl walk up to me. "What does the sign say?" the girl asks. "Touch me," her mother says. "The sign says touch me."

So the child reaches out a hand and touches my own.

☝

Have a good week or two of writing. Massage your transformation lines. Write at least 2-3 pages a day. Then, in a week or two, come back to this book. I'll be here waiting for you, ready to take you through the next concept. I know you may be tempted to read the next chapter, but don't rush through this one. The next concept is very technical. It's best to wait until you've had a few weeks of working on the emotional and psychological techniques of the first two concepts. Not only are you practicing writing like you talk, you're practicing letting go of the need to make your journal entry "good." Focus on the exercise, not on whether or not you find a good story, idea, or theme. This may be harder than you think, since once you put on your writing cap and assume the writer's pose, you may be tempted to ACKT. Follow your voice, and when you hit the Slauson Cut-Off (a good transformation line), take it, massage it. See where it takes you. Avoid preconceived notions. I've had students tell me they didn't write because they couldn't think of anything to write about. If in the middle of writing your journal entry, someone approaches and asks, "What are you writing about," tell them, "Who the hell knows?"

Remember, without a craft, a series of techniques, a "method," the actor may give a performance that lacks specificity and authenticity. We call this "playing an attitude." Of course there is "flow," that term we love to invoke, as if going with the flow is all that lies at the heart of the creative process. But in the hands of a professional, going with the flow follows a grounding in the fundamentals—techniques that teach the actor to stay in the moment, to make specific choices about actions and intentions, while remaining open to impulse and improvisation. The same is true for the writer. The motor that invisibly powers a particular piece of writing is voice. When you write, focus on the voice, how to move it from reporting to deep, how to massage your transformation line. A thousand practice swings.

One could do worse than be a swinger of birches.

NEXT CHAPTER: Striking While the Transformation Line is Hot! ⇨

Chapter 6

CONCEPT #3:

IMAGE-MOMENT

Striking While the Transformation Line Is Hot

Before you delve into the arcane mysteries of the Image-Moment concept, read over the graphic spread on pages 126–127. That's the concept in a nutshell, your cheat sheet, you might say. Do it now, then come back and continue reading. The function of the Image-Moment is to create a cinematic effect. Good writers do this all the time. The scenes they create are so vivid, they make you feel like you're watching a movie. Once you learn to master this basic concept, you'll find there are endless variations, and Image-Moment will become the basic building block of all your narrative sequences. But it's not something you'd naturally do when telling a story, it's not intuitive. When you read this chapter, it's best not to let it wash over you, like you would a story. Pay attention to each section and make notes if you have to. Move on to each succeeding section only after you are clear on the concept explained up to that point. I've noticed that most of my students rush through this chapter, and though I may repeat a basic concept multiple times, they seem not to get it because they weren't really paying close attention. I say this to prepare you. This concept will make your writing vivid and compelling, but you may have a tendency to gloss over it, and in the end, it will not work. Image-Moment works, but you must work it, as well.

Image-Moment is a mechanical device with several moving parts, but in the end, it's really quite simple. Here's the concept in a nutshell: Between two lines of dialogue, you insert **static description** or between two lines of action, you insert static description. **An action must be instantaneous, no more than two seconds.** It's as simple as that. If it's so simple, why do so many of my students struggle with this, why do they often get it wrong? I don't know. The only conclusion I can draw is that my explanation is faulty, or that they read the text but didn't pay close attention. For instance, you've just read the words that an action must be instantaneous, that it can't last more than two seconds. And yet, at some point, you will write what you consider an action, and it will not be instantaneous, it will last longer than two seconds, like someone walking across a room, or going up the stairs to get a book, or traveling to Bench Point, Iowa, or going to college and getting married and having five kids. Those are not actions, though I must admit, as I sit here and write this, going to college and getting married and raising our son Josh seems like it all happened in a flash. But common sense must prevail. Slapping the table or throwing a ball or biting into a baloney sandwich are all actions; walking across the ballroom floor, driving down the street, going to Paris, those are not actions, they're events, which are made up of dozens, if not hundreds, of actions. Another theory of why this concept poses problems is that it has to do with our inability to walk and talk at the same time—meaning when we're writing, we become so engrossed in the story we're trying to tell, that we don't pay attention to the particulars of the exercise, of the concept. Who knows, maybe it's a combination of all those reasons. In any case, as I often say, do the exercise, forget your story. Here are two examples in which I've made bold the dialogue and/or action that serve as bookends to the moment. First, the dialogue example:

> **"When are you coming home," my mother asked.** [bookend]
> She was wearing a red apron, standing in the kitchen. Sunlight filtered through the yellow curtains on the windows. There was a bent paper clip on the table, as if she'd used it to pick a lock. Her hair was tied in a tight bun. Such a sad look on her face, I dared not tell her the truth.
> **"In a little while," I said.** [bookend]

Notice that between those two "bookends" in bold there was nothing but static description: a red apron (costume), the kitchen (set), sunlight (mood), yellow curtains (set dressing), a paper clip (prop), mother's hair (character description), and the opinion that her face was sad and that I didn't want to tell her the truth (commentary). All of that is description, but no action. No action whatsoever. No one moved or said anything between the bookends. In cinematic parlance, it was a freeze-frame. **Nothing happend** between those dialogue bookends, only **static description**. Here's an example of static description between two sentences expressing an action:

> The guy in the pin-striped suit **brought the gun up** and **pointed it** at my face. He was tall and had a scar on his left cheek (character description), a food stain on his blue, silk tie (costume). The heat (mood) of this boiler room in the basement of the hotel (set) was all the more oppresive (commentary, thought) because it was the middle of summer (also commentary, exposition). There were a few drops of moisture on the wooden desk in the corner (set dressing), and the only object on the desk was a small deck of cards (prop), wrapped in cellophane. This was not how I planned to die, but what difference did it make. I could feel the poison I had taken earlier work its way through my veins. The hit-man was just my backup, in case the poison didn't work (all commentary: thoughts, feelings, exposition). Then **he squeezed** the trigger.

Between those two sentences indicating an action (pointing the gun and squeezing the trigger), there was only static description: what the hit-man looked like (tall with scar), what he was wearing (a blue tie), where they were (a boiler room), the sensory mood (humid oppresive heat), what was in the room (a desk), a small object (the deck of cards), and the character's thoughts or feelings commenting that he'd taken poison and wanted to die. I might have gotten credit for the pin-striped suit as costume, but it appears outside the bookends of the Image-Moment. Mention was made of the seven elements of Image-Moment: the set, the set dressing, props, sensory mood, character, costume, and commentary. **Nothing actually happened** between those bookends, just the static description. Let me repeat: static description. **No action between the bookends.** Between those bookends, NOTHING HAPPENED. "Why are you repeating that nothing happens between bookends?" you might ask. Because sure as shootin', you're going to create an Image-Moment in which between your bookends someone is going to turn their head or lift a finger or sit down or stand up or recite the Gettysburg Address while remodeling the entire room. So be sure that when you create your Image-Moment, you refrain from the temptation to write a sentence in which something happens: just write static description, and you'll be fine. Attach an elecretic wire to your hand and plug it into a nearby socket, and as soon as you write a sentence between two bookends that expresses an action, you'll get a shock that will knock you off your chair. That should prevent you from writing action sentences between your bookends. **You can start with a line of dialogue and end with an action, or vice-versa. Any combination of action or dialogue will work.** That's the basic idea. Tattoo it on your forearm so you can see it when you write. Inscribe it on your doorposts so you'll be reminded everytime you enter a room: **"An Image-Moment is composed of static description between either dialogue or action in which nothing happens."**

Now, before reading the rest of this chapter, look over pages 126–127 again and answer these five questions:. 1) What are the four levels of narrative structure? 2) What's an action? 3) What's a moment? 4) What are the seven elements of Image-Moment? 5) What are the three parts to Commentary? After you've familiarized yourself with those basic definitions, come back to this page and proceed to the rest of this chapter.

Story: Event: Moment: Image

Okay, you're back. Can you answer the five questions I posed above without looking back at those pages? If not, re-read those pages again and then answer those five questions. (I'm waiting for you. It may take you a few minutes, so I think I'll get a bowl of soup. Cabbage with chicken, if you're interested.) Okay, good, you're back. The soup was good, and while slurping up the tasty broth, I read a few pages of Tolstoy's *War and Peace.* Guess what? Every page had at least four or five Image-Moments. We can now proceed with "the four levels of narrative structure."

It's not what you say, but how you say it. The tone is what hooks the reader and creates a connection, a sense of intimacy. Once the reader is hooked, it's time to bring in scenes filled with vivid *images.* This is what narrative is all about, not just the *story,* but the *events* (or scenes) and the *moments* that make up those scenes. Those are the four levels of narrative structure. Like those Russian dolls, one doll inside the other, stories contain events and events contain moments, and moments contain images. Most of us concentrate on writing our story, going from one event to another. In those events or scenes, there's usually descriptive images. Where we fail, and this is the crucial point, is usually where we failed to create vivid moments, because we failed to create the cinematic equivalent of an Image-Moment. When we remember a scene from a book or movie, it's a moment within the scene that stands out. We say things like, "Remember the scene where he chases his grandson around the tomato patch, and he's got that piece of orange peel in his mouth?" Or "Remember when they're sitting on that bench together and he recites the letter to her that she's holding in her hand, and she realizes that he's the one who wrote it?" Even if you forget the plot, you never forget those vivid moments. This chapter shows you how to make a scene indelible by creating moments that come alive. Image-Moment is a cinematic technique that stamps those moments in the reader's mind.

Joseph Conrad once said that the novelist must create an *impression* on the reader while staying rooted in what Virginia Woolf called "materialism," the depiction of the world as it is. "My task," wrote Conrad, "is, by the power of the written word, to make you hear, to make you feel—it is, before all, to *make you see.*" [My italics.] It is the image that engages the reader's senses—the picture worth a thousand words. The deep voice creates a sense of intimacy, and the images create a sense of immediacy. Pick up any book on writing and you will find the author stressing the importance of specificity, of detail. But the mere description of images can be static. I often skip through long paragraphs of description because it feels as if the story has come to a standstill while the author breaks for a commercial to describe something in painstaking detail. Image-Moment is the mechanism by which details are used to create compelling moments of tension and drama. Without those bookends (remember? Bookends are sentences that either express an instantaneous action or a line of dialogue), the images do not create tension. They're just static description. But when placed between bookends, the drama and the suspense are heightened. Action alone does not create suspense. As a matter of fact, it can be just the opposite. The suspension of action is what creates suspense, the expectation of something about to happen is what creates those compelling moments.

In a review of *Le Samourai*, a film by Jean Pierre Melville, Roger Ebert includes this little aside about action in movies: "The movie teaches us how action is the enemy of suspense"—he is pointing out how **action releases tension** instead of building it. Better to wait for a whole movie for something to happen (assuming we really care whether it happens) than to sit through a film where things we don't care about are happening constantly. Melville uses character, not action, to build suspense. While you may think that stopping the action of a scene with the mechanical device of **Image-Moment** will slow your story down, in fact, it enhances it, it dramatizes it. It **creates suspense**. The reader is waiting for the next line of dialogue or the next action/gesture. They're waiting, so to speak, for the other shoe to drop.

So let's consider a scene from the film Ebert spoke of in his review of Melville's 1967 *Le Samourai* where an underworld hireling calls on Jef Costello, a hitman, to apologize to him and to hire him for another job. He pulls a gun from his coat and points it at Jef's head and waits for him to speak. Jef says nothing. The dialogue that follows is spare, with a short pause between each line of dialogue, heightening the tension.

"Nothing to say?" the goon says.

"Not with a gun on me."

"Is that a principle?"

"A habit."

That's a classic example of movie Image-Moments. Four (dialogue) bookends = three moments (and no action between). In the movie, the characters might pause before saying the next line of dialogue. In the moments of those slight pauses lie the *cinematic* Image-Moments. During those moments, the pauses are filled with camera shots and images—in this case, two clean shaven men in a gray-walled room with two windows, one curtainless with a broken pane, the larger one with its patterned gray and white curtains closed. There's also a double bed and bolster pillow with a coverlet and pillow case that match the curtains. Daylight filters through the curtains, revealing a night table on which sit a black rotary dial phone, an alarm clock, a bottle of mineral water with a red and white label, a blue and white tissue box, and a yellow tin of Cachone Lajaunie licorice drops next to a neat stack of metro tickets. (The *tin* of drops is a prop. The *stack* of tickets is a prop. A single drop or a single tickets is a prop. But several tickets or several drops scattered on the table is set dressing.) There's also a couple of lamps, a muted-gray chintz armchair, a couple of bentwood cane café chairs, a gray armoire with two rows of empty mineral water bottles across the top of it, a small gray bird in a gray cage on a gray wooden table, and a few staples on the shelf of the galley kitchen. The dark-haired man, the one with the gun pointed at his head, wears a black, thin-collared overcoat over a white dress shirt and dark tie. His signature gray fedora with a black grosgrain ribbon sits atop his pretty-boy face. It casts a shadow over his blank, empty blue-gray eyes. The other man, the goon holding the M1911 Colt pistol, wears no hat so we can see that his straight blond hair is parted to the side and is just long enough to touch the pulled-up collar of his buttoned and belted classic beige trench coat.

Did you notice how all that static description I just gave you became somewhat boring to read, that your tendency was to skim over it to get to the end? We do this often when reading a story: when we see a long descriptive paragraph coming down the pike, we're liable to read it without paying close attention, or we put the book down and get ourselves a bowl of soup. But when writing your prose story, if you take some of that static description and place it between those bookends (either a line of dialogue or action), the reader will slow down and read every word. Why? Because they are colluding with you in experiencing dramatic tension. One part of them wants to rush ahead and read the next bookend (that other shoe about to be dropped), but another part of them wants to experience the delicious tension, the suspense of waiting to see what's going to come next. In a movie, of course, we see all that descriptive information. The director and film editor are showing it to you. All the actors have to do to create that tension is pause. But in a prose story, the writer has to create that tension, that suspense, and using the technique of Image-Moment is what does it. In order to provide cinematic suspense, give the reader some of those details between bookends of dialogue or action. Doing this transforms the second or two of spoken-word real time into suspenseful psychological time that would seem to last forever, time in which NOTHING happens. In a book, that scene above with only those few lines of dialogue might look something like this (I'll write from the point of view of the underworld hirling, in first person. I'll also make bold all bookends, actions or dialogue. I may not mention every detail that one would see on the screen, just a few to create that psychological time.):

> I **knocked** on the door and heard a voice say, **"it's open."** When I **entered**, Jef was sitting in a chair behind the door. It startled me. I **pulled** my gun, **leveled** it at his head. Jef didn't flinch, just stared at me with blank, empty eyes, calm as a cucumber. I liked holding a gun on people. It gave me a sense of power. That moment just before I pulled the trigger, life got so big I felt I could slice it up and eat it. I **cocked** the gun. Jef just stared straight ahead as if he were about to fall asleep with a book in his lap.
>
> **"Nothing to say?"** I asked. Jef remained gray and calm as the room. He seemed rather cozy in the bentwood cane café chair, like he was waiting for the waiter to bring him an order of fried scallops. On the opposite wall was a rather ornate mirror, and I could see myself as if I were looking at someone in the next room, through a window. I was hatless and clean-shaven. Handsome, except for my broken nose. I coulda been a contender. Or a movie star. Rather fashionalble, too, I thought. My classic beige trenchcoat was buttoned and belted tight. Its collar pulled up across the back of my neck touching my blonde hair. You couldn't see I was holding a gun to a man's head. In the mirror, I might have been a model, or a gigolo.
>
> Jeff answered, **"Not with a gun on me."**
>
> The large one-room ground floor apartment was gray-walled, and a gray

afternoon light came through the curtainless window. Glass from its broken pane was scattered on the floor. Either someone tried to break in, or Jef had tried to break out. Men like Jef are always breaking out, I know. When I pull the trigger, I figure I'm helping them make their final break. This room, it looked like he was getting ready. How neatly the double bed in the corner was made up, and I wondered if the bed was for sleeping or show. It didn't look like a man had made the bed. It didn't seem to fit the room. There was a bolster pillow tucked tight and a coverlet and pillow case that matched the closed curtains on the larger window, a chintz armchair in muted grays, another café chair, and a gray armoire. On the night stand next to the bed was a bottle of mineral water with a red and white label. A black licorice drop nestled against its tin, next to a neat stack of metro tickets, the only strokes of color in this drab room.

    "Is that a principle?" I asked.

    He kept his eyes on me, didn't blink or look away, as if the gun to his head could just as well have been a feather. On top of the armoire were several empty minteral water bottles arranged in a neat row, almost as if he were planning an art installation. In the movies, when they show scenes like this, there's always a bottle of whiskey and a highball glass. Maybe he lives here with a woman, or a boyfriend.

    "A habit," he said.

    I **uncocked** the gun, **brought** it down and **slipped** it into the pocket of my coat. Jef **smiled, stood up,** and **offered** me a glass of water.

I would have liked to have worked in more of the details, but since we're creating psychological time, the length of the Image-Moment and the number of words have to be adjusted, depending on how long you want to make the pauses seem. Remember, if you say "there was a long pause," you're telling instead of showing. Show the the details and you create the pause, that psychological time that seems to last forever. I would love to have mentioned the bird, the M1911 Colt pistol, the brim of Jef's crisp gray fedora with the wide, black grosgrain ribbon, perhaps comment on why he'd be wearing it inside, but it would have made the Image-Moments too long. As the scene would continue those other details could be dropped in as well in between other Image-Moments, or just as part of basic description. Some Image-Moments are short, with only a few words between those bookends. Later in this chapter, we'll discuss the two shortest Image-Moments possible.

    Did you notice that nothing happened between the bookends in the scene from *Le Samaurai*, most of which were dialogue. Cocking the gun was an action, so that's a bookend as well. In the movie, the characters would pause slightly before saying their dialogue. In that slight pause, there lies your Image-Moment. In the moment, the pause is rendered with images, camera shots. In a book, you'd have to fill in your images (or commentary), which stretch the real time between the bookends (only a second or two) into the psychological time (which seems like forever).

    What counts is that **nothing happens between bookends**. Action is the enemy of suspense. Action releases tension instead of building it. Learn to work the mechanism of Image-Moment and your scenes will be compelling, not just formless narrative.

    Notice, I said *mechanism*. Unlike the Massage of the Transformation Line, which requires a willingness to plum the depths of emotional and psychological truth, Image-Moment is a mechanical device. To make it work you have to understand its parts. My students often resist the mechanical nature of this concept. They worry that pausing to attend to the specific functions of each part of Image-Moment will rob them of the creative spark. Trust me, it won't. Once you get this mechanism down pat, there will be hundreds of ways you can tweak it, bend it, shape it. The creative possibilities will be endless. But first you have to get the basic steps of the dance down pat, one step at a time. At the heart of it lie those descriptive details, though how you use them makes all the difference in the world. **If your action lasts longer than two seconds, your Image-Moment will be lifeless.**

Warning: Be prepared to read this chapter as if you found it in *Popular Mechanics*. So get out your slide rule. Pretend you bought an Image-Moment kit at the Ikea store, and if you don't follow the directions precisely, the structure will fall apart, and those planks of wood will end up in the fireplace. Okay, so it's technical, and most of you reading this book are artists and writers, and being one of those myself, I know that many of us sat in algebra carving our initials in our desks. So I feel your pain. I can hear you whispering, "Maybe I'll just skip this chapter." But if you take this chapter one concept at a time, you will write better. Leo Tolstoy will raise his glass of vodka to you.

If you find yourself getting overwhelmed with the technicalities, take a break. Throw some cheese on a bagel, do a crossword puzzle or Sudoku, watch your favorite *film noir* on television. Take a bubble bath. Take a cold shower. Walk the cat. Book a freight train to Margaritaville. Then come back when you're fresh and read another section. When your brain starts to melt, take another break. But make sure you understand each concept before you move on to the next. In time, each part will make better sense when attached to the whole.

I've been teaching the concept of Image-Moment for several decades and have observed how my students go through this chapter without taking the time to clarify each part of the concept before moving on to the next. I don't want to overwhelm you now with this warning, but I feel it's better than having you speed read through this chapter and becoming overwhelmed by the details. I know there are a great deal of moving parts to this Image-Moment mechanism. But each part fits together and allows the whole to function in a way that will enhance the story you are writing. None of the definitions are that difficult, but you may become overwhelmed by the totality of it. Think about each definition before moving on. This is not a chapter you can read the way you read a swift-paced narrative. Don't be in a rush. For instance, there's a section that discusses the difference between an "action" and an "event." **An action lasts no more than two seconds. It's instantaneous. An event is anything that takes longer than two seconds.** Don't read further until you are clear on that concept. If you confuse the two, your Image-Moment will not work. There's also a difference between an "action" and a "continuous" action. **A continuous action is a repeated series of actions** such as twiddling your thumbs, pacing back and forth, curtains waving in the breeze, rain running down a windowpane, a hamster running on the wheel in its cage. Make sure you are clear about the difference before reading further. There are four levels of narrative structure: Story, Event, Moment, and Image. Take the time to make sense of that before moving on. And finally, there are the seven elements of Image-Moment. I know—this is beginning to sound like one of Julia Child's French recipes. But if you want your Beef Bourguignon to be the hit of your dinner party, you can't confuse a radish with a carrot, a potato with a leak, or an onion with a mango.

Neither can you buy all the proper ingredients, and without following the recipe, throw them all in the pot. If you're going to make Julia Child's famous Beef Bourguigon, you have to follow her recipe, step by step. And if you're going to make Image-Moment work, you have to follow the recipe, step by step. But if you persevere and get each moving part working correctly, you'll be able to create a narrative world from the ground up, moment by moment, scene by scene, detail by detail, all because you mastered the concept of Image-Moment.

To Detail or Not to Detail

Let's start with something that every book on writing talks about: specificity. Details build a dynamic picture, the way a film goes from a wide shot of a forest to a close up of ants crawling down a tree. The narrator's eye can zoom in and out, drawing our attention to a trivial detail that becomes memorable as the story moves forward. In his *Essay on Method*, Gérard Genette uses the term "descriptive pause" to identify that moment in a story when the author slows down the narrative (or stops it altogether) to focus on the painting on a vase or the texture of a character's skin or the spine of a medieval manuscript. "Oh, before I tell you the rest of the story," the author seems to say, "let me describe the delicate way he held the gun, as if it were a crystal glass—that way, you'll understand how he felt about shooting another person in the face."

Nevertheless, any good writer will remind you that as crucial as the image is to good storytelling, it can interrupt the compelling flow of narrative. A good writer, like a good storyteller, has a feel for when description goes on too long, or is irrelevant to character and plot. The images—vivid as they may be—can slow down the dramatic flow of the narrative. Without description, however, your story will be vague. So what's the solution? The recipe calls for salt, but not too little, not too much.

Show, Don't Tell

Good writing makes a movie in the reader's mind, and to make a movie, you need detail, but like a director or film editor, you must be selective. There's no formula, but you can develop an ear for narrative pace. You develop that ear by reading, reading, and more reading. Pay attention to how a writer builds a story, scene after scene, and how she uses description. When does the writer shift from description back to narrative action? When the does the writer shift from commentary to dialogue? Look for that in the writing, and you'll develop an instinct for it. That can only be learned by reading other writers. But what I can teach you is how to create compelling moments by using the Image-Moment technique. This is not Genette's "descriptive pause," which stops the narrative flow. **It's the use of detail within a moment to stretch real time into psychological time.** When you create psychological time, you create tension, drama. As Ebert said, action doesn't create tension, it releases tension. The image beween action or dialogue is what creates tension, that psychological time in which nothing is actually happening. Image-Moment technique is one of the basic building blocks of all narrative, and gives a scene tension and suspense. The deep voice draws your reader into the story, but story becomes tedious without compelling scenes and specific events. No matter how deep the voice, at some point you have to close the deal. To repeat an adage you've probably heard a thousand times, "Show, don't tell."

Story and Event are basically the same thing—each has a beginning, a middle, and an end. We assume that our story is interesting, whatever story we wish to tell, but it's the moments within events that bring the story to life. I've read pages and pages of writing in which the writer rushes through their story—"We did this, we did that, then this happened, then that happened."— but there are no moments in which I can get a foothold into the characters or their inner conflicts. It's all action and narrative, story and event. It was as if the writer was so focused on the story, that he failed to slow down and bring the images and moments to life. Afterall, to concentrate on one scene at a time and each moment within each scene—well, that takes focus and stamina, and lots of patience. You can't rush it. Writing is like sculpting, with each scene sculpted from a mass of marble. The compelling moments are what we hold onto—in some ways, they *are* the story. Clark Cable says to Scarlet O'Hara, "Frankly my dear, I don't give a damn." Humphrey Bogart looks at Ingrid Bergman and says, "We'll always have Paris." Marilyn Monroe's dress rises up above the sidewalk grate. Roy Scheider walks back into the cabin of the boat after seeing the shark for the first time, and deadpans, "You're gonna need a bigger boat." Meg Ryan simulates an orgasm in a coffee shop and the lady at the next table says, "I'll have what she's having." Gary Cooper holds his badge in his hand, looks at the townspeople for a long Image-Moment, then throws it into the dirt. Jack Nicholson sticks his head through the hole he's made with an axe in the bathroom door and says, "Heeeeerrrree's Johnny!" Jimmy Stewart feels in his pocket for Zuzu's petals. Betty Davis says, "Fasten your seat belts, it's gonna be a bumpy ride." Arnold Schwarzenegger's Terminator deadpans, "I'll be back." Lauren Bacall says, "You know how to whistle, don't you Steve? You just put your lips together and blow." Emily Blunt promises, "I'm one stomach flu away from reaching my goal weight." Julie Hagerty apologizes for the sudden turbulence on a commercial jetliner, saying, "There's no reason to be alarmed and we hope you enjoy the rest of the flight. By the way, is there anyone on board who knows how to fly a plane?" Great moments can evoke a vivid sense of the entire story: "I'll make him an offer he can't refuse." "You had me at hello." "I see dead people." "You want the truth? You can't handle the truth." "Luke, I am your father." "I love the smell of napalm in the morning." "Major Strasser's been shot. Round up the usual suspects." "Here's looking at you, kid." "You got the wrong guy. I'm the Dude, man." Without such moments, scenes fall flat, and without compelling scenes, our stories are boring.

So where's the balance between too many details, and enough detail to bring a moment to life? Is there a number of imagistic details beyond which we should never go? Are we supposed to count them? Nah. That would be too easy.

Here's how the mechanism of Image-Moment works:

The Descriptive Pause vs The Dramatic Pause

What makes the narrative forceful is not the *image*—static description—but the *moment*. By moment, I mean *that pause between two bookends that lasts just a few seconds*. We're not talking about the wonderful weekend that *seemed* to last a moment, or the year in Paris that *seemed* to last but a moment. **A moment is not a minute, it's *less* than a minute, usually just a few seconds**. Why can't a moment last 60 seconds? Because I can spell. This concept is not called Image/Minute, it's called Image-Moment. A moment begins and then it ends. It's a pause, a freeze-frame. Like pressing the pause button on the video, time seems to freeze. It's more than a "descriptive pause," it's a dramatic pause filled with *expectation*. Here's a typical scene you might encounter in a novel:

Tom walked into the study and faced his old nemesis, the Earl of Claridge, who stood nonchalantly by the pool table. Tom pulled out a gun and pointed it at him, his finger on the trigger. They stood there, facing each other, retribution hanging in the air like a thundercloud. Killing him would be too easy, thought Tom. He placed the gun next to the eight-ball on the pool table and walked out.

Tom pulls out a gun and points it at his nemesis. That's two definite actions. He pulls out a gun—one second—then he points it—another second. Two quick actions. Then there's a pause. In that pause, the reader feels the drama, the expectation of what is about to happen. Will Tom pull the trigger? Will the gun misfire? Will the Earl of Claridge run for his life? Will someone else enter the room? In that dramatic pause, we feel the tension mount. After the pause, there is another action, Tom placing the gun on the pool table, a definite action. Between those two actions—pointing the gun and placing it on the pool table—time seems to freeze. Sometimes, a moment is created when an ongoing action—such as walking or running—suddenly stops.

> I saw her from a distance, carrying a suitcase, her handbag slung over her shoulder. I walked faster. It had been years since I'd seen her, and as I got closer to her, I felt the longing. When we were three feet from each other she saw me and we both suddenly stopped and stood for a moment before I gave in and hugged her.

That moment starts once they stop in front of each other. There's an awkward pause. Will they hug? Will she turn away? Will they speak? Will he turn away? As they walk toward each other, there's no sense of a moment. But once they stop, it's as if a bell goes off, signaling the beginning of the moment. They pause. Then they hug—end of moment. The moment begins with each of them suddenly stopping, there's a pause, then it ends when they hug. Between the beginning and end of that moment lies the dramatic pause in which **nothing happens**; it's the pause, the *expectation* of action or dialogue that provides the drama, A few moments like that strung together become an event; events strung together become story. But the drama is not in the **story**, or in the **events**, it's in those dramatic **moments** when time seems to stand still as we wait to see what will happen next. Here's an example from Jhumpa Lahiri's collection of short stories, *Unaccustomed Earth*. After the bookends of a line of dialogue, the moment begins with the action when she stops walking. The moment is framed by the action at the beginning and the dialogue at the end, which bookend the moment.

> "Don't marry him, Hema."
> She stopped walking. They were on a street of steps, lined with cypress trees, working their way down. Those behind her in the collective procession murmured *permesso* and pressed past. She felt the lurch of a head rush. The boy who had not paid attention to her; the man who'd embarked on an affair knowing she could never be his. At the last moment he was asking for more. A piece of her was elated. But she was also struck by his selfishness, by the fact that he was telling her what to do. Unlike Navin, he was not offering to come to her.
> "Don't answer now," he said.
> —from "Nobody's Business"

The story here pauses to give us a moment that reveals this character's inner life and her dilemma. We are held waiting in suspense, invested in the choice she will make since the unveiling of her inner life has drawn us closer to her. It's a mistake to think that narrative action is what creates a "page turner." Not true. What keeps us immersed in the story are the dramatic moments contained in the pauses between an *action* or a line of *dialogue*.

The Way You Wear Your Hat,
the ay You Sip Your Tea

English novelist, poet, editor, and critic Ford Maddox Ford, best remembered for his novels *The Good Soldier* and the *Parade's End* tetrology, wrote an essay on Joseph Conrad. Conrad is considered one of the greatest novelists of the twentieth century, a master prose stylist who wrote many great novels including *Heart of Darkness* and *The Secret Agent*. In his essay, Ford wrote that impressionism is "the record of the impression of the moment." In other words, a moment experienced through the senses. We do this by inserting static images within the framework of that dramatic pause between an *action* or line of *dialogue*.

A description of a person or a room or a landscape can convey mood and psychological truth. When a character walks down the sidewalk on a dreary afternoon, leaves covering the lawn, dark clouds gathering above the houses, these images evoke a sense of inner turmoil. The description of a pencil sharpened to a fine point and the manicured fingernails of the man writing with it can tell us more about the person than a long explanatory paragraph "telling" us the man's character. Such images don't describe for the sake of description. They convey the mood of the character, the voice of the narrator, the conflict in the story itself.

> He tried to remember how heavy the coffin had been that morning, the weight of it spread out over his left shoulder as he helped Roland carry it up the stairs and into the parlor, the shape of Roland's back, hunched in front of him when they set it down on the table. How heavy had it been, the coffin? He thought of Roland's hands, patient and callused, clasped around the waist of the little white dress that was laid out for Nyah in the guest nursery, the little white dress and the little white shoes sitting on Roland's lap at the funeral tomorrow, and the empty velvet in the pine box going into the ground; Mrs. Halima's words, *It came in to take her,* no blood anywhere, anywhere at all, and the stagnant heat of the African night coming in through the windows and doors and the cracks in the floor. He went into the kitchen and dragged one of the flour bags out.
>
> —Téa Obreht, "The Laugh"

Obreht's paragraph above conveys both the inner mood of the character and the outer mood of the scene, each detail adding to the overall effect. Nothing is really happening, it's just the character's thoughts, and the imagistic details. Not until that last sentence, when he goes into the kitchen (*action*) are we thrust back into the story. In the hands of a lesser writer, an accumulation of detail can bog the reader down. But a few details can show a great deal. One sentence showing us how a woman wears her hat speaks volumes. You can tell us everything about the character sitting across from you, but show us how she sips her tea, and we know all we need to know at that point in the story.

In the movie *Three Days of the Condor*, the screenwriter could have spent pages of dialogue revealing how repressed the character played by Faye Dunaway was. Instead, the writer has Robert Redford's character look at a series of photographs framed on the wall: beautifully shot, well-composed scenes of snowy landscapes, empty benches in a park, leafless trees lining a gray street. Each photograph an image, static description. But oh, what they reveal about the person who took them. Then Redford says, "There's no people in these photographs." The line seals the deal. You want story? There's your story, embedded in a few images and one line of dialogue.

We are talking here about the four levels of narrative structure: Story, Event, Moment, and Image. It's nearly almost impossible to write a story that doesn't have details, description, images. When you consider the fact that Story and Event are basically the same thing—events are the smaller stories within the big story, and both have a beginning, middle, and end—what we're left with are static description and moments. Description is pretty cut and dried, a picture, an image, a detail. Moments are tricky because we're dealing with *psychological time, that pause between two actions or lines of dialogue* in which time seems to stand still. To call up the analogy with method acting, it's in the pauses that we shape the drama, not in the speaking of the lines. When Stanislavski talks about the number of beats in a scene, he's calling attention to those moments when the action stops; there's an inner conflict; something's going on, but it's internal, not external; then someone finally speaks and we move into the next beat. This is where the drama lies, in those beats, those dramatic pauses between lines of dialogue or action.

No Ideas But in Things

In the middle of *Spring and All*, a book-length poem by William Carlos Williams published in 1923, the poet combines story with critical theories, at one point making the famous pronouncement that there were to be "no ideas, but in things." By things, he meant actual objects. Let the "idea" you want to express be conveyed through the materiality of the object. It's another way of saying "show, don't tell," but Williams was also saying that the objects themselves tell the story. Those words were a call to arms. Except for the revolutionary impulses of Walt Whitman and Emily Dickinson, American poetry had suffered from a bland and quaint abstraction, romantic thoughts and feelings rarely grounded in everyday reality. This is what led Ezra Pound to declare that "poetry must be as well written as prose." As founder of the Imagist movement, Pound advocated the "direct treatment of the thing," without straining for effect. Give details about a scene and the details will convey the ideas. "No ideas," said Williams, "but in things."

"God is in the Details"

The battle for imagistic clarity continues to be waged on various fronts. A few decades back, Louis Simpson declared, "Write truly about visible things." And most of us are familiar with the adage "God is in the details,"expounded by architect Mies Van der Rohe. It doesn't matter if you're writing a story, directing a play, or building a cathedral. The marvel of St. Denis, one of the great edifices of Gothic architecture, lies in the detailed work evident in both the plans of the designer, Abbot Suger, and in the intricate solutions to architectural problems worked out by an unknown master builder. Anyone who has looked at it can truly say that "God was in the details." I don't know who first coined the counter phrase, "the devil is in the details," but it means that being overly attentive to trivial details can result in the whole thing falling apart from the weight of its components. George Allen, a noted football coach, was meticulous about every little thing. One day during practice he flew into a rage because he spotted a gum wrapper on the sidelines. His attention to detail made for well-coached teams, but some say his over-attention to detail explains why his teams never won a Super Bowl. It's the difference between "God is in the details" and "the devil is in the details." Images and details are important, but don't go overboard.

Writing like you talk makes you receptive to emotional truth.

The **transformation line** moves the voice below the level of reporting into emotional truth.

Massaging the transformation line gets you into the deep voice.

Once there, **Image-Moment** moves the reader from intellectual understanding into experience by engaging the senses.

IMAGE-MOMENT

Moments contain Images.
Events contain Moments.
Story contains Events.

We can't see love, fame, death, happiness, sadness, grief, loneliness, or longing. Those are abstractions. But we can see the tall blonde kissing the guy on roller blades next to the park bench; we can see the wilted rose in a glass of water by the window; we can see an old woman's hand reaching for that rose. Don't write about your character's freshman year at college, show us a moment from that experience, one detail at a time:

> My pen fell behind the desk, the pen my father gave me. I lay there on the bed, too tired to get it, listening to him snore, the roommate who won't talk to me. Listening to the bed creak as he rolls over. Watching the numbers on the digital clock flip over. Thinking, I should get up and find that pen before I forget it's even there. Before I forget, fall asleep, and wake in the morning to this stupid desk, stupid ceiling, stupid world.

Let the details bring your characters to life. I don't mean a handful of adjectives, I mean a clarity achieved through specificity. The glass of water in which the old woman's rose is so carefully placed—it reveals something about her. If the rose were in a vase, it would tell a different story altogether. That's what I mean by specificity.

An image is a picture. The starfish button on the coat. The scar on the finger. The smudged eyeliner. The crumpled piece of paper. The broken pencil next to the coffee cup.

A moment is . . . well, a moment. Someone stands "for a moment" at the window looking out at the rain. A woman takes a sip of sherry and pauses for a moment to savor it. A moment is not an event or a story, it's a short duration of time, a few seconds at most. **Image** and **Moment** are two of the four basic levels of narrative structure, the other two being **Event** and **Story**. You could say that images and moments strung together form events. Events strung together create your story.

IMAGE ⇨ MOMENT ⇨ EVENT ⇨ STORY

Every sentence will fall into one of the above categories. "An old Chevy, its wheels missing, stood on cinder blocks in the backyard; birds nested in the weeds and vines that grew up into the car." That's an image. Nothing happens. It's a photograph. "It was when John was five years old and in first grade that he was first noticed." That's a story or event. It's not a single action or a still photograph, an image. It's a sweeping summary of something that happened. There are no details. "The summer after my freshman year of college, I moved in with a girl who worked as a waitress at a local diner." This is story. No details, no images, no moments. We have no idea what the girl looked like, what the diner looked like, what the apartment looked like, what they did each day, or on any particular day. All we know is the general **story**, which when told, will be composed of various **events**. The events themselves will contain specific **moments**, and the moments will include **images**. Those are the **four levels of narrative structure**, like those Russian dolls: images within moments, moments within events, and events within story. Combine a vivid image with a compelling moment, and the reader will keep turning the page from one moment to the next, one event to the next, all the way to the end of your story. Notice how an action or line of dialogue in the text quoted below functions as a bookend.

> It was when John was five years old and in the first grade that he was first noticed; and since he was noticed by an eye altogether alien and impersonal, he began to perceive, in wild uneasiness, his individual existence.
>
> They were learning the alphabet that day, and six children at a time were sent to the blackboard to write the letters they had memorized. Six had finished and were waiting for the teacher's judgment when the back door opened and the school principal, of whom everyone was terrified, entered the room. No one spoke or moved. In the silence the principal's voice said:
>
> "Which child is that?" *[This line of dialogue begins a moment]*
>
> She was pointing at the blackboard, at John's letters. The possibility of being distinguished by her notice did not enter John's mind, and so he simply stared at her. Then he realized, by the immobility of the other children and by the way they avoided looking at him, that it was he who was selected for punishment.
>
> "Speak up, John," said the teacher, gently. *[another bookend]*
>
> On the edge of tears, he mumbled his name and waited. The principal, a woman with white hair and an iron face, looked down at him.
>
> "You're a very bright boy, John Grimes," she said. "Keep up the good work." *[another bookend]*
>
> Then she walked out of the room. *[another bookend]*
>
> —James Baldwin, *Go Tell It on the Mountain*

What happened in that classroom is an event within a larger story. The event itself is comprised of several moments, and the moments begin and end with what I call a "bookend"—a line of dialogue, or an action/gesture. The images within each moment convey the emotional content of the scene. When the principal asks, "Which child is that?", Baldwin could have written, *There was a long dramatic pause before the teacher spoke again.* But that sentence would be telling, not showing. Baldwin created a moment that dramatized the child's apprehension. He doesn't tell us what to feel, or even what the boy was feeling; instead he creates a moment that *evokes* the feeling, and crystalizes the story's meaning. That's what people remember.

> The way you wear your hat.
> They way you sip your tea.
> The memory of all that.
> Oh no, you can't take that
> away from me.

What Goes between the Bookends of a Moment? Images

In Baldwin's story, the structure of that moment is simple. I call those two lines of dialogue *bookends,* because they contain, between them, a psychological pause, in which a few telling images show us what the character is experiencing. Another way of looking at that structure is to imagine that it's a baloney sandwich: The piece of bread on top and the piece of bread on the bottom are the bookends (an action or line of dialogue). Between them are the images and thoughts (the slices of baloney). **Nothing actually happens between bookends,** just images and thoughts. This is crucial. The slightest action or gesture will break the tension. No one can lift as much as an eyebrow, much less a finger or an arm. No one can look up or look away, or heave a sigh, or shift their weight from one foot to the other. Blinking is *verboten.* Taking a breath is a no-no. Shrugging is tantamount to the Normandy invasion on D-Day. Nothing, absolutely nothing, happens. Images and thoughts or feelings are not actions. Thinking is not an action; feeling sad, mad, glad, or bad is not an action. Even as small a movement as leaning across a table is tantamount to a volcanic eruption. That's all that's allowed between bookends—static description and commentary in the form of thoughts and feelings. This is not the first time I've emphasized that nothing happens between two bookends, and it won't be the last. Yet, your tendency will be to allow some action to occur, thus breaking the tension and effectively ending the Image-Moment. So pay attention when constructing your Image-Moment. Allow nothing to happen. Looking *at* something is not an action. But looking *away*, looking *up*, looking *down*—these imply movement, thus they are actions. **Nothing happens between bookends**.

I know, I know, you're going to tell me that in the story you are writing about your mother, she reached for the doorknob between the two lines of dialogue. Forget the true details. You are creating the Image-Moment for the purpose of enhancing the drama of your story. Don't let your mother and "what really happened" ruin the psychological time of your Image-Moment. Sorry, Mom, you can *reach* for the doorknob *before* the opening bookend or *after* the opening bookend, but *not* between. And mom, while we're at it, you can't look *up*, look *down*, or look *away*. Those are movements. You can *feel* sad, mad, glad, or bad, since feelings and thoughts are not actions, but leaning across the table is tantamount to a volcanic eruption. So, one more time: **NOTHING HAPPENS BETWEEN BOOKENDS!**

A "continous action" is allowed between bookends, but we'll discuss that at further length on page 111. But for now, remember that an action is swift and sudden; it takes no longer than two seconds. A continous action can last throughout the moment, such as pacing back and forth, twiddling one's thumbs, doing pushups, etc. But be careful! As soon as a "continous" action stops, that's an action. It's also an action when it starts. Starting and stopping take one second. Hence, they're actions.

This simple structure forms the basic building block of all narrative. Every scene or event in a story is composed of such Image-Moments, and a good writer builds the tension and drama of a scene or event with the skillful use of those slices of baloney (the images that go between the two slices of bread). Every good scene in a longer narrative has dozens of baloney sandwiches, enough to feed an army.

After you've massaged your transformation line, try not to tell a story; go, instead, to a scene, and in that scene create at least one good Image-Moment. Let the details do the work. The story will tell itself through the moments. Out of the image or the moment may come more transformation lines. Massage them, too, if you like. Remember to look for details that convey character, though often it's the seemingly unimportant, even trivial details that have symbolic or psychological power. When composing that first draft, those details may seem arbitrary, but eventually they will attain mythic proportion, even if they don't seem crucial to the story. You can always cut some of them later if you think your piece is better off without them. But don't worry about that now. You're not editing, you're writing. Maybe there's an empty bottle on the counter. Your brother's shirt with the ripped pocket. The way his hand rests on the table, the fingers always moving, tapping out some tune. When the event or scene shifts to moment, it's a few seconds of film. Like the moment in the Baldwin story where time, for the boy, seemed to slow down or stand still. The more details you give within the moment, the longer the moment seems to last; the greater the tension, the more vivid the moment.

Review of Clint Eastwood's *Unforgiven*

"Eastwood suggests that the only human value capable of sharing the scene with violence and not being upstaged is generosity. He conveys this not in the narrative of his film, but in its art. For instance, in *Unforgiven*, when Eastwood's character leaves his two children to ride off and take up the gun, the camera holds on the children—a boy and a girl. Then the camera moves toward the girl, then the girl takes a step toward the camera, then the camera moves a half step toward her again. It's the last we'll see of that little girl, so most script analysts moves toward the girl, then the girl takes a step toward the camera, then the camera moves a half step toward her again. It's the last we'll see of that little girl, so most script analysts would not consider her an important character. Yet, we remember her, *because the moment is full of content*—full of generosity toward her spirit at that place in the story. According to the moves of the camera, she has changed three times in that moment of her father's leaving, and changed on levels inexpressible through words. A moment so full is, inherently, generous. There is so much to be savored, remembered.

"*Unforgiven* is full of such moments. Characters seen only briefly are offered to the camera with an openness and a sense of importance that brings them utterly alive. It's a way of saying that life wastes nothing. That even in the most senseless, compulsive acts, where we have good reason to think everything is wasted, the life of life is there, like a camera, like Eastwood's camera, blessing, by virtue of its focus, every move, every reaction, every moment."

—*Los Angeles Times*

When you write your journal entries, follow the sequence of the exercise.

1) Begin without a subject or idea. **Write like you talk**. No forced, elaborate descriptions, no literary language.

2) Get the voice to go deeper using the transformation line. If a good transformation line doesn't pop up after a paragraph or so, make one up.

3) Massage the **transformation line** to get the voice even deeper.

4) Now give the reader an **Image-Moment.** It could be anything that pops into your head, it could be an image or moment directly related to the transformation line, or something you see as you write. The point is, give the reader an Image-Moment while you're still in the deep voice. That's the key. You're showing the reader a moment using specific details, but the voice is coming from a deep place, and this will unconsciously affect the way you write. Allow a few sentences to set up the scene, then focus on the moment.

Cinematic Moments and Psychological Time

When I was in my twenties, determined to be an actor and a writer, I began going to see foreign films—we called them "art" films then. Fellini, Bergman, Varda, Kurosawa, Goddard, Wertmuller, anything that was playing, the more esoteric the better. I collected them like notches on a gun belt. That way, at parties, when the talk came around to art and culture, I'd be ready. What I didn't expect was how I would be affected by those films. It wasn't the themes or grand vision or even the literate scripts; it was the simplicity of the moments that struck me. Toshiro Mifune's face and posture in Kurosawa's *Seven Samurai*, for instance, or the old man in *Ikiru*, standing by the swing set in the park in the middle of winter, at the end of his life, bewildered by it all. I drove home after the movie down the Gentilly Highway alone in my car, feeling that I had been changed by what I saw. I was discovering something important about the way great art works. Robert Bresson's films, and those of Jean Renoir and Vittorio de Sica, had the same effect. Especially Renoir's *The Grand Illusion*, de Sica's *Bicycle Thief* and Fellini's *La Strada*. It was the way those directors respected the moment that struck me then and continues to resonate with me today, so unlike most of the Hollywood films at the time that careened along the roller coaster of plot. Giulietta Masina's face as she watches Anthony Quinn scoop up his plate of beans in *La Strada*. Bruno's face as he watches his father stand in the square without his bicycle, helpless and frightened. So little dialogue, so little exposition. The clarity of those images evoked waves of emotion. I had no defense against them. I wasn't able to intellectualize my way to a safe distance when drawn in that way, through my senses. Many of those films were a part of my becoming a man as my grasp of human nature, and of my own nature, grew. That's what I look for still. To be drawn in against my will. For those worlds to be drawn into me.

I know you have a story to tell; I know you believe that your story is compelling and will hold your reader spellbound. But story is but an accumulation of events, and events are nothing more than an accumulation of moments, and moments themselves become dramatic when **real time is stretched into psychological time**. Your story will not engage the reader; compelling moments—compelling Image-Moments—will. There are moments in novels as imprinted in my mind as those cinematic moments. Years after reading them, I may have forgotten the plot and structure, but I remember certain scenes and moments—the smell of the mutton kidneys cooking in Leopold Bloom's kitchen as the cat brushed against his leg (*Ulysses*, James Joyce); Benjy in Faulkner's *The Sound and the Fury* looking up at his sister's muddy underpants as she sits in the tree trying to see into the second floor bedroom; the disorienting isolation of Jane Eyre, sitting hour after hour on an ottoman in the red room of her aunt's house as it grows dark, contemplating her fate; the scene in Zora Neale Hurston's *Their Eyes Were Watching God*, in which Joe Starks hugs another man's yellow mule to save it from abuse, then later on, in his kitchen, when he hits his wife because he doesn't like her cooking; or *The Godfather's* Michael Corleone visiting his father in the hospital when he discovers that all the staff and police had deserted them. When I read that scene in the book, my heart was pounding so furiously that I had to get up and walk around the living room before getting back to the book. That scene was delicious, the way Mario Puzo drew it out, filling it with images that conveyed Michael's dawning realization: his father is in danger and no one is there to protect him. Such moments are small, but the impact is lasting.

Not much "happens" in a moment. A girl slips her foot into and out of a new pair of shoes. Someone leans over to smell a corsage. A simple gesture conveys so much about character, emotion, story. When you're writing, you're the director, the cinematographer, the set designer, the actor. When you point the camera at a rose sitting in a glass of water, the longer you want the camera to hold on that object, the more words you have to use so that the reader looks at it longer. **The more words you spend describing an image, the longer it lingers in the reader's mind.** This is the essential mechanism of how Image-Moment works. You, the author, tell the reader how important a moment is by how long you ask them to consider it. Conversely, asking a reader to linger over something with little importance, simply because you got carried away with detail and image, misleads the reader into thinking that a moment is more important than it really is; or worse, it bores the reader. Description, like anything in writing, must be used with discrimination. Too little, and you fail to bring the reader into the scene; too much, and the reader grows weary. But note this: There is a difference between description for the sake of description, and **description that takes place between the bookends of a moment in order to create psychological time.** That's a crucial difference.

Take this poem by Dorianne Laux. It describes a moment, just a few seconds. Watching from a distance, we'd think that nothing was happening. But despite the lack of narrative action, the images convey an entire story, even if the nature of that story is somewhat ambiguous. There are several ways to interpret what is going on in the poem that follows, but its foundation of Image-Moment engages the reader with the emotional truth of character, and the poet even tells us that it is the moment, not the story, that the girl will remember all her life, the moment "when she learns what she will love."

Homecoming

At the high school football game, the boys
stroke their new muscles, the girls sweeten their lips
with gloss that smells of bubblegum, candy cane,
or cinnamon. In pleated cheerleader skirts
they walk home with each other, practicing yells,
their long bare legs forming in the dark.
Under the arched field lights, a girl
in a velvet prom dress stands near the chainlink,
a cone of roses held between her breasts.
Her lanky father, in a corduroy suit, leans
against the fence. While they talk, she slips a foot
in and out of a new white pump, fingers the weave
of her French braid, the glittering earrings.
They could be a couple on their first date, she,
a little shy, he, trying to impress her
with his casual stance. This is the moment
when she learns what she will love: a warm night,
the feel of nylon between her thighs, the fine hairs
on her arms lifting when a breeze
sifts in through the bleachers, cars
igniting their engines, a man bending over her,
smelling the flowers pressed against her neck.

—Dorianne Laux, from *What We Carry*

The event in this poem is an internal one, very little actually *happens*. A transformation line tells us: "This is the moment when she learns what she will love." Even though it's in the third person, it has the effect of a transformation line because of what it reveals; ultimately, it's the center of the poem, carefully set up by the images. The father leans against the fence while she stands there. Despite the "continuous action" of her slipping her foot in and out of a new shoe as she fingers the weave of her French braid, nothing is happening... yet. We don't know what they are talking about. Then, against that background of nothingness, the father bends over her and smells the flowers pressed against her neck. Laux leaves it to the reader to interpret what that action implies, what that scene is about. The poem is not an event, it's a moment, a seemingly insignificant moment after a football game, before the girl will head off to the homecoming dance. Even the title—"Homecoming"—has deeper implications. What Laux has so skillfully done is render that moment with images between bookends—the father leans against the fence, then he bends over her—that create the drama of psychological time.

A poem like Dorianne Laux's "Homecoming" contains sentences that are not—strictly speaking—like one talks. If you were talking, you'd simply say "In cheerleader skirts," but Laux adds the adjective "pleated." I might say the same thing about some of the other adjectives, such as "glittering earrings," or some of the verbs, such as "cars igniting their engines." Laux is a deft poet who skillfully blends the natural voice with the eloquence of poetic language. This blending of voice and style is what gives signature to her writing. At this point, however, you're still writing like you talk, staying true to your natural voice, but eventually we'll focus on how to extend that voice to include poetic/literary flourishes. I bring the poem to your attention to point out how she uses image and moment.

Real Time vs. Psychological Time

A sixteen-year-old girl sits in her room, thinking about something that happened in school that day. Her mother walks in, followed by her father. The mother holds a diary in her hand. She holds it out toward the girl. "What's this about, young lady? Are you going to stab yourself?" she asks. The girl stares at the diary, wondering if her mother has read it all or just a portion of it, enough maybe to prompt that question. Her eyes go from the diary, to her mother, to her father, and back to the diary. It's only a moment before she answers, but it seems longer. "No, I'm not going to stab myself, now give me back my diary."

This example illustrates "psychological time" as opposed to "real time." You can tell the reader that "time passed slowly" but that would be TELLING, not SHOWING. The trick is to make the reader feel the passage of time. But images alone won't do it. The trick is to combine both image and moment into one: Image-Moment. This is a technical skill, and not something one does naturally when telling a story. It's **counter-intuitive**, like swinging a golf club. No one would pick up a golf club and grip it the way one is taught. It's not natural. It feels forced and mechanical. When telling stories to friends, we don't usually provide Image-Moments, but a skillful Storyteller might. You can learn this skill just as one learns how to grip a golf club. Once you learn to hold the club correctly, your ability to hit the ball with power and focus increases dramatically. All you have to do is practice. Image-Moment is the same thing. Once you get the mechanics down, the real creative work begins.

BOOKENDS: A line of dialogue or an action/gesture

Let's begin with some definitions. Unlike a story, a moment has no middle, just a beginning and an end. It begins with an action/gesture or a line of dialogue, and ends with an action/gesture or a line of dialogue. Those are the *bookends*, which makes it clear that a moment has begun and ended. That gives the reader a sense of time, a pause. What is a bookend? **A bookend is a sentence in which there is an action/gesture or a line of dialogue.** What is an action? **An action is instantaneous and takes no more than two seconds. If it takes longer than two seconds, it's an event.** So many of my students confuse **action** with **event**. A bookend is a clear, decisive action. Putting on chapstick is an event (it takes more than two seconds). You have to take it out of your purse or pocket, open it, apply it, re-cap it, and put it back in your pocket or purse. The application alone takes more than two seconds. Uncapping the tube of chapstick is instantaneous, putting it to your lips might be instantaneous, but the whole process is a series of small actions that take more than two seconds. Therefore, it's an event, not an action.

Now might be a good time to take a break. Walk the dog, and as you walk, keep saying to yourself, "An action is instantaneous, it takes no more than two seconds; an action is instantaneous, it takes no more than two seconds."

A bookend begins the moment decisively. *John looked at the window* is not a forceful bookend. Looking or seeing are passive. Anytime you describe something, it goes without saying that you are looking at it. If you want looking or seeing to come off as an action, better to say *John turned his head and looked at the window*. The action of turning the head tells us a moment has begun. It's decisive. **Looking is not an action**, but looking *up* is an action, looking *down* is an action, looking *away* is an action; but looking by itself is merely seeing. Seeing is what you do when you describe anything, but it's not an action.

The mother enters the room. That signals the beginning of a moment. It takes a second to enter a room. *The mother holds the diary out toward the girl.* That's also a bookend. If you were to write *the mother holds the diary*, that would not be an action because **holding something is not an action**, it's a statement of condition. One could hold something forever. But if the mother holds *out* the diary, it becomes a decisive action, and therefore, a bookend.

Two bookends in a row define a moment,
but without images between,
it's only a moment.

But two bookends with images between
is an Image-Moment,
and that's what we're going for—
the creation of psychological time.

The real time between bookends is a pause, just a few seconds. But when you add the images, you stretch real time into psychological time. As people often say, "I was standing there for a few seconds, waiting to hear what the doctor had to say, but it felt like forever."

Every bookend that closes a moment can be the opening bookend of the next moment. The mother holds out the diary to her daughter—the closing bookend of the previous moment, but also the opening bookend of the next moment, which ends with the line of dialogue, "Are you going to stab yourself?" That moment ends with another line of dialogue, "No, I'm not." Between those two lines of dialogue, we hold the moment. The camera pans the room. The tension between mother and daughter builds. "Are you going to stab yourself?" asks the mother, and we wait to see what the daughter will say or do. That's an Image-Moment. Don't confuse a direct quote with an indirect quote: "I will be home in one hour," said Joe. That's a direct quote. But if you wrote: Joe said he'd be home in one hour, that's indirect, and cannot be used as a bookend. Dialogue means someone actually speaks, with quotes around it. Garbo talks. Simon says.

MOMENT: a few seconds between bookends

*A moment is a suspension of time **between** two bookends.* Bookends are what define the moment, like walls define a room. Without walls, you have undefined empty space. Without bookends, you have empty nothing, maybe static description. Two bookends, one after the other, creates a moment. When you fill the space between those bookends with images, you now have an Image-Moment. The first bookend creates tension as we wait to see what will happen next; it's as if time freezes. The second bookend resolves that tension. As soon as something *happens*, the moment has ended. The smallest action or gesture, a line of dialogue, and your moment is over. That's why I make a point of saying that **nothing happens between the bookends of a moment**. Had James Baldwin described the principal's white hair before the beginning of the moment, it would have had no dramatic effect. But he called our attention to that detail while we waited to see what the boy would do when she asked who had written the letters on the board. Description outside of your bookends is merely static description. When it comes between the bookends, it's no longer static, but prolongs the tension created by the first bookend. The time it takes to read the words between the bookends delays the end of that moment, signalled by another line of dialogue. Real time stops as psychological time ticks on. We're riveted, waiting for the other shoe to drop. But we're not just waiting. We're reading words, and that takes time; thus we *experience* the psychological time between the bookends.

Where do the images come from? They're right in front of your eyes. No need to memorize the seven elements. You know where you are: set. You know what the large objects are: set dressing. Objects smaller than a deck of cards: props. Your senses detect the mood. It's not enough to identify a character, provide at least one piece of physical description. What are they wearing?: costume. It's all in front of your eyes.

 ### The Seven Elements of Image-Moment

1) The **set**: Where are we? The kitchen, a bedroom, a dentist's office, the beach, a classroom, the backyard, inside the car, a dungeon, etc.

2) **Set dressing**: furniture, chairs, large objects that take two union stagehands to bring into the room. If it's an outdoor set, objects like trees and fences, even clouds are considered dressing. The same set might be dressed as a Victorian reading room or a modern library.

3) **Mood**: light, sounds, smells and other **sensory data**: the feel of the leather upholstery or the denim shirt, the smell of spaghetti cooking in the kitchen, the glare of fluorescent lights, the sound of rain, the taste of chocolate.

4) **Props**: small objects **no larger than a deck of cards**: a paper clip, a bottle cap, a comb, a nickel, a coaster. A hammer is not a prop. Neither is an axe. A few pennies is not a prop—it's set dressing. A single penny is a prop.

5) **Character**: physical description, face, hands, fingernails, lips, etc.

6) **Costume**: what the characters are wearing, the overalls, the torn pocket on the shirt, the hat, the gloves, the scarf.

7) **Commentary**: the narrator's *thoughts* and *feelings*. Commentary can also consist of *Exposition*—background information, something that happened before the moment, but exposition or background info should be kept to a minimum, lest you lose the reader's involvement in the moment.

How to Make $1400

Pretend a producer promises to pay you $1,400 for the fully realized scene in that girl's bedroom, but you failed to mention the set (the room). Was it a rundown attic bedroom or a newly painted boudoir? The director tries to contact you but you're home sleeping and turned your phone off. The director has to pay someone else $200 to come up with the set. You saw the room in your mind, but you were in such a rush to tell the story, you left out the details. They deduct $200 from your fee, and now you're only making $1,200. Still, not so bad. But what did the mother and father look like? Did the mother have a delicate face and lots of makeup, or the face of a gargoyle with steel-wool eyebrows? Was the father tall, dark and handsome, or did he have a beer belly and a craggy face? The casting director, who's being paid $200, comes up with a skinny bespectacled actor to play the father and a white-haired old lady from Pasadena for the mother. Not what you had in mind at all. Not only is your story being changed, but you've lost another $200. Same goes for the lighting. Was the room dimly lit, or lit from the sun coming through the curtains or from flourescent lighting? What about costumes? We can learn so much about your characters just by what they're wearing, but if you leave out any mention of costume, that decision will be made by the person in the costume department, and you've lost another $200. **And don't forget props, those small objects no bigger than a deck of cards.** A single object is a prop; more than one of the same object is set dressing. A roll of pennies is a prop. A few pennies scattered on a table is set dressing. A small tin of marbles is a prop. So is a single marble. But two or three or many marbles lying on the floor is set dressing. John lost his marbles—that's commentary. Without any details between the bookends of your moment, you'll be lucky if the producer gives you $50 for the concept.

You want readers to see in their minds the same film you see in yours. If you don't give the details and images, they might see a different film. But Image-Moment is about more than giving the reader descriptive details, it's about *creating tension by converting real time into psychological time.* The reader doesn't just see the moment, the reader experiences it.

WORDS, WORDS, WORDS: The more words you use, the longer the moment lasts.

For the purposes of the exercise, I want you to *practice using all seven elements.* Eventually, you may only use a few, or even just one image to stretch the moment. Some writers can stretch a moment longer with one image than another writer does with all seven. How is that possible? Because it's not about using all seven elements, it's about how many words you use. *The more words you use, the longer the moment seems to last.* I want to repeat that: ***The more words you use, the longer the moment seems to last.*** I say "seems" because the actual moment you're describing doesn't last longer in real time, it lasts longer in psychological time, and therein lies the drama. The pause becomes more dramatic. But I want you to use all seven elements because it's good practice. Using all seven now is like taking your thousand practice swings a day with a golf club; you're practicing your form. Wax on, wax off.

> As writers, we tell a STORY and the EVENTS of that story. But you are becoming more than a teller of stories, you are becoming a STORYTELLER who holds an audience spellbound as only a STORYTELLER can do. That is done by focusing on the MOMENT and the IMAGES contained between the bookends of a moment.

How Will I Know Which Moment to Pick?

It'll pick you. Whatever you're writing about, one or two moments will stand out. But here's something curious about this exercise. The Image-Moment exercise will make even the most trivial of moments more compelling. I was working with a group of sixth-graders last year, and these kids did the exercise by the numbers. Their opening bookend was a sentence in which something "happened," a definite instantaneous action, or a line of dialogue. One or the other. Then they went through the list, adding details about the set, the set dressing, the mood, physical description of a character, costume, etc. I told them that it wasn't enough to name a character—Mom, Jerry, Uncle Moe—they also had to include some description of a physical detail. A scar on the cheek, a mustache, short and fat or tall and slender. I also reminded them to include a prop. **A small object that has nothing to do with the scene can end up being the most memorable:** a peanut on the arm of a sofa, a red false fingernail next to the sink, a pushpin next to your uncle's slippers. Remember, for our purposes, **a prop doesn't have to be used by a character**. As a matter of fact, it's better if it's not. It can be lying on the floor, sitting on a bookshelf, stuck between the pillows of the sofa. I realize that we tend to think of a prop as something being handled. A student will have a character pick up a sledge hammer. "That's my prop," they'll say. "No," I reply, "it's too big, it's bigger than a deck of cards." They counter: "Yeah, but my character is using it." Then I have to remind them that for our purposes here, a prop is not defined by its use. That's not a consideration. Size matters. If the object is no bigger than a deck of cards, it's a prop, even if it's a penny lying in the corner of the room, a penny that is totally irrelevant to the scene. So keep this in mind: **A prop is a small object. Smaller than a deck of cards. The smaller the better.** A key. A paper clip. A dime. An eraser. A single leaf. A button. A bottle cap (not the bottle, which would be set dressing). An ice-cube (but not the highball glass, that's too big to be a prop). A pen knife (but not a Bowie knife, that's too big). A roll of stamps. Notice the distinction between a single stamp (a prop), a roll of stamps (a prop), and several individual stamps lying on a table (set dressing). Props are small objects. But despite its size, the prop can become the touchstone to the scene's emotional truth. One student's story involved a boy who felt abandoned by his parents. He had all seven elements, but the one that everyone remembered was the crumpled gum wrapper under the coffee table. Another piece involved a boy who had climbed a tree. His prop was a shiny quarter he had lost then saw partly hidden under a rock. Two props that gave the piece a special quality. Props convey emotional truth. *If you can't see a prop in the scene you're writing, make one up.* After getting all seven elements between two bookends, the kids closed the moment with another action or line of dialogue. As they read their pieces aloud, a hush fell over the room. The teachers were awestruck at the result. The kids sounded like professional writers. To tell you the truth, I was amazed myself. For years I have taught this exercise to adults, but this was the first time I'd had eleven-year-olds do it. I felt like Archimedes as he ran through the streets of Athens yelling "Eureka!" How did these kids pull it off like pros? They did it by the numbers. They made their fourteen hundred bucks.

Write Like You Talk

Find a Juicy

Transformation Line

Massage It

Get to the Deep Voice

Strike While

the Transformation Line Is Hot

Image-Moment

Make $1,400

and Buy a New Wardrobe

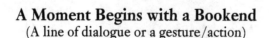

Make sure you bookend the moments:

A Moment Begins with a Bookend
(A line of dialogue or a gesture/action)

A Moment Ends with a Bookend
(A line of dialogue or a gesture/action)

What Happens in between the Bookends?
Nothing happens! Only images—no action, no dialogue.

Master storytellers use this technique instinctively, but students often resist it, believing that it interrupts the flow. They want to get on with the STORY. But story by itself is boring. Just as narrative without changes in tone (tonal dynamics) can lull us to sleep, a story without images or moments leaves the mind to wander. Teachers talk about the descriptive paragraph, but description is static. Too much description and the eyes glaze over. Even a story written in extremely beautiful prose is tedious without dramatic tension. **Many writers confuse dramatic tension with dramatic action**. They think that if something is always happening, if the action is fast and furious, the reader will be hooked. Not true. It's **dramatic tension** that grabs us. Don't confuse action with tension. When a scene in a story moves from one action or line of dialogue to another, we think we're creating drama. **But the dramatic tension lies in the pauses between those actions and lines of dialogue**. In method acting, we talk about moving through the scene "moment to moment." Some moments are fraught with inner conflict, problematic subtext. As actors, we bring out the drama of the scene not by how we say the lines, but by the pauses between the lines of dialogue or action. It's what we mean when we say some actors listen well. We love to watch them listen. What the actor and the camera allow us to see in the actor's face creates psychological time. The moment is filled with the nuance of expectation, conflict, inner life. The same thing is required of us as writers, but if we rush headlong through the story without bringing the moments alive, the story ends up boring the reader, not because it's too slow, but because it moves too quickly.

Before we move on, let's take a look at the journal entry about the diary. It was written by Peggy Geisler, a writer in one of my classes. When she wrote it, she was doing the exercise by the numbers, including all seven elements, stretching real time into psychological time, just as James Baldwin did in his story. (I've made bold several bookends. I've also italicized the seven elements: the set, set dressing, mood, props, character, costume, and commentary.)

The Diary

When my brother was nine years old, he found his cat in the park across from our house. It had been torn apart by some dogs in the neighborhood. He came running home and collapsed on his bed. I sat there with my arm around him and wept, too. I was seven years older than him. I knew there wasn't much I could do, so I just sat there. Mom poked her head in every now and then. She kept whizzing by, doing laundry, making beds, never slowing down long enough to feel anything. I was the one who comforted her children. I wasn't helping her. I was doing her job. She was useless when it came to feelings, and on some level she knew it. Because Mom was so cold, it took a lot to get a response out of her. Something extreme. And even if it was over the top, she'd just make an entrance and then get back to her nonstop activities.

[This paragraph sets the moment. The writer is giving background information: exposition, story.]

She made one of those appearances when I was in high school.

[This sentence signals the shift from general story to specific event.]

I was making my bed. I heard a shuffling behind me. When **I turned my head** I saw Mom and Dad in the doorway. **I stood up** and saw that she had my diary in her hands. **I glanced quickly** at the closet, to my sweaters on the shelf, **then back down** at the diary in her hands. **She held the diary out**, as if she were a policeman showing the criminal a piece of evidence.

"What about this, Peggy?" she said. **"Are you going to stab yourself?"**

[dialogue as bookend]

I didn't know what to do. My parents never wanted to know what I thought or felt or hoped for. So in that moment, Mom's question felt like a violation. I stared at the *diary*. I was stonestill. My back to the window. The *sun* coming in through the *lace curtains*, warm on my calves. My mother held the diary open, exposed, so I could see my writing on the pages. Mom had found the pages that revealed my fear that I was pregnant and didn't know what to do. My eyes glanced at words that uncovered my fantasy of taking one of the knives from the kitchen and stabbing my belly, over and over. As I read the words, I wondered why I'd spelled everything out. I knew shorthand. Why, of all the pages in my diary, did I write those in longhand?

My closet was between us, just to my left. The door was open. I could see some *skirts on hangers* and *sweaters* folded on the upper shelf. That's where I had hidden the diary, underneath some sweaters that Opa had sent. Opa was Mom's father. He sent packages from Germany throughout the year. He called them "Care Packages." He sent them because he resented needing the packages sent by the United States after the Second World War. He sent his Care Packages to us to get even. Dad stood behind my mother, an *eyebrow* raised as usual, his *lips* tight, both hands on his hips. He wore *jeans*, running *shoes*, and a *T-shirt*. Usually Dad wore long-sleeved shirts, so people couldn't tell how dark he was. But when he wore a T-shirt, I could see his *redneck tan*—brown face, neck and hands—and the *pale-face* behind the tan. Mom wore *yellow cotton pants* with an elastic waistband. She bought them from a thrift store. She loved going there. It took her back to her days growing up in Germany during the war. She had survived the war. That fact was a source of pride for her, and wearing clothes from the thrift shop kept her permanently connected to it. I think it kept her alive. She also wore a *blue sweater* from one of Opa's care packages, *bobby socks* and *sandals*.

I don't remember what I was wearing. Probably some *shorts, a cotton top*, and *sandals.* It didn't matter, though. What mattered was that I felt naked, ripped open, humiliated, the secret out. Mom and Dad waited for my answer. I looked them right in the eyes. I knew if my mother had read the journal, she knew I was having sex. She knew who the boy was. She knew what my fantasies were about him. She also knew I was sad and scared and lost.

I held my breath and answered her question. **"No . . . no, I'm not going to** stab myself." *[bookend]*

And Mom said, **"Well, then . . . . O.K.!"** *[another bookend]*

She handed me my diary, **turned,** and walked back down the hall to the kitchen. Dad followed her, shaking his head. **I closed** my bedroom door, **sat** on the lower bunk and wept. I held the diary in my hands. That's when I realized that it wasn't the humiliation I was feeling, but the loss. Maybe that's why I wrote the words in longhand. I wanted her to know the secret. I wanted her to know how I felt. I felt awful when they confronted me, but worse when they left. Now they knew, and they had walked away.

Look back over Peggy's journal entry. I've made bold twelve bookends, four of which are lines of dialogue, and eight of which are actions. The first five are all actions: I turned, I stood up, I glanced quickly, then back down, she held the diary out. Those are five clear and decisive actions, each one taking no more than 2 seconds. Making her bed is not an action, it's an event. Shuffling is not an action, it's a continuous action. The last two actions—She handed me my diary, and she turned—are clear and decisive. Two later bookends actually make up a bread sandwich (no baloney between). She handed, she turned. Boom! Bam! No images between. **So two bookends in a row with no images between make up a moment, not an Image-Moment.** If she were to cash in that last moment, she'd get nothing, zero, zilch. Maybe $50 for the concept if the cashier was feeling especially generous. Same for the next two—she closed, she sat. What about wept? Not an action, that's an event, it takes longer than two seconds. The mother walked down the hall—that's also not an action, it's an event because it takes more than two seconds. But there's some money to be made with the first five bookends, which consist of four Image-Moment baloney sandwiches. (Remember, the closing bookend of one moment can also be the opening bookend of the next moment.) Each of those actions—bookends—make a small baloney sandwich, four small baloney sandwiches, to be precise. There's one or two images between each set of bookends, so in effect, we have four very small Image-Moments. If we were paying Peggy for those Image-Moments, she'd get $200 or $400, depending on how many images she had between the bookends. If she could only cash in one of them, she'd probably choose the one that consisted of glancing at the closet, and then back down at the diary. The closet is part of the set, the sweaters are costume, and the shelf is also part of the set. So we have a nice little baloney sandwich there, enough money for lunch at Craft. But the real money is to be made with the next three bookends, which are lines of dialogue: "Are you going to stab yourself?", "No . . . no, I'm not going to stab myself," and "Well, then . . . O.K.!" The second one is worth about $200, since all we have between those two lines of dialogue is "and Mom said," a conjunction and an attribution. Very small baloney sandwich. Maybe worth an In 'n' Out burger. But the real money lies in the Image-Moment between the other two lines of dialogue: "Are you going to stab yourself?" and "No ... no, I'm not going to stab myself." That Image-Moment is the big winner, worth every penny of $1400. La Tour D'Argent, here we come.

Keep in mind that an action or gesture must be quick, decisive, instantaneous. When she was making the bed, that's an event, since it takes a good minute or more to make the bed. Same for when she heard shuffling behind her. It takes more than two seconds, and is actually what I call continuous action, something we'll talk about later. At the end, after Mom and Dad turn to go, they walk back down the hall. Walking back down the hall takes more than two seconds, so it's an event, not an action. The good thing to remember about dialogue is that it always makes a clear-cut bookend. Why? Because no matter how long the dialogue lasts (it could be the Gettysburg Address), when it comes to a stop, that's clear-cut. No matter how long someone is speaking, as soon as they're finished, as soon as you put that period to the sentence and close the quotes, the dialogue stops. **Dialogue is always a bookend**, you can't go wrong with dialogue. But if you choose to bookend a moment with an action, be sure it's an instantaneous action, and not an event (or an ongoing continuous action). Those are pitfalls we'll discuss later.

So if Peggy were going to cash in just one of her baloney sandwich Image-Moments, the big money maker is the one in which she mentions all seven elements:

prop (the diary);

set dressing (lace curtains, sweaters in the closet, skirts on hangers in the closet, etc.);

costume (jeans, bobby socks, t-shirts, sandals, running shoes, etc.);

character (rednecktan, brown face, etc.);

commentary (the exposition about Mother in Germany and Opa's care packages, her feelings of being ripped open).

Ooooops, she only mentioned five. She mentioned set earlier (her bedroom), but not in between those two bookends. I know, she said she was making her bed, but for all we know she could have been making the bed in the garage or the living room. So she didn't explicity tell us it was her bedroom, and the finicky guy whose job it is to "cash-in" her Image-Moment is not giving her $200 for set. Furthermore, there's no mention of mood (the other four senses) either. Where's the mood (lighting, sounds, smells, taste, touch)? Read back over the entry and see if you can find a sentence between those two bookends of dialogue that cover mood. There's one possible indication of mood: when she writes that the sun was coming through the lace curtains. We get the sense of a sunny day, bright sunlight giving the room a glow. So let's give her credit for mood. Another $200. But methinks if she'd gone back and worked in a sentence or two about what kind of light the sun created, our sense of mood would have been heightened. She could also have brought to our attention the sound of cars going by outside, the smell of spaghetti sauce cooking in the kitchen—it would have added to the sense of isolation she felt, the sense of drama. And to make the full $1400, she should have included mention again that it was her bedroom. Remember, I want you to use all seven elements for now between your bookends; it's good practice. But the real point of Image-Moment is not how much money you make, it's the words that you use to stretch real time into pyschological time.

Most of us telling this story—of being confronted by parents who had read our diary—would not have filled that pause between the two bookends. But telling the reader that there was a long pause doesn't make the reader *feel* it. When you add the images between those bookends, it creates an experience for the reader. It takes time to read those sentences. The very act of reading them creates a real pause (psychological drama) between those bookends. We are waiting for the other shoe to drop. What's Peggy going to say? What's going to happen? Look how much drama is contained in that "descriptive pause" between bookends.

When you're done reading this chapter, open your journal to a blank page and begin writing with no subject in mind. When you get to the Slauson Cutoff (a juicy transformation line), take it, massage it. When you feel your voice has deepened, give the reader an Image-Moment—the whole package: start with a line of dialogue or gesture/action, then write a few sentences in which you mention all seven elements, then close your Image-Moment with another bookend, either dialogue or action. Make $1,400. If you don't get caught up in the flow of your "story," but make the deliberate attempt to mention all seven elements between your bookends, you'll find it's really easy as pie. It's an easy as making a baloney sandwich with seven slices of baloney between two pieces of bed.

When you're done, go back over it and identify your Image-Moment. If you have more than one, that's okay. But identify each one. You should know where they are, because it's something you did deliberately. Keep the Image-Moment graphic display on pages 126–127 handy, so you can refer to it. **Make sure you get all seven elements.** However, read the rest of the chapter before doing your journal entry. There's still some concepts that need to be clarified.

The Four Questions

A good way to verify how well you've done your Image-Moment is by answering the following four questions—be sure you read the answers as well:

1) *What were your bookends?*

Was it dialogue? "Oh Rhett, what will I do, where will I go?" Or an action/gesture. *A door closes. She points to the river.* Going to the store is not an action, it's an event—a common mistake. *Then he drove home.* That's not an action, it's an event. It takes more than a few seconds to drive home. If your bookend takes longer than a second or two, it is not a bookend. The closing bookend is also an action/gesture, or a line of dialogue; in this case, it's a line of dialogue: "Frankly, my dear, I don't give a damn." Weak bookends, or worse, bookends that are events or continuous action will not work. The mechanical device known as Image-Moment will not function unless your bookends are clear and decisive.

2) *How much time elapsed between bookends (in actual real time)?*

A few seconds. Technically speaking, it could be as much as 59 seconds, but not 60 seconds. Why? Because I can spell. Image-Moment, not Image/*Minute.* If it's longer than that, you've got a problem. How much time elapsed between Scarlet asking Rhett what she should do and Rhett's response? A few seconds. What about an opening bookend like *He dropped the gun,* and a closing bookend like *He ate a sandwich.* Dropping a gun takes no more than two seconds, but eating a sandwich takes at least a few minutes. It's an event, not an action. If you wrote, *He began to eat his sandwich.* that would work, since beginning to eat takes a second. But for all we know, there might be 15 minutes between his dropping the gun and eating a sandwich. A moment lasts only a few seconds. It's hard to create a pause that lasts nearly a minute, most situations do not consist of a freeze frame of 60 seconds. So technically speaking, I'll grant you 59 seconds between bookends, but not 60 seconds, not a whole minute. We're not talking about the time it takes to write your sentences between the bookends, or the time it takes the reader to read those sentences. We're talking about the actual time that transpires in the scene you're writing about. The pause between the bookends in the real, actual time of the imagined scene must be no more than a moment, a few seconds. "What happened between?" I asked. "Well, they had dinner and talked for three hours." Sorry, that's not a moment. That's an epic poem!

3) What happened between your bookends?

Nothing. No one says anything, no one does anything. Nothing means nothing. Nothing doesn't mean something. Nothing happens, period. No walks in the rain, no emptying the trash. No turning of the head, no looking up, no looking down, no head movements of any kind, no blinking, no action, no dialogue. The only thing between your bookends are images. Description. Images are not actions. Static description between bookends is dramatic because it creates psychological time. If you have backstory/exposition (which is part of commentary) between your bookends, the action in backstory does not count as action because the action occurs prior to the moment. Avoid exposition between bookends, or keep it to a minimum. It's okay to say he bought the jacket yesterday for his birthday, but stay with the images in the scene. A whole backstory about how he bought the jacket takes the reader out of the drama of the scene.

Okay. You've read the above paragraph, but you weren't paying close attention. You were petting the dog or listening to your iPod. So I'll say it one more time for emphasis: NOTHING HAPPENS between the bookends of a moment. No one exits a room, no one turns up their collar, no one blinks, breathes, bawls, or blows their nose. It's a freeze frame. No one sits down or stands up. The dog doesn't bark, the parakeet doesn't tweet, the door doesn't open. Furthermore, no events occur. Events are a series of actions. Finding your keys is an event (you have to look around, bend over, check behind the body slumped against the bookcase, etc.). Getting a pack of cigarettes is an event (you have to walk up the stairs, open the door to your room, rummage through the pockets of the bloke lying against the dresser, retrieve the pack of cigarettes, come back down the stairs). Going to Europe for the summer is an event (you have to lug the body into the trunk of the car, drive to the docks, board the ship, etc.). There are no actions, between bookends, no events, no dialogue, no nothin' but words that describe the set, the set dressing, one or more props, the mood, a character, what they're wearing, and commentary—thoughts, opinions, or backstory.

4) How many of the seven elements of Image-Moment did you get? How much money did you make?

Set, set dressing, props, mood, character, costume, commentary. Seven possibilities. No dialogue. No action. Just description. This is where your skill as a writer comes into play, your ability to create drama for the reader. A few words creates a small pause, more words creates a bigger pause, and a whole bunch of words creates an even bigger pause. As you read your paragraph back to yourself, feel the pause and decide if you need more words or fewer words. You're sculpting psychological time.

What Are the Two Shortest Image-Moments Possible?

I'm not sure why people forget this section. Maybe they read it and don't pay attention. Will you be one of those who reads this section without really paying attention? I hope not—it's quite important. The shortest Image-Moment—one word—was discovered in 1917 while archeologists were digging for dinosaur bones. The field of paleoanthropology was still quite new, but as Selma Stein (Gertrude's sister) once said, "A bone is a bone is a bone." Louis Leakey established the tradition of palaeoanthropology and was directing a dig in the Olduvai Gorge in Africa. Quite absent-minded, he once had everyone looking for spectacles that were around his neck; often he wore pants with the buttons off and shoes with holes in them. But he was completely happy searching for dinosaur bones. One morning, as the archeologists were digging under a prominent outcropping of rock, out came the fossilized word "and," along with several stray letters—one was either an "O" or a "Q"—there is still some dispute to this day about that. For archeologists, the discovery of the word "and" was no big thing, but for writers, it was an international sensation. Before that, writers were straightjacketed by simple declarative sentences, such as *He put on his socks*, or *He put on his shoes*. One bookend after another. But by inserting the word "and" between those two sentences, they were able to create the shortest Image-Moment possible:

> He put on his socks and he put on his shoes.

Granted, there's only the slightest pause between those two bookends, but to paraphrase Selma Stein and Gertrude Stein, "A pause is a pause is a pause." In this case, it's the smallest pause possible. Prior to that discovery, most Image-Moments were at least four words long, such as:

> He put on his socks with a flourish, then he put on his shoes.

This was like discovering that molecules were made up of atoms and atoms were made up of protons and protons were made up of quarks. Writers around the world were delighted by the discovery and partied into the night. Some are partying to this day.

Let's look at one more example of a one word Image-Moment, and how by adding words between bookends we can stretch psychological time.

> **John picked up the gun.** [no images between] **He pulled the trigger.**

That's a moment. Two actions, no images between. But with our conjunction "and" we can make a very very short Image-Moment.

> **John picked up the gun** and **pulled the trigger.**

The "and" between the two clauses creates the slightest pause in the reader's mind. We could add more to it, stretch the moment out a bit longer.

> **John picked up the gun** without taking his eyes off his victim and **pulled the trigger.**

> or

> **John picked up the gun** without taking his eyes off his victim, who was still standing in the doorway in his tuxedo and top hat, and **pulled the trigger.**

Obviously, we could keep adding words between those two actions and make the moment last even longer. But what about dialogue? This is where the second shortest Image-Moment discovery comes in. It was the summer of 1965. A young songwriter named Paul Simon had just released his first album with Art Garfunkel in 1964, which turned out to be a flop. So Simon moved to England to pursue a solo career, touring folk clubs and coffee houses. At the first club he played, the Railway Inn Folk Club in Brentwood, Essex, he met Kathy Chitty who became his girlfriend and inspiration for "Kathy's Song," "America," and others. With "America," he was trying to write a song with non-rhyming lyrics about the journey of two companions in search of the true meaning of America. The song describes a trip east through America which leads to New York City, as Simon's lovers travel from Saginaw, Michigan to Pittsburgh and then onto the New Jersey Turnpike. The lovers' initial hopefulness turns to a sense of angst and maybe sadness. Paul had written at one point:

> "Kathy, I'm lost; I'm empty and aching and I don't know why."

But he felt the line needed an Image-Moment, a short one, between "Kathy, I'm lost," and "I'm empty and aching and I don't know why." But he was not sure how to create that pause. One afternoon while walking about north London, he ventured into Camden Passage in Islington, full of Georgian-Victorian ramshackle buildings and warped shop fronts selling all manner of thrift, vintage, and antique collectibles. An old man standing in the doorway of one curiosity shop mysteriously waved him in. For a moment, he hesitated. The old man's eyes twinkled, his clothes full of dust, a pair of spectacles dangling from his shirt pocket. As if in a trance, Simon stepped in, and walked to the back of the store. There, among pieces of broken furniture and brass plates, stood an old Dickensian armoir. While rummaging through its cobwebbed interior, he came across a piece of parchment that appeared to be hundreds of years old. Written in faded ink was the two-word attribution, *I said.* Simon was ecstatic. "Eureka!" he yelled, running through the streets of London wearing only his boxer shorts, "I have discovered the second shortest Image-Moment." He rushed home and wrote:

> *I said,* "Kathy, I'm lost, I'm empty and aching and I don't know why."

Wait, that didn't work, he thought. Something was wrong. He tried putting the attribution at the end of the line.

> "Kathy, I'm lost, I'm empty and aching and I don't know why," *I said.*

Hmmm? That didn't work either. There's no Image-Moment, just one line of dialogue, one bookend. Then he hit upon a crucial idea: if I put the attribution *between* the lines of dialogue, he thought, I will have created two bookends with the two-word attribution between. That should do it!

> "Kathy, I'm lost," *I said,* "I'm empty and aching and I don't know why."

He sang it aloud, but realized he needed to stretch the Image-Moment to delay the other bookend, the closing line of dialogue. So he added the phrase *though I knew she was sleeping.*

> "Kathy, I'm lost," *I said, though I knew she was sleeping,* "I'm empty and aching
> and I don't know why."

By putting the two-word attribution *between* the two lines of dialogue, he created the slightest pause; not as short as the word *and*, but certainly the second-shortest Image-Moment possible. Later, in the same song, Simon had another line that needed a short Image-Moment. At first, he wrote:

"Kathy, Michigan seems like a dream to me now."

The solution was obvious: just insert the two-word attribution between the lines of dialogue.

"Kathy," *I said*, "Michigan seems like a dream to me now."

Again, he felt the need to stretch that psychological time, so he added another five words.

"Kathy," *I said, as we boarded a greyhound*, "Michigan seems like a dream to me now."

Like a cook tasting the soup, before adding more salt, he felt he needed another two words to extend the psychological time even more.

"Kathy," *I said, as we boarded a greyhound for Pittsburgh*, "Michigan seems like a dream to me now."

Perfect!

Prior to the song's release, a version was sung by the band The Clouds at the Marquee in April 1967. The Simon and Garfunkel version was released in 1968. Several cover versions have been produced since then, including a ten-and-a-half minute version by the progressive rock band Yes in 1971, and a memorably minimalist performance by David Bowie to open The Concert for New York City in October 2001. The song was also featured in the soundtrack to the film *Almost Famous*, where the main character's sister uses the song to represent her reason for leaving home to become a stewardess. Today it's almost impossible to sing those lines without the Image-Moment between the bookends. They make dramatic and musical sense.

Let's take a look at a few more examples of using a two-word attribution—*I said, she said, he said, we said, they said*, etc.—to create pauses, and then ways to extend that pause with a few more descriptive words.

"If I find out you had an affair with Zelda Sleeklegs, I'm leaving you for good," *she said.*

There's only one bookend in the sentence with the attribution at the end of the dialogue. Let's reconstruct that sentence another way.

She said, "If I find out you had an affair with Zelda Sleeklegs, I'm leaving you for good."

There's no Image-Moment there either. It's just a line of dialogue with the attribution (she said) at the beginning, before the dialogue. But if we break the dialogue in half, putting the attribution in the middle, we have a two-word Image-Moment, a very short pause:

"If I find out you had an affair with Zelda Sleeklegs," *she said*, "I'm leaving you for good."

Eureka! And if we wanted to make the pause last longer to create more psychological time, we'd add more words after "she said."

> "If I find out you had an affair with Zelda Sleeklegs," *she said, holding the photograph of his mother against her chest,* "I'm leaving you for good."

A scene can have dozens of moments, and some of those moments can be Image-Moments. Some will have a short pause between bookends, and others will stretch psychological time to the utmost. The more you work with the seven elements, the more you'll get a feel for the various permutations and combinations possible and how they can be used to stretch real time into psychological time.

Before reading further, take stock of what we've covered so far. Are you clear about what a bookend is? Are you clear about what constitutes an action, as opposed to an event? Are you clear about filling the space between your bookends with words—it could be one word, like *and*, it could be two words, like *she said*, it could be several sentences. Are you clear about what the seven elements are? You know: the set, the set dressing, etc.? Okay, we've got a few other concepts to nail down so your Image-Moment will work like a well-oiled machine. We'll start with a few pitfalls.

A Common Pitfall: When Is an Action an Event?

An event takes longer than two seconds, and is composed of many actions. It doesn't have the *force* of a single action. This distinction may seem trivial, but it's not. A bookend must create a sense of expectation—the reader waits for the other shoe to drop. An event will not create that sense of expectation. Whether the event takes five weeks or five seconds, it dilutes the force of the bookend. If I write: *Waldo went to Paris,* there's no suspense. Where the hell is Waldo? Is he disembarking from the plane? Is he checking into his hotel? Is he hailing a cab? At what point can one say he finished "going" to Europe? If I were to say Waldo stepped off the plane and began to walk down the ramp, or Waldo slammed the door of the taxi, or Waldo opened his suitcase, I'm waiting for the next bookend. There's a sense of immediacy. What will he find in his suitcase? Don't confuse an action with an event. That's a common pitfall. The following sentences, for example, describe events, not actions.

> John left the house.
> (How many actions does that require? Walking to the door, turning the knob, opening the door, walking out, closing the door, walking down the steps, etc. Too many to count. It won't function as a bookend because it doesn't have the *force* of an action, no boom-bam-bang. The same is true for the events that follow.)

> Shirley went to her room and got the book.

> Phil went to the store for cigarettes.   Brenda went to Europe for the summer.

> Professor Quigglemeister toured the Alps and wrote a travel guide.

> Bradley flew to Jupiter and met his wife.

> Olivia walked past the bank. (This takes at least 10 seconds, it's a big bank.)

When is an action an event? *When it takes more than two seconds.* Make sure your bookends are instantaneous. The time **between** bookends can last as long as 59 seconds (though most likely only a few seconds), but a good opening bookend is decisive and creates drama. What's going to happen next. When people talk about a novel being a page-turner, it's because there are Image-Moments that leave us waiting for the other shoe to drop (the closing bookend).

When Is an Image-Moment Like a Baloney Sandwich?

When the two bookends of bread have baloney between them. The baloney must go *between* the two slices of bread, just as the images must go *between* the two bookends. Every Image-Moment is a baloney sandwich.

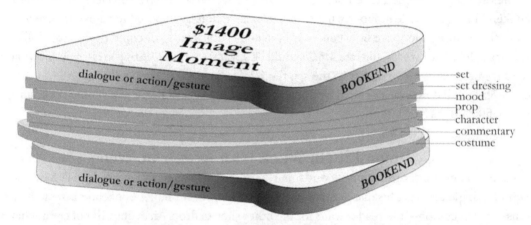

As practice, I want you to make a baloney sandwich using all seven slices of baloney (all seven elements of Image-Moment). The images must go *between* the bookends—you wouldn't put your baloney outside the slices of bread, would you? If the images are outside the bookends, they're just description, which can be boring. *But images between bookends stretch real time into psychological time.* How long that psychological time lasts is up to you, the writer. The more words you use between bookends, the longer it takes for the other shoe to drop.

Sculpt your Images/Moments to create vivid scenes. Sometimes the narrative requires the action to move from one bookend to another. Bookends without images between them are just moments. A scene can proceed moment to moment, dialogue following dialogue, action following action. No Image-Moments, no baloney sandwiches, just one slice of bread after another. The following is a series of moments.

> "Did you bring the suitcases?" she asked.
> "No," he said, "I left them in the car."
> She took off her raincoat. He sat in the armchair and crossed his legs.
> "Our passports were in the luggage, you idiot!" she yelled. "The luggage was in the trunk of the car. The car's at the bottom of the river. What are we supposed to do now?"
> "Go fishing," he said.

Any baloney there? Nope. Just slices of bread—bookends. (I'm ignoring those two-word Image-Moment attributions "he said" and "she asked" for now.) Here's the sequence of the scene: dialogue, dialogue, action, action, action, dialogue, dialogue. Seven bookends, six moments. In the following version, I added some images and continuous actions between a few pairs of bookends, turning what was a moment into an Image-Moment. (I've made bold the bookends below.)

> **"Did you bring the suitcases?" she asked.** The hotel room was stuffy. She could detect traces of smoke from the previous occupants. It was supposed to be a non-smoking room, but someone had broken the rules. She watched the rain hit the window that looked out onto the park below. Raindrops coalescing as they ran down the glass. Cars were whizzing by on the street below. She could hear them and was momentarily distracted by the thought of all that exhaust coming in through the cracks. The curtains were waving in the breeze. She could see him in the mirror now, standing there, his tanned face sullen and hopeless.
>
> He thought, she might as well know the truth. **"No," he said, "I left them in the car."**

[Now we have an Image-Moment. Two bookends (two slices of bread). Let's count the images (slices of baloney).

> the stuffy hotel room—**set** ($200),
> the smell of cigarette smoke, exhaust fumes—**mood** ($200),
> the reference to disobeying the rules—her thoughts, **commentary** ($200),
> raindrops on the window, the curtains—**set dressing** ($200),
> the mirror—**set dressing** (we've already gotten paid for that),
> his tanned face, sullen and hopeless—**character** ($200),
> his thoughts about fessing up—**commentary** again.

> Let's total it up.
> Set · · · · · · · $ 200
> Mood· · · · · · $ 200
> Commentary · · $ 200
> Set Dressing· · $ 200
> Character · · · · $ 200
> TOTAL · · · · $1,000

In that one Image-Moment, we made $1,000. Not bad for a few sentences. (Note the continuous actions: cars whizzing by, raindrops coalescing, curtains waving: since they're not "actions," but continuous actions, they can be included between bookends.) If I had wanted the pause between her question and his answer to last longer in terms of psychological time, I'd have added more words. Let's continue:]

> "No, I left them in the car," he said.
> She took off her raincoat.

[Two bookends: a line of dialogue and an action. But since there are no images between the bookends, it's not an Image-Moment, it's just a moment. (Once again, I'm ignoring the two-word Image-Moment attributions "she asked" and "he said.") Remember, the bookend where she takes off her raincoat is the closing bookend of the moment before it, but it is also the opening bookend of the next moment: one man's ceiling is another man's floor.]

She took off her raincoat. She was wearing a Glynnis O'Brien dress that tapered to her waist, the cut of her neckline showing her ample cleavage. A few freckles stood out on her chest, delicious buds he wanted to lick. But it was too late now for love, too late even for sex. All of that had been lost in the last few days. They were going through the motions, trying to survive. **He sat in the armchair** and **crossed his legs.**

[She took off her raincoat and he sat down in the armchair—in between we have a series of images. There's the description of her dress—costume ($200), her figure and chest with freckles—character ($200), his thoughts—commentary ($200), and then the closing bookend when he sits in the armchair (set dressing, $200). We've made a total of $800.

Like a film editor, you construct a series of shots between the dialogue or actions of a moment to create the effect you want. Let's say there's a line of dialogue: "I've always loved you," (bookend) You decide to cut to a shot of the lamp in the corner of the room (set dressing); then you cut to the paper-clip on the floor (prop); then a close-up of the man's face with the bushy eyebrows and a scar on his cheek (character); finally a realization that looks aren't everything (commentary). Then you close the moment with an action/gesture: the man closes his eyes and turns his head (bookend). That's an $800 Image-Moment.

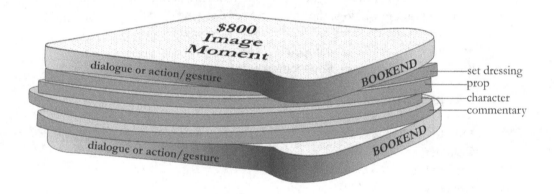

But as a good film editor, you're also aware of time, pacing and drama. How long will you hold on the shot of the lamp, or the scar on his cheek? A film editor counts frames to hold the camera on the lamp for one second or two or three. One second = 24 frames, two seconds = 48 frames., etc. But the writer counts words. The more words you spend describing the lamp, the longer the reader looks at it. You are, after all, making a movie in the reader's mind. You're the director, the characters, the set-decorator, the prop master, the lighting director, and even the voice-over, should you decide to provide commentary. With the mechanism of Image-Moment, you'll shape psychological time as well. If you think the Image-Moment was too long, if it gave too much importance to an inconsequential moment, cut a few words; if you think the suspense should be held longer, add a few words. If you want the reader to notice the penny on the table, to feel the oppressive heat in the room, to see the plush sofa, add those details. The mechanics of Image-Moment is your starting point. Now you're writing like a professional, constructing each moment within a scene and each event within the story.

Another Common Pitfall: Continuous Action

Image-Moment involves static images between bookends in which nothing happens. There are seven categories of images. So let's posit three categories of narrative movement: Action (no more than 2 seconds), Event (more than 2 seconds), and last, but not least, Continuous Action. A continuous action is a repetitive action like pacing a room, curtains waving in the breeze, cars passing by on the street, someone drumming their fingers on a table, rain streaking down a window, the pendulum of a clock swinging back and forth. A continuous action is not someone making a ham sandwich or painting a wall, because those involve numerous different movements. But twiddling one's thumbs is a simple movement repeated over and over. Patting one's belly or spinning in a circle or banging one's head against a wall—those are Continuous Actions. How long can a continuous action last? Well, within the bookends of a moment, they can neither start nor stop. They last as long, if not longer, than the Image-Moment itself. If they started or stopped, that would be an action, since starting or stopping takes less than two seconds. So don't confuse an action—boom! crash! bam!—with Continuous Action—la de da, de da, de da. A continuous action is not a bookend, because it lasts longer than two seconds. This is a common pitfall. Don't begin your Image-Moment with a continuous action. If you do, your Image-Moment will not work in creating psychological time. However, a continuous action can exist within the bookends, because it's an ongoing repetitive action, since it neither begins nor ends. You could still say that nothing happened! And what about Event, our second category of movement? Well, an event can neither function as a bookend, nor can it fit between bookends. Got it?

So why don't I list Continuous Action as one of the seven elements? Because it's not a static description. The sound of the continuous action could be considered mood, but only if you mention the sound. Remember, mood includes the other four senses beside sight (since what you can see are the set, dressing, props, etc.): taste, smell, sound, feel/touch. Continuous Action is not one of those senses unless you describe the action in terms of its sound, etc. The ticking of the clock could be mood, but the pendulum swinging back and forth is Continuous Action, not mood. Your Image-Moment will still function if there is a continuous action between the bookends, but technically speaking, it's not part of static imagery. So I would be careful introducing a continuous action between bookends. I don't want to encourage it, which is why I don't list it as one of the seven elements, but if you can get away with it, more power to you. But be careful. Continuous Action is another common pitfall. It can function as a bookend, but unlike action, it can still be placed between bookends as long as it doesn't stop. If uncle Harry stops pacing, or begins pacing, that's an action. So be careful how you handle continuous action. And what about Event, our second category of narrative movement? Heaven forbid, an event can function neither as a bookend nor between bookends. Nothing happens between books, and certainly not an event. Got it? Good.

Yet Another Pitfall

Pennies on a table, rose petals scattered on the floor, leaves on the ground, drops of water on the hood of your car—those are not props, but set dressing. A roll or stack of pennies is a prop, however, since it's the roll that constitutes the prop. A thousand pennies scattered across the San Bernardino Freeway is not a prop. A single penny lying by the side of the road is a prop.

can be part of the seven elements: mood, character, props, set, set dressing, costume, etc.

♦ "His bony fingers were fiddling with the pen."

That sentence combines character and props. You make $400 with that sentence.

♦ "The child with the blond hair rocked back and forth in the antique rocker near the window of the living room."

That sentence is worth $600. Character, set dressing, and set.

♦ "The lightbulb swung back and forth over the table, throwing shadows across the old man's face as he continued shuffling the cards, humming the opening bars of Beethoven's 5th Symphony."

That sentence is good for $800: set, mood, character, and props.

When Is an Image-Moment like a Swiss Watch?

When all the parts click. Once you are clear on all the parts, the simplicity of the whole becomes clear. But this concept is counter-intuitive and easily misunderstood. We often think the creative act is one of "flow," and to suggest that we stop the flow of our story to create an Image-Moment may seem antithetical to being in the moment. Pitchers talk about the mechanics of throwing a curveball, golfers talk about the mechanics of the backswing, film editors must decide the number of frames with which to compose each shot—will it have 48 frames lasting 2 seconds or 72 frames lasting 3 seconds? The combinations are endless. Does she cut to the close-up of the face, then the medium shot of the two lovers standing in the rain, or does she cut first to the wide shot filmed from above, a shot meant to emphasize how small they are in relation to the buildings around them? And if she cuts to that shot first, for how many frames does she hold that shot? A scene like that could involve half-a-dozen angles and numerous decisions as to the order of the cuts and the length of time each shot will last on screen. I'm sure there's an intuitive flow to how the editor cuts the scene, but the editor is not "flowing." It's a deliberate, mechanical process. If, however, you are not clear about the mechanics of Image-Moment, you will not create an Image-Moment that works. If your bookends aren't truly bookends; if your actions are events, not actions; if your moment lasts too long in real time; if you aren't clear on the seven elements, your Image-Moment will not *work*. It might be good writing, you might have good description (images), but the concept will not function as it's meant to, it won't effect the reader the way a good Image-Moment can.

Another Pitfall: Verbs of Condition vs Verbs of Action

Take the sentence: *He looked at me.* Looking and seeing are not necessarily actions. They're statements of condition, and depending on the context, a sentence like that will not function as a bookend. On the other hand, if you were to write—*He looked up at me*—now you have an action. Looking is not the same as looking up. The same goes for sitting. *He sat there watching the fire.* In that case, sitting is not an action. But if you were to say—*He sat down to watch the fire*—now we've got an action. What about, *He held onto the gun.* That's not an action. He's holding the gun, but there's no action. If he held out the gun, that's an action. If he grabbed hold of the gun, that's an action. What about, *He clutched the book.* That's tricky. If he reached out and grabbed the book, then he clutched the book to his chest, clutching would be an action. But if he clutches the book, meaning he's holding on to it, that's not an action. *He stood by the door.* Again, depends on the context. If you mean he levered his body into a standing position by the door, then it's an action. But if you mean he's just standing there, then there's no action. Remember, an action takes one or two seconds at most to complete. If it takes longer than two seconds, it's not an action, but an event. If someone walks *across the room*, that's an event. If someone walks *into* the room, that could be an action.

Verbs of condition can function between bookends and not break the dramatic tension. Someone standing by the door, holding a gun, clutching a book, looking at the fire, will not interfere with the dramatic pause.

Round up the Usual Suspects

It's obvious by now that Image-Moment is a cinematic technique. The words I've used for the seven elements are cinematic: set, props, lighting, etc. If you were writing a screenplay, your focus would be on the dialogue. You could spend hundreds of words on descriptions of the characters, on what a particular scene looks like, but in the end, none of that is in your control. The director will shoot the movie her way. No matter how much description you give in a screenplay about the lighting or the set, in the end, it will fall into the hands of a lighting designer and set designer. All you can hope for is that the actors say your words. That's why it's common to hear someone say, after seeing a movie made from a book, "The book was better." The movie they imagined as they read the book was better than the movie they saw on the screen. But with poems, stories, or novels, you're the actor, the set designer, the lighting designer, the director, and the film editor. Writers have been making movies for nearly three thousand years. You can find Image-Moments throughout the *Iliad*. Take the scene near the end when Priam sneaks into the enemy camp to ask Achilles to give him back the body of his son, Hector. He finally confronts Achilles, who has just finished his evening meal in his tent.

Clasping Achilles' knees, Priam kisses the "dread and murderous hands that had slain so many of his sons." This action/gesture sets up the drama of that scene. What will Achilles do, a man famous for his explosive wrath? Will he draw his sword and kill Priam? Homer creates a psychological pause as the reader awaits the other bookend. Achilles stares at Priam in wonder. "Is he a god?" thinks Achilles. Homer cuts to Achilles's companions, warriors both. We see the table still set with food and drink. We cut back to Priam waiting for Achilles' response. Finally, Priam speaks, ending that Image-Moment, but beginning another. Priam begs for the body of his son. He tells Achilles that of his fifty sons, not one is left alive, and now Hector, the only one who could have saved the city, has been cut down by Achilles' sword. "My Hector," he says. "It is for him that I have now come to ransom his body from you. Think on your own father, and have compassion upon me. I have sneaked into the enemy camp, risked my life, borne what no man who has walked this earth has ever yet borne. I have kissed the hand of the man who killed my son." In this most cinematic of moments, Homer pauses as the reader waits to see what will happen. Homer stretches the time between the two bookends, intensifying the drama. Like a film editor, he chooses which shots to cut to, and how long each will last before cutting to another image, then another, before cutting to the action/gesture (or the next bookend).

> Sorrow for his own father
> Welled up in Achilles. He took Priam's hand
> And gently pushed the old man away.
> The two of them remembered. Priam,
> Huddled in grief at Achilles' feet, cried
> And moaned softly for his man-slaying Hector.
> And Achilles cried for his father and
> For Patroclus. The sound filled the room.
>
> When Achilles had his fill of grief
> And the aching sorrow left his heart,
> He rose from his chair and lifted the old man
> By the hand, pitying his white hair and beard.
> And his words enfolded him like wings:
>
> "Ah, the suffering you've had, and the courage.
> To come here alone to the Greek ships
> And meet my eye, the man who slaughtered
> Your many fine sons!"

You'll be happy to know that Achilles returns the body to Priam. Brave and gallant Hector, "breaker of horses," is finally accorded a proper burial as the sun comes up. The poem ends with a glorious feast.

Homer composed the *Iliad* and the *Odyssey* nearly three thousand years ago, yet it's as cinematic as any movie made in the 20th century. In the movie *Casablanca*, near the end, as Humphrey Bogart and Ingrid Bergman prepare to board a plane for Lisbon, Bogart pulls his gun from his trenchcoat and shoots Major Strasser, the German officer who has come to arrest them. The prefect of police, Claude Rains, witnesses the event. Just then, a car drives up, filled with gendarmes. Rains says to them, "Major Strasser has been shot." Were the film editor to cut to the next line of dialogue, all the drama of that moment would be lost. Will Claude Rains identify Bogart as the man who shot Strasser? Will Bogart shoot Claude Rains to prevent him from exposing him? In that pause, the film editor builds dramatic tension by cutting back and forth between close-ups of Rains's face, then Bogart's face, a shot of Bogart's hand in the pocket of his trenchcoat, holding the gun, then back to the master shot of the gendarmes waiting for instructions, then back to Claude Rains. On screen, it takes only a few seconds, this pause between bookends, but what we experience is not real time, but psychological time. Each image is filled with information: the look on their faces, the clothes they're wearing, the early morning fog rising in the background, the plane beginning to taxi down the runway. After a few seconds that seem to last a lifetime, the other shoe drops: "Round up the usual suspects!" Whew. That was close.

What Is a Beat?

An actor or director sculpts the pace and rhythm of a scene by defining the various beats, or units of drama within the scene. Every scene has rising and falling action, stops and starts. Actors call these units "beats." Each beat is a mini-scene. It's as simple as counting the significant pauses that indicate one beat has ended and another is about to begin. When rehearsing a scene, actors think in terms of the character's actions and objectives, but the scene also has a pace, a rhythm, a tempo; it doesn't just run from one line of dialogue to the next. It's not enough to tell your story, you must sculpt the beats, and within the beats are moments. You sculpt the drama of your scene—the pace and rhythm of your beats—by varying the length of your Image-Moment, by the number of words you include between each set of bookends.

They say a picture is worth a thousand words. The real art of Image-Moment is in choosing which element to use first, then second, and so on. Your goal is to create psychological time. How many words will you use to describe Bogart's face? The more words you use, the longer the shot lasts. Obviously, a shot can last too long. This is where the art comes in, your sense of timing and pace. Make your readers see what you want them to see, then decide how long you want them to look at it. The more words, the longer the look. The longer the look, the more important it is to the story. So the Image-Moment creates more than dramatic tension, it tells the reader what's important by how long we ask him to pay attention to that image, to consider its meaning.

The Four Aspects of All Narrative

There are four "levels" or "degrees" of narrative structure as shown on the left column on page 126. There are also seven "elements" to Image-Moment, as shown on page 127. Another way to categorize all writing is according to the four "aspects" of all narrative: Action, Dialogue, Description, Commentary. Every sentence you write will be one (or more) of those four aspects. There is no fifth aspect. Only those four. A sentence can show the reader an action, someone is doing something, something is happening, etc. A sentence can invovle dialogue, Garbo speaks. A sentence can describe something—no action, just description. And finally, a sentence can involve commentary, thought, feelings, analysis, etc. Can you think of another aspect? No, you can't. Those four, that's it. A single Image-Moment can contain all four of those aspects. Bookends: Action or Dialogue, that's two. The seven elements between those bookends include static description and commentary, that's the other two. Four total.

What is a bookend?

A sentence that is either a line of dialogue or an action/gesture.

What is a moment?

A short span of time, less a minute, but usually only a few seconds, *between two bookends, in which nothing happens.*

A moment is two bookends, no images between (or two pieces of bread, no baloney between).

What is an Image-Moment?

A moment that has images between the bookends. It's a baloney sandwich. It can have one slice of baloney or it can have many slices of baloney. How many slices is up to you.

What's the function of an Image-Moment?

It stretches real time into

psychological time.

What do you use to accomplish that?

WORDS. The more words, the longer it

takes the reader to get to the closing

bookend of the moment. And the longer it

takes the reader to read it, the longer the

psychological time seems to last.

What can the words be about?

Set, set dressing, props, mood, character,

costume, commentary (thoughts, feelings,

or exposition).

Here's Looking at You, Kid

Below is what a story board from *Casablanca* might have looked like. Except for the opening bookend (dialogue) and the closing bookend (dialogue), you'll notice there's no action or dialogue. Just static shots. In one context, these shots—or the writer's description of these shots—could be tedious and boring, but placed between the dramatic bookends of a line of dialogue or an action, the static shots create tension and psychological time.

"Major Strasser's been shot!"
  [We're on a master shot. The whole *set*. You would write a sentence that gives the reader an image of the airport and landing field. You could also give info about *set-dressing*, which in this case includes the car and the hangar.]

[Cut to medium shot of *character*. We can describe the face, eyes, mouth, etc. *Costume* could describe the coat, the hat, the tie. *Commentary* includes thoughts, feelings and back story (exposition), but keep exposition to a minimum. The more words you use, the longer the shot lasts.]

[Cut back to Claude Rains We've got *character* and *costume*, but we could also do *mood*: fog in the background, the glare of the runway lights.]

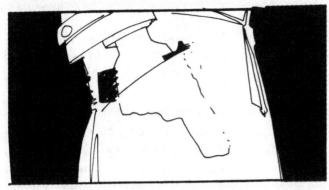

[Close up of the gun in the pocket of Bogart's trench coat. *Prop.* The scar on his hand reveals *character*, and the tear in the coat is part of *costume*.]

Note: technically speaking, the gun in the illustration is too big to be a prop. Just imagine it's a tiny Derringer.

[Back to Rains' face. *Character* again, if we want to add more details about his face, but we can also include details about *costume*, *set-dressing, mood* (sounds of plane engines in background). *Commentary* would deal with thoughts and feelings, what's going through his mind, his inner conflict.]

"Round up the usual suspects." [Closing bookend. The moment is over, but a new one begins. Bogart looks back at Rains, who acknowledges that he has no intention of spilling the beans. They walk off. It's "the beginning of a beautiful friendship."]

The filmmaker and editor have used various shots between the bookends of dialogue to create tension. In the writing, we've used all seven elements of Image-Moment to accomplish the same effect. We made our $1400. While it's not necessary to use all seven every time you create an Image-Moment, it's good to practice doing so until you master the technique. Ultimately, it's not about how many of the seven elements you use in creating your Image-Moment, it's how many words you use. That's how you create psychological time, that's how you bring out the drama of the moment.

Image-Moment shows the reader what cannot be expressed by mere telling. We could reverse the procedure and look at a page from the screenplay of *Casablanca*. Notice how often the screenwriter has a character pausing or thinking, but a screenplay cannot give the Image-Moment; that's up to the director and film-editor. In a prose work, it isn't enough to say someone pauses or thinks. That's telling; it doesn't convey psychological time (the drama). Here's a close-to-final version of one of the scenes from the film. There are half-a-dozen Image-Moments on that one page. Where the script says they are **silent, depressed,** the film editor would make a few cuts showing their faces, what they're seeing, what they're hearing. While the screenwriter can't show it, the prose writer would, thus creating an Image-Moment. When Rick **looks** at Ilsa, there's probably a pause before he finishes his line. Another Image-Moment. Where the screenwriter says Ilsa **thinks,** that's another Image-Moment. They both **pause** before the last line of the scene. Another Image-Moment. The screenwriter wants the viewer to experience psychological time. There's no dialogue, but he's assuming the actors will fill those pauses with expressions of feelings and thoughts. The screenwriter, though he doesn't control these effects, hopes the director and cinematographer will shoot the scene in such a way that the film editor can emphasize those pauses. Here's the scene exactly as it was written. (I've put into bold the words that would be made into an Image-Moment and indicated the beats.)

```
           MED. SHOT.    AT THE OPEN WINDOW

     as Rick and Ilsa come into the scene. The loudspeaker is blaring
     in German.


                         RICK:

           My German's a little rusty--


                         ILSA:

                       (sadly)

           It's the Gestapo.  They say they expect

           to be in Paris tomorrow.  They are telling

           us how to act when they come marching in.
```
They are **silent, depressed.**   [beat]

```
                         ILSA:

                  (smiling faintly)

           With the whole world crumbling

           we pick this time to fall in love.


                         RICK

                  (with an abrupt laugh)

           Yeah.  Pretty bad timing.
```
     (**looks** at her)   [beat]

Where were you ten years ago?

                    ILSA:

                (TRYING TO CHEER UP)
Ten years ago? Let's see--

                   (THINKS)
Oh, yes. I was having a brace put on my
teeth. Where were you?

                    RICK:
I was looking for a job.

                                        [beat]
Pause. Ilsa **looks** at him tenderly.

                    ILSA:
Rick--Hitler or no Hitler, kiss me.
Rick takes her in his arms, kisses her hungrily. While they are
locked in an embrace the dull boom of cannons is HEARD. Rick and
Ilsa separate.

                    [end of beat, end of scene]

There are four main beats in the scene above, indicated by the screenwriter with "pause," "he thinks," or "they are silent." Those are large Image-Moments, but within the beats are smaller Image-Moments and it's up to the actors and director to determine those. In prose, it's your job to sculpt those beats with Image-Moment. For now, it's a question of practice. Like a painter who creates dozens of sketches for a larger painting, start by creating Image-Moments using all seven elements. Practice the different permutations and combinations. Then do a few using only six elements, then five, and so on. After awhile, focus not on the number of different elements but on the number of words. Create an Image-Moment that lasts for half a page, then do one that lasts a quarter of a page, and another that lasts only a few short sentences. Create an Image-Moment that is only two words. If you decide you want a longer pause, stretch the psychological time with more words.

So much depends on how you set up the first bookend, then the various images before the other shoe drops. Sometimes, the drama is about the other shoe *not* dropping. Here's a piece I wrote about seeing De Sica's *The Bicycle Thief* with my wife and son. There's an Image-Moment at the end in which the other shoe does *not* drop, but the expectation of it dropping informs the drama of that moment.

FINE

My great fantasy when I was in my early teens was that my dad and I would go bowling on a Saturday morning, then go out to breakfast together. Maybe to one of those broken down waterfront joints next to the wharf. They served coffee in thick, white mugs. It would be just the two of us. We'd watch the big ships come down the Mississippi. He could tell me stories of when he was young, tramping around the country during the Depression, eating in places like this.

Why bowling? I don't know. Maybe because I thought I'd have him all to myself. The only time it was me and my dad was when he took me fishing. And even then, we didn't talk much. He'd wake me up at two in the morning, and I'd sit in the back of the car, half asleep, still in my pajamas. Every so often I'd open my eyes to see where we were. We're on the Airline Highway, passing the airport. We're driving through the bayous with cypress stumps sticking up out of the swamps. We're on a dirt road passing the shacks by the oil refineries. Fire shooting out of a big smokestack in the middle of the night. The car comes to a stop and we're in Grande Isle just as the sun's coming up.

By the time it was light, we'd be out on the water in the Gulf of Mexico with a bunch of men who were all grizzly and unshaven, loud and playful. The smell of diesel fuel mixed with the odor of fish heads used for bait. The boat went up and down, smacking the choppy waves that got higher and higher the further we got from land. Finally, we came to the oil rigs. When they cut the engine and threw anchor, I had to hold on as the boat rocked and rode the waves. The men were smoking and drinking and yelling back and forth, throwing their lines into the water, pulling up the fish. They seemed to come flying on board as if their fins were wings. Spade fish and red snapper. There wasn't time for my dad and me to talk in all that confusion. It was mostly the slime and blood of the fish, and my worrying that he was sneaking a drink and would end up drunk by the time we got back to shore. On the way home I watched how he drove the car, so that if he was so drunk he couldn't drive, I'd be able to get us home. I was eleven, and had no idea how to drive a car, but if I had to, I thought, I could figure it out. And I worried that my mother would yell and threaten divorce if she smelled the whiskey on his breath, and then maybe they'd fight and the mirror in the medicine cabinet in the bathroom would get broken again and Mom would start slapping us kids, and then Dad would go on a binge that would last for days and we wouldn't know if he would ever come home again.

So bowling seemed tame. Afterwards, we could get French Market doughnuts, maybe talk about his life before he met my mom, that life of adventure during the Depression when he "rode the rails and slept in hobo jungles," when he saw Dempsey fight Firpo and get knocked clear "outta the ring," and when he was a cowboy out west. I liked it when he told us stories of his days as a cowboy, getting shot in a gun battle and being nursed back to life by a Mexican woman named Juanita. I was 14 before I realized the cowboy stories were made up.

If my dad were alive today, I'd want to take him and my 12-year-old son bowling. I'd want my dad to know Josh, want Josh to know his grandfather. I'd want my dad to see how Josh and I go out every Friday night to see a play, that we've been doing this since he was 10, and how before that we went to the Silent Movie Theatre on Fairfax every Friday since he was eight. Josh always has more popcorn and candy than his mother would like, but what the hell. We've seen Shakespeare and Thornton Wilder, Chekhov and Neil Simon, Molière and Arthur Miller, Sophocles and Eugene O'Neill, Ibsen and Samuel Beckett, Ionesco and Bertolt Brecht, Neil Simon, Pirandello, and Edward Albee. It's better than bowling.

So anyway, Josh and I saw Strindberg's *Dance of Death* last weekend at the Company Rep in North Hollywood. An adaptation by Friedrich Duerrenmatt. A battle of the sexes, to put it mildly. The play figuratively takes place in the boxing ring of their living room. The husband enters the stage and sits up left while the wife enters and sits down right. An announcer steps into the center of the ring and says, "Round One, Conversation before Dinner." Then they sit there for five minutes saying absolutely nothing. Tick tock. Tick tock. Silence. I've never heard silence get such a laugh. It came in waves. Silence, then laughter, then tired silence. Waiting. You figure, okay, joke's over. But no, the silence goes on. Then laughter again. Then silence. Then laughter. Then silence and more silence. Acceptance of the profundity of their lack of communication. Everyone, actors and audience alike, finally lapsed into this sad and weary silence.

On the way home I told Josh about Strindberg's life, how he married several times, always to very young women.

"Sounds like he was a player," Josh said.

Last night Lori, Josh and I went to see De Sica's *Bicycle Thief* at the New Beverly Cinema. A bad print, and the bulb kept going out in the projector, but it was still exquisite. Father and son searching all over Rome for the bicycle stolen from the father that morning after he finally gets a job that requires a bicycle, the bicycle he got out of hock by selling all the family's linens. "We don't need sheets," his wife says as she strips the bed. Bruno is about 10 years old. So many moments in that film, silences between dialogue. The purity of De Sica's shots that seem more interested in the human face than cinematic composition. I don't want to give the end away for anyone who hasn't seen this masterpiece of Italian Neo-Realism, but at the end, as the film fades to black, the two walk away from us into the world awaiting them, a sad ending, surely, but to say the ending was sad would be to trivialize its profound complexity. Bruno takes his father's hand and we see them from the back as they disappear into the crowd, trudging their weary way homeward, leaving the world to darkness as the Italian word FINE appears in white on the black background. After having read the English subtitles throughout the film, there was an odd confusion when that final word appeared. As if De Sica were commenting on the ending, father and son walking off into the rest of their lives together, the son burdened at such an early age with the awareness of his father's desperation and imperfection—yet De Sica seemed to be saying that everything would be fine, not to worry. FINE. But no, you re-adjust. The word is Italian. It wasn't fine, it was FINE, THE END, FINITO. Everyone in the audience sat there, silent. No one got up to go. We sat staring at the black screen, at the word FINE. A long silence before one or two people began to clap. Then the slow, deliberate applause of everyone in the theater, then silence again, as we sat there, going nowhere. And why did we sit in the darkened theater without moving? Because we had lives to go home to, just as Bruno and his father had to face the rest of their lives, and it wasn't FINE, it wasn't the end. But for a moment, just for a moment, we sat there, in the silence of the theater, somewhere between the life on the screen and the life waiting for us outside.

When we left the theater, just before we crossed the street to our car, Josh took my hand. A casual kind of thing, something he hadn't done in years, since he was little and used to take my hand whenever we crossed the street. Hugs and small embraces had become rare, as Josh took off into that teenage macho thing. But there was his hand taking hold of mine. I wasn't sure how obvious I should be about it, so I just let my hand dangle a bit, let him hold me without me holding back. Then as we stepped off the curb, I grasped and entwined, and we crossed the street together, holding hands, like when he was a little boy. We continued to hold until we got to the car, talking the whole time about the film.

Josh has his bedtime ritual with his mom, and I still haven't learned the sequence, good night, good night, sleep tight, sleep tight, bed bugs bite, bed bugs bite, then these little sounds that are impossible to describe: hawwooo, hawwooo, uuuwaaahh, uuuuwaaaaah, weeeeoooh, weeeeooooh. It's like a song two animals might sing to each other. I've tried but never get the sequence right, so I'm not exactly allowed to do it. So he and I have our own ritual. It's a bit of a joke, and Lori always cracks up when we do it.

"'Night."

"'Night."

"Love you."

"Love you too."

Then there's a perfectly timed pause, and both of us say at exactly the same time, "Just kidding!" Then we laugh, and it feels good. We get to be sentimental and mushy, but we get to undercut it as well.

So last night, after the movie, we did it again, all the way through the "just kidding" part. Maybe it was the movie, that heartbreaking movie, and the father and son thing. But after the "just kidding," I walked to the door, and just as I was closing it, said, "Love you," a frail whisper sent like a paper airplane into the darkened room, and he answered back, just as quietly, "Love you too."

I decided to wait, to see if he'd say "just kidding." We'd turned off the light so I couldn't see anything, just the shadow of him in bed, under the covers, his hands holding the duvet up to his chin. The dog's rustling into position at the foot of his bed. I could hear Lori in the kitchen close the dishwasher with that little snap. I waited another second, let the silence grow larger. Was he thinking the same thing I was thinking? Was he waiting to see if I was going to say "just kidding" again? I let the silence hang a bit longer, as if to clarify our joint decision not to say anything. We were both going to endure the silence, a silence that was not about separation or disconnection, but an affirmation of the love between us.

I closed the door, leaving that little crack as usual. Then into the kitchen to help Lori with the rest of the dishes.

"Don't bang the dishes," she said.

"No, I'll be quiet."

And we cleaned up around the kitchen, whispering to each other until we were sure he was asleep.

FINE

The Four Levels of Narrative Structure:

STORY

Story is the whole narrative. "The summer I spent with my father changed my life." That's story. "We rented a car and drove across country." That's story. Stories are composed of events and events are composed of various moments.

EVENT

Events are just smaller stories within the big story. What happened at the rental office is an event. The episode with the flat tire is an event. Going to the store or going to Paris is an event. An event lasts *more* than two seconds; thus, it cannot be a bookend and cannot appear between bookends. Each event is composed of moments.

MOMENT

A moment is a short span of time, *less than a minute*, usually *a few seconds*, between bookends, *in which nothing happens*. A bookend is an action/gesture or line of dialogue. An action is one or two seconds, instantaneous—a glass drops, a door slams. "Dialogue is dialogue," he said. A moment is *a suspension of time, framed by the action or dialogue of a bookend.* Like a piece of film, Image-Moments are composed of a series of images between bookends in which nothing happens, just static description.

IMAGE

An image is a picture. When that description comes between the bookends of the moment, it creates tension. *Thus, the combination of IMAGE & MOMENT becomes the crucial building block of narrative.*

7 Elements of IMAGE-MOMENT

Creating Psychological Time

While the Transformation Line Is
HOT

All right, you've massaged your transformation line, your voice is now in a deep place, and the reader is connected to the story or event. Set the moment up with a line of *dialogue* or *action/gesture*. Close the moment with a line of *dialogue* or *action/gesture*. Between compelling or dramatic bookends, stretch real time (a few seconds) into psychological time by giving the reader the Seven Elements of Image-Moment. Use all seven:

1 SET: Identify where you are, the place: you're in a library, in the kitchen, in the backyard, in a car, in a train depot, in a bunker, etc. Parts of the set are either set-dressing or props.

2 SET-DRESSING: Movable objects: furniture, a rug, a lamp, paintings, chairs, tables, etc. If outdoors, is there a tree, a barn, a skyscraper, a fountain, an automobile parked by the curb? Set pieces are larger than props.

3 PROPS: The little things: a paper clip, a penny on the floor. It doesn't have to be used by anyone, and may be related or irrelevent to the story. A prop is a small object, **no bigger than a deck of cards.**

4 MOOD: *Lighting* gives the reader a sense of mood. So do *sounds* or *smells*. Harsh bright lights, dim yellow light, morning sun, afternoon sun, what? Same for the other two senses: *taste* and *touch*.

5 THE CHARACTERS: Who are the people and *what do they look like?* Describe **physical features:** the face, eyes, nose, chin, hair, arms, hands, fingers, the general shape of the body, height, weight, etc.

6 COSTUME: What are people wearing? We learn a lot about a person just from the kind of shirt they're wearing, their shoes, how they are dressed. Little details tell a lot. A necklace or pair of glasses counts as costume (though if on a table, they're props).

7 COMMENTARY: *Thoughts, feelings, exposition;* no images. What's going through the character's mind at that moment, what feelings are being aroused? *Exposition* (or *backstory*) is also part of commentary, but it should be kept to a minimum. Telling what happened before the moment can distract the reader from the drama, so keep your *exposition* short. You can work in expositional information—"He was wearing the shirt he bought in France"—but it's best to keep it out of the moment itself, otherwise the reader loses the sense of tension, of psychological time. When doing an Image-Moment, it's better to focus on the images in the scene itself, not on exposition or backstory. If you do create a lengthy backstory, be sure to reset when returning to the moment. "So there we were, . . . ", etc.

After a few sentences, you've stretched real time (seconds) into psychological time (which can feel like forever). Thus, instead of TELLING you are SHOWING. Real time is stretched into psychological time by the words you use bewteen the bookends. **The more words, the longer the moment lasts.**

RECAP

1) Transformation Line vs Image-Moment

Learning to massage a transformation line requires a certain amount of psychological and emotional accessibility. Though I've given you some examples ("I was hiding the birthday cake"), there's no simple formula. Get rid of the birthday cake and know the difference between a horizontal and a vertical massage: the former will take you somewhere, but the latter will take you deeper and provide the greatest surprises. But there's no substitute for practice. Your intellect will not help you as much as your emotional availablity, and the more you practice your thousand swings a day, the better you will get at this. Keep trying to find the deeper truth. Eventually, you will get the hang of it, and discover how dramatic the massage of a transformation line can be for the reader. Suddenly, idle chit-chat in a crowded restaurant becomes the intimate whisper of one human being making contact with another human being.

Image-Moment, on the other hand, is a mechanical structure, a machine with many moving parts, and if one part of the machine fails to function properly, the whole contraption falls apart. Once you understand how the machine works, you will discover countless ways you can apply it, but first get the basic mechanism down pat.

2) What are you doing when you introduce an Image-Moment?

You are stretching "real time" into "psychological time." A moment lasts a few seconds, that's why we call it a moment, and not a minute. But some moments are so filled with tension and drama, they *seem* to last forever. When editing a film, the real time is stretched into psychological time by inter-cutting several shots between the bookends of the dialogue or action. As a writer, you do it by using words. The more words between the bookends of your moment, the more time it takes the reader to read those words. The more time it takes the reader to read them, the longer they have to wait for the other bookend (the other shoe to drop). It's like an actor taking a dramatic pause. How long should the pause last? Some will be short, others long, and most will be somewhere in the middle. If you feel your Image-Moment needs to last (for the reader) a few more seconds, then add a few more words. If you feel your Image-Moment is going on too long, then cut a few words. The words can only be about the seven elements: set, dressing, props, mood, character, costume, commentary. They can't be dialogue or action/gesture, because sentences like that are bookends. NOTHING can happen between bookends of an Image-Moment. Nothing. No one can blink, turn her head, lift his finger, look down, look up, lean against a wall, wiggle their nose, etc. Even the act of taking a breath is an action. Nothing can happen. Nada. Rien. Nichts. Non. Niente. Nothing. See the moment in your mind as if you were watching a film. Did anyone move? Did anyone do anything? Did someone speak? If so, cut it. You can't have action/gesture (unless it's a continuous action/gesture) or dialogue between the bookends of your moment.

3) What about "continuous action"?

Make sure it is continuous. Remember, a continuous action becomes an action when it starts or stops. So it's okay for someone to be pacing up and down the room during your Image-Moment, but they can't START pacing, they can't STOP pacing. "He drummed his fingers on the desktop." Is that okay? Yes, as long as he didn't *start* drumming his fingers on the desktop after the first bookend.

4) Event vs. Action

A bookend must be dialogue or action, but what if your action is really an event? This will cause a problem. Your Image-Moment will not work. There's no sense of finality to an event. An event requires several actions. An event takes more than a few seconds to complete, and the reader will have no sense that something has just happened. A bookend must have a sense of finality. **An action is quick, it takes one or two seconds to complete**. More time than that, and it becomes an event. There is no difference between saying, "He went to his room," and saying "He went to Europe." Both are events. Going to his room requires him to get up, take a step, take another step, another step, and so forth. By the time he's in his room, many seconds have gone by. It's not an action. So make sure your opening bookend is a clear-cut action, not an event. "My boss called me into his office." Is that an action or an event? It's an event. Unless the writer is more specific, it could take more than a few seconds to be "called" into his office. Was it on the intercom, did the secretary appear at the door and inform him that the Boss wanted to see him? We don't know. So it's an event. What about this sentence: I tried to calm my brother down. That's not an action, it's an event. Who knows what actions you took to calm your brother down, or even how long it took to calm him down. Events are part of story, they are not part of moment. If you open an Image-Moment with an event, the whole mechanism falls apart.

5) What about those pesky props?

Yes, props can be a ticklish proposition. In a theatre context, a prop is considered to be any object handled by an actor. A sword or a hatchet or an iPad would be considered a prop. So might the tractor trailer that Superman lifts with one hand. But for our purposes in creating an Image-Moment, keep in mind that *a prop is a small object, no bigger than a deck of cards*, whether or not it's handled in the scene you're writing. A pack of cigarettes is a prop; a single cigarette is a prop; several cigarettes scattered on a table is set dressing; a lamp is not. A pair of glasses is a prop; a suitcase is not. A marble is a prop; a hammer is not. A package of mints is a prop; an armoire is not. A watch is a prop; a pitcher of milk is not. A paperback book is a prop; a hardback book is set dressing. But remember, the pair of glasses, when worn, is part of costume; the watch, when worn, is part of costume. **The prop doesn't have to be used by anyone in the scene and it doesn't have to be in someone's hand to be a prop**. It doesn't ever have to be used. That's it. The prop can be anywhere: a paper clip on the floor, a key under the sofa, a battery on the coffee table. A rock, a coin, a lightbulb. Not a television set, or a printer, or a trash can, or a tree, or a candelabra or a casaba melon. Those are set dressing, like furniture.

6) Can you have action or dialogue within exposition?

You betcha, you can. You can have all the action and dialogue you want in your backstory, because none of that is actually happening between the bookends of your moment, it's what already happened in the past, and the character is thinking about it. So cars can crash in your backstory, houses can burn to the ground, Joe can run the 100-meter dash, Evelyn can go to

Europe, Ben can go to his room, Sylvia can break every plate in the kitchen, as long as it's happening in the past, in exposition, in backstory. You can have dialogue in backstory, you can have all the dialogue you want. If it's part of commentary, you can write *War and Peace*. However, I would advise you not to have your backstory go on for too long, else the reader will lose touch with the drama of the moment. Keep backstory to a minimum, but if you must go into a long exposition, remember to RESET before jumping to the closing bookend. Remind the reader where you were. "So there I was, standing on the edge of a cliff, and Hortense was pointing a gun at me asking, "Where are the jewels, you lying, backstabbing thief?"

7) How do you know you have a moment?

A moment is defined by two bookends. Two lines of dialogue in a row define a moment. Two actions in a row define a moment. A moment is not an Image-Moment. A moment has no images between the bookends. Just two bookends. Narrative is usually a series of bookends, one after the other, with no images between. Below are four bookends, one after the other, creating three moments, no images between::

John opened the door.	[bookend, action]
"I've come for the money," she said.	[bookend, dialogue]
"I gave it to Sally," Joe said.	[bookend, dialogue]
She tossed the book onto the coffee table.	[bookend, action]

When you put images between two bookends, you've got an Image-Moment. Don't confuse the two.

8) What's the purpose of Image-Moment?

To create drama. Most people rush through their story, but remember what you should have posted over your writing table: *My story is boring*. The reader is not hooked by the reportage of narrative events, but by the compelling tone of the deep voice and dramatic tension inherent in Image-Moments. A reader can stop in the middle of story, but they turn the page in the middle of an Image-Moment. Image-Moment works like a well-oiled machine. Readers see a big descriptive paragraph and they tend to skip it and jump ahead. Not when the description is part of Image-Moment. When writing your Image-Moment as an exercise, be precise: Film editors don't "go with the flow," they're precise and deliberate when cutting a scene; you should practice the same kind of approach to your sentences and images. Be deliberate and precise. When done, be diligent and make sure all the parts of the machine are in place. How many elements did you use? Did you get all seven? Were your bookends clearly actions or dialogue? Did anything happen between those bookends? Let's hope not, or you'll have cut your Image-Moment in half. Of course, in the future, you will write hundreds of Image-Moments in which all seven elements are not used. You're only using all seven now to get some practice. Eventually, it won't be about how many elements you use, but how many words you use. That's the whole point of Image-Moment. *You're stretching real time into psychological time, and the more words you use, the longer the moment seems to last.* Eventually, your artistic sensibility will come into play when you have to think like a cinematographer/ editor: Which image do I start with? Which image do I cut to next: the close up of his face or the long shot of the set? And which image finally leads into the closing bookend: the shot of his hand on her knee, or the commentary about her inability to love? There's an infinite number of permutations and combinations. But practice the basic mechanism so when you are "going with the flow," so to speak, you're adept at making those decisions on the fly (see Chapter 9, "Going with the Flow vs. The Triangle Offense").

Here are a few practice exercises:

1. Do an Image-Moment that has all seven elements, but use no more than 75 words.
2. Do an Image-Moment that has only three elements, but use more than 125 words.
3. Do an Image-Moment in which you start with props, go to character (physical description), then end with commentary before the closing bookend. Do this in less than 50 words.
4. Do an Image-Moment that starts with character (close up of a description of character's hands, say), then mentions two different props, one held by the character, the other on the floor in the corner of the room (the prop should be small and have nothing to do with the "story"), then commentary (just feelings—maybe transformation line massage—no thoughts, no exposition), then set dressing, and finally a sentence or two about mood (sounds, lighting, etc.). You can use as many words as you want.
5. Do a very short Image-Moment. Use a line of dialogue to open, then two elements of Image-Moment, then close with another line of dialogue. Use no more than one sentence of no more than 15 words between bookends. The majority of your Image-Moments will be short ones. It will depend on the dramatic set-up of the first bookend. If the opening bookend is not very dramatic, your Image-Moment will not need to be long. But if it is dramatic, you can toy with the reader and make them feel that pause as if it lasted an eternity.

"Oh Rhett, what will I do, where will I go?"
       image: the set
       image: set dressing
       image: mood (lighting, sounds, smells, etc)
       image: character, physical description.
       image: costume, what he's wearing. Clothes on a chair counts as dressing.
       image: commentary—thoughts, feelings, backstory.
meanwhile, nothing is happening
continuous action is allowed, but no action or dialogue, just description, image.
       then:
"Frankly my dear, I don't give a damn."

The Permutations and Combinations of Image-Moment

Obviously, a writer has to have an overall vision for his or her work. It doesn't have to be an outline of every scene and event, but a general sense of the story. How that vision plays out—how it morphs and changes—is determined by the writer's openness to the creative accidents of genius. Process, by its very nature, is a way of working, not a blueprint for product. The artist must find a way of working—a process that will serve him or her through all the vicissitudes of deadlines and remunerations. When all is said and done, the creative process remains an elusive concept. All I can say is, stay in the process of the creative act and sometimes you will get lucky. If your aim is to be good all the time, you will learn to be good all the time. If your aim is to create something great, something that comes out of the accidents of your genius, then you have to risk writing crap sometimes. That's what Voltaire meant when he said that the good is the enemy of the best. Risk failure, and the accidents of your genius will emerge. As Beckett said:

> Ever tried.
> Ever failed.
> No matter.
> Try again.
> Fail again.
> Fail better.

But whatever your vision is, whether it be a story or novel or poem or screenplay, the delivery system for that vision is always going to be voice and character:

Voice creates character.
Character creates plot.

Massaging your transformation line and getting your voice deep takes emotional and psychological acuity. The more you practice this, the more compelling your work will be and the deeper your voice will go. Image-Moment, on the other hand, is not about emotional or psychological acuity, but about mechanics. We tend to trust "going with the flow" more than mechanical construction, but as artists our work always entails a combination of "flow" and "technique." Your ability to master this device will pay off when you construct scenes, and it's the scenes that carry the story's vision.

The Magic Number: 5040 x Infinity = Infinity

You might think that because Image-Moment is mechanical, it requires no artistry, but it's in the application of Image-Moment that your creative choices are called into play. How many different ways can one arrange the seven elements of Image-Moment between bookends? You've got seven elements to give the reader in some combination. How many possible combinations are there? Ready? There are five thousand forty possible combinations that determine the different ways you can arrange the seven elements of Image-Moment. It's a simple question of applying the formula for permutations and combinations.

$$(7 \times 6) \quad \times \quad (5 \times 4) \quad \times \quad (3 \times 2) \times 1 = 5040$$
$$42 \quad \times \quad 20 \quad \times \quad 6 \quad \times 1 = 5040$$

I apologize if this reminder of 10th grade math makes you feel like I slipped a mickey into your drink. I'm not trying to render you senseless, but I want to show you how the basic baloney sandwich of seven elements can be used in limitless variations. The possibilities are endless, but it's crucial that you become proficient in the assemblage of the basic mechanism. This is how you control the pace of your narrative. This is how you create tension and dramatic expectation in dialogue or action. A scene, especially one with dialogue or action, is like a musical score in which half-notes and quarter-notes and full-notes and rest-stops bring the scene to life. How you arrange the images is important and create a cinematic flow. The more words you use between bookends, the more you stretch real-time pauses into psychological time. How you stretch that time depends upon the combination and sequence of the images between your bookends. Like a film editor, you create the movie in the reader's mind—the pace of each scene and its emotional tension.

Every scene can have dozens of narrative moments and dozens of Image-Moments. Each Image-Moment can be rendered in thousands of different combinations. Do you start with a close up of the face and the scar on her cheek (character), then a shot of the set, then a shot of the button on her blouse, then a thought or feeling (comment), then back to a medium shot of the set so the reader can see the chairs and curtains (set dressing), then a shot of the deck of cards (prop) on the table (set dressing)? The possible arrangements of the seven elements of Image-Moment equal five thousand and forty. That's a lot of possibilities. There's a great deal of leeway for artistic maneuvering. The reason I want you to be able to write one good $1400 baloney sandwich of Image-Moment is so you will begin to understand how this device works. It not so much about getting all seven elements, but in which order, in what combination do you show them. Therein lie your creative choices.

Okay, get a cup of coffee. We're not done. That's only the arrangement of the seven elements. How many words can you spend describing those images? **The more words, the longer time the reader must spend reading those words, and the longer the psychological time seems to last.** If you were to systematically practice every possible combination of elements and every possible number of words, it would take you forever. So any amount of practice will be a drop in the bucket, but that is no reason not to practice. Eventually, you will know instinctively how each Image-Moment should be handled, depending on the scene, the characters, and the pace of the narrative. (See the essay on "The Triangle Offense vs. Going with the Flow," page 161.)

Story is boring. Narrative without scenes is boring, and scenes without Image-Moments are boring. Stories are a dime a dozen. Scenes and Image-Moments and compelling voice, those are rare indeed. Practice writing in the deep voice. Practice the mechanics of Image-Moment. Your reader will thank you.

FREQUENTLY ASKED QUESTIONS

Dear Jack,

I'm still not clear on the difference between "action" and "event." What's the big deal anyway, why is that so important? You say action, I say event. Let's call the whole thing off!
—*Busted Flat in Baton Rouge*

Dear Busted,

An action is instantaneous. It takes no more than two seconds. If you hit a table, drop a book, punch a wall, break a glass, look up, step down, slam the door, it takes a second or two. If it takes longer than that, it's an event. Smoking a cigarette is an event. Pouring a glass of milk is an event. Eating a sandwich is an event. Setting the table for dinner is an event. **So action is instantaneous, and event takes more than two seconds.** Someone in class wrote, "I was driving down the freeway," and called it an action, a bookend. "How long did that last?" I asked. "Twenty minutes," she replied. Sorry, that's not an action. That's an event. If it takes longer than two seconds, it's an event. Case closed.

Dear Jack,

This whole bookend thing is driving me crazy. I want to create one of those dramatic moments, but why can't I just segue into the moment? I got so many bookends on the page, I might as well open a used bookstore. Help!
—*Dizzy Diogenes in Denver*

Dear Dizzy,

A moment is a pause in which nothing really happens. Time seems to stop. But how do we define that moment? **The pause occurs between two bookends. No bookends, no pause**. We need a bell to signal the beginning of round three, but we also need a bell to signal the end of round three. And what happens between those two bells is what we came to watch. The sentences that operate as bookends cannot be events or continuous actions. "Mom was eating her soup" is not an action, it's an event, but "Mom picked up her spoon" is an action, as is "Mom began to slurp her soup." (The operative word there is "began." That's why it's an action. Beginning to splurp takes one second, but slurping her soup is not an action, it's either a continuous action or an event.)The space between two well-defined bookends is the moment.

Dear Jack,

I've got two decisive bookends. But you say that a moment lasts less than 59 seconds.Why can't the moment, the time between the bookends, last 60 seconds?
—*Languid in Laguna Beach*

Dear Languid,

Why can't the moment last 60 seconds? Because I can spell. This concept is not called Image/Minute. A moment usually lasts only a few seconds, but out of the goodness of my heart, I will allow you 59 seconds. But not 60. That's just too long. The drama is psychological. Those few seconds seem to last forever, but in reality, it's only a few seconds. When the girl's mother asks, "Are you going to kill yourself," the pause before she responds will probably last 5 seconds that feel like forever. "No," she says simply, but in those five seconds, there's a great deal of tension, what I call psychological time. Real time = a few seconds. Psychological time = forever. Remember: "nothing" happens between the bookends of a moment. It's a freeze-frame. If you can construct your Image-Moment with decisive book-ends, with a moment that lasts only a few seconds, filled with expectant psychological time, you'll hold the reader's interest.

Dear Jack,

How do I gauge how long that psychological time should last, and how do I make the psychological time seem to last longer, how do I stretch the psychological time?
—*Slide-rule Sammy*

Dear Slide-Rule,

Use words. You stretch psychological time by using words. The more words you use be-tween your bookends, the longer it takes for the reader to read them, and the longer that psychological time seems to last. So this is where your instinct as a writer comes in. If you feel the moment has to last longer—psychologically speaking—just add more words. If you feel you're giving too much importance to a relatively inconsequential moment, use fewer words.

Dear Jack,

My background is theatre. A prop is something characters hold in their hands, something that is used in a scene. According to your definition, it can be any object, whether used or not. I don't get that. I was in a dinner theater production and had to enter from stage left car-rying a candelabra. According to you, that's not a prop because it's larger than a deck of cards. But the candelabra was on the "prop table." I don't get it. A prop is a prop is a prop. What gives?
—*A. Thespian*

Dear A.,

In the theatre, props are put on "the prop table" and the actor who has to use it picks it up before making a grand entrance. Once in acting class I did the opening scene from Arthur Miller's *Death of a Salesman*. Willy enters, carrying a heavy, battered suitcase. I picked it up from the "prop table" in the wings. It certainly wasn't smaller than a deck of cards. However, in Method Writing, a prop is no larger than a deck of cards, so the suitcase would be consid-ered "set dressing." The penny lying on the floor under the coffee table; the marble sitting in the ashtray on the mantelpiece; the piece of chocolate from Brussels on the counter next to the coffee maker; the paper clip next to the book on the dining room table: all props. **I would encourage you to find a prop that has nothing to do with the scene.** Something trivial. Here's why: it will end up being the most memorable image in your scene. The poet T.S. Eliot called this the "objective correlative." The object correlated with an emotional truth. Carl Jung considered such objects to have symbolic power. And here's the beauty of this: you don't even have to know what the "objective correlative" is, nor do you need to know what the object might symbolize. Just pick any small object—better yet, make it up—and your subconscious will do the rest. Like the madelaine cookie in Proust's novel *Re-membrance of Things Past*, the paper clip will capture the emotional power of the scene and remind the reader of the experience of the book. So when I choose an object to be my prop, I scour my cluttered imagination and come up with any object at random. Maybe the penny really was on the floor, but if not, I might just put it there. I might not even know why. But I trust my subconscious to make the right choice. And the reason I say that the object must be no larger than a deck of cards is because most of us writing a scene will pick props that are larger and connected to the scene. **But the smaller the object, the more psychological power it will contain.**

Dear Jack,

I notice that you divide "commentary" into three parts: thoughts, feelings, and exposition (or backstory). Does it matter which one I use? If I use all three, do I get more than $200.
—*Cassandra from Khartoum*

Dear Cassandra,

I'm afraid you only get $200 for commentary, no matter which or how many parts you use. But don't let that stop you from using all three. Commentary is where you allow the reader to enter the mind of the character. What's she thinking, what's he feeling? And backstory? It's a chance to provide context, to inform the reader of a pertinent fact. Be careful, though. If you're in the middle of a dramatic Image-Moment, don't distract the reader with too much backstory. If you go into too much detail, the immediacy of the scene will be diluted. When exposition or backstory becomes top-heavy, consider moving it—before or after the Image-Moment might serve your pupose better. If you feel, however, that the backstory must be presented to the reader just before the murderer is about to pull the trigger, remember to remind the reader where you were. I call that "resetting." —So there we were, standing on the edge of the cliff, ...

Dear Jack,

When calculating how much money I make for an Image-Moment, why can't I just count the elements from different sets of bookends? Why does it all have to be confined to just one moment?
—*Hodge-Podge from Hudson Point Nebraska*

Dear Hodge,

If you went into a delicatessen and ordered a baloney sandwich, and the bread was scattered across the table while the slices of baloney were sailed across the room like frisbees, I think you'd find the service questionable. A moment is specific and discrete. Two pieces of bread. Two bookends. No images between. But once you start putting images between your bookends, you've got an Image-Moment. One baloney sandwich. Each Image-Moment is a baloney sandwich. One might have four slices of baloney (four of the elements), in which case it's worth $800. Until you really get the hang of this, however, I'd like you to start by doing $1400 Image-Moments. Use all seven elements.

Dear Jack,

I signed up to be an artist, not an accountant; a writer, not an engineer. Whatever happened to going with the flow?
—*Selma from Slippery Stream, Montana*

Dear Selma,

Read chapter 9, "Going with the Flow vs. The Triangle Offense." Here's the big secret, but don't tell anyone: **Amateurs go with the flow; professionals know what they're doing every step of the way**. They learn their **craft**. Their **technique** is welded to their brain stem through practice, practice, practice. Writers know grammar and sentence structure, but they also know the structure of plot and the arc of a story, they know how to make scenes work, how to make characters come alive, how to make events snap, crackle and pop. This is not an instinct that good writers are born with, but a grounding in craft. You might hear an actor or writer say in an interview, "Oh, I'm well-versed in technique, but when I start writing, I just go with the flow." The amateur hears that and skips the thousands of hours of practice required to ground oneself in craft. They're like children in a sandbox shoveling sand. Castles do not magically appear. **You have to know what you're doing before you can forget what you're doing.**

Dear Jack,

I overheard what you just told Selma, and I want to add that when I'm writing in my journal and practicing the techniques of Method Writing, I don't have that sense of excitement that I get when I just let 'er rip. It feels so mechanical. I wanna feel that fly-me-to-the-moon exhilaration. Will I ever get that?
—*Tiny Dancer from Tupelo*

Dear Tiny Dancer,

How many times have I done a play with an actor who felt he was dancing with the stars only to be told his performance was more like swimming with the fishes? How many times have I heard an actor complain before the show that she felt uninspired, only to go out and give the performance of her life? Same for sports. One time I was so psyched-up for a football game, I thought I could score ten touchdowns, only to miss every pass. But in the championship game, a slight drizzle coming down, with no sense of focus, what happened? I was fleet-footed Mercury! I saw the field as if I were having an out-of-body experience. Where did that come from? From the body, from the hundreds of practice hours, from the thousands of repetitions. My **technique** and **craft** came to my rescue. You can't count on instinct, you can't rely on inspiration. I'm not saying that instrinct and inspiration play no part in the creative process. I'm saying don't *rely* on it. **Rely on the techniques of craft, techniques you've practiced over and over**. You should be able to sling Image-Moments like a short order cook. You should be able to massage a transformation line like a master prestidigitator. You should be able to distinguish the difference between a sentence that is "written" and a sentence that is "spoken," like an FBI agent who can hold a dollar bill up to the light and tell whether it's real or counterfeit. These concepts are the wings that allow you to glide over the terrain of your story, whether you're going with the flow or not. Practice these techniques and you'll see what I mean.

Dear Jack,

I'm writing this from a cabin in the woods, reading Norman Mailer's *The Naked and the Dead*. Honestly, I just don't get the point of all this Image-Moment stuff. Can't I just read my books and write my story.
—*Dazed and Confused*

Dear Dazed and Confused,

Sure you can just read your books and write your story. But you're going to have to know how to construct narrative scenes and events with moments that provide tension and pace. This is what all great writers do when they construct a story. I'm just giving names to the devices they use and breaking the whole into parts. Whatever you want to call it, it still has to work. I call it Image-Moment. You say you're reading Mailer's novel of that doomed patrol in the Japanese Pacific. Mailer himself claimed to have four books on his desk while he wrote *The Naked and the Dead*: Tolstoy's *Anna Karenina*, Thomas Wolfe's *Of Time and the River*, John Dos Passos' *U.S.A.* trilogy, and James T. Farrell's *Studs Lonigan*. Those books are full of Image-Moments; there's not a page that doesn't contain at least one, and on some pages, you can count a dozen. True, they're not all $1400 baloney sandwiches—some are worth only $200—but the Image-Moments are like bricks used to build a story's foundation, and the foundation is what holds up the house. Here, at random, I've opened my copy of Norman Mailer's *The Naked and the Dead* to page 23. I count six Image-Moments on that one page. Here's a short one:

> The air was chill, and the sun at his left was still low and quiet without any heat. He stamped his feet, breathing the curious odor of the ship's deck, oil and tar and the fish smell of the water.
> "When do we get into the boats?" Hennessey asked.
> The shelling was still going on over the beach, and the island looked pale green in the dawn. A thin wispy line of smoke trailed along the shore.
> Red laughed. "What! Do ya think this is gonna be any different today. I figure we'll be on deck all morning."

Before the line of dialogue, there's description of the set and mood (the smell of the oil, etc.). Then comes the line of dialogue—"When do we get into the boats?"—which is a bookend. The closing bookend is Red's laugh (an action!), followed by another bookend, more dialogue. Between the dialogue and Red's laugh there are several elements of Image-Moment. The shelling going on is continuous action, but it's also mood (sound, $200). The mention of the beach is part of the set ($200), and the pale green island is set dressing ($200). The wispy line of smoke is also set dressing. So the whole Image-Moment is worth $600. Then Mailer closes that moment with another bookend, Red's laugh. I could open to any page of Tolstoy's *Anna Karenina*, or *War and Peace*, and find several Image-Moments on each page. One of the biggest influences on my own writing was Thomas Wolfe's *Of Time and the River*. The book is filled with Image-Moments. Same for Dos Passos' *U.S.A.* trilogy. Mailer asserted that in writing his novel, "the overspirit was Tolstoy, the rococo comes out of Dos Passos, the fundamental slogging style from Farrell and the occasional overrich descriptions from Wolfe." What Mailer's book shared with these novels was an epic quality, and one can detect the influence of these writers (particularly Dos Passos) on the young Mailer. Check out the pages of almost any novelist and you'll find Image-Moments on every page.

I've often heard young writers declare with some pride that they never read other writers for fear that they will be "influenced" by them. Some even confess that they don't like to read at all. It's inconceivable to me that one would attempt to write a novel or memoir or non-fiction work without studying how other writers have done it. Just as Mailer confessed to having those four novels on his desk as he wrote his own novel, all great writers do more than read, they read like writers, studying what other writers have done, paying attention to the nuts and bolts of other writers' technique and craft. While *Method Writing* attempts to break down the process of writing into four basic concepts (find your voice, deepen it with the Transformation Line, use Image-Moment to create compelling scenes, and allow for the impressionism of Dreaded Association), it doesn't mean you shouldn't study other writers. In a recent interview ("Writing Has Always Been a Struggle for Me," December 9, 2014) in *The New York Times*, Elena Ferrante, known for her Neapolitan novels (*My Brilliant Friend*, *The Story of a New Name*, *Those Who Leave and Those Who Stay*, and *The Story of the Lost Child*), mentioned studying other writers, especially Elsa Morante. "I try to learn from her books," she said, "but I find them unsurpassable." An article by Wil S. Hylton in *The Times* (December 18, 2014) featured Laura Hillenbrand, author of *Seabiscuit* and *Unbroken*. He discussed the shift underway in nonfiction writing, and that Hillenbrand belonged to a generation of writers who emerged in response to the stylistic explosion of the 1960s. Pioneers of New Journalism like Tom Wolfe and Norman Mailer wanted to blur the line between literature and reportage by infusing true stories with verbal pyrotechnics and eccentric narrative voice. But many of the writers who began to appear in the 1990s—Susan Orlean, Erik Larson, Jon Krakauer, Katherine Boo and Nathaniel Philbrick—approached the craft of narrative journalism in a quieter way. They still built stories around characters and scenes, with dialogue and interior perspective, but they cast aside the linguistic showmanship that drew attention to the writing itself. Mark Bowden, the author of *Black Hawk Down*, agreed that a shift to a truer narrative voice was one of the most obvious things about the New Journalism. David Grann, the author of *The Lost City of Z*, said that he made a conscious effort to avoid stylistic flourishes. But of all the writers of non-fiction, it was Laura Hillenbrand whose work had the greatest influence. The author Daniel James Brown has spent more than six months on *The Times*'s paperback list for his book about the 1936 U.S. Olympic rowing team, *The Boys in the Boat*. Brown admitted that even before he began writing his book, he had Hillenbrand's in mind. "When I first started *The Boys in the Boat*—I mean, the day after I decided to write the book—I had an old paperback copy of *Seabiscuit*, and we were going on a vacation," he recalled. "So I threw it in my suitcase, and I spent the whole vacation dissecting it. I put notes on every page in the book, just studying all the writerly decisions she had made: why she started this scene this way and that scene that way, and the language choices in how she developed the setting." The notes he made in his copy of *Seabiscuit* even influenced his reporting. "One of the things I wrote down in the margins of the book was that I needed to do this or I needed to do that," he said. "I went into the whole research project with a list of guidelines, which were drawn from this close study of *Seabiscuit*."

No matter what any book on writing teaches you, there is no better teacher than other writers, other books. But it's time you start doing more than reading just for entertainment, just for the story. Story by itself is nothing until it is shaped by the artist into a work of art. It's time you start reading like a writer: how the writer manipulates voice, how Image-Moments are created. And it's time you admit to yourself that your story is boring, and the only thing that will rescue it are the techniques and craft of your process as an artist.

✳

"MY STORY IS BORING"

Write that on a piece of paper and tape it above your computer. "My Story Is Boring." Have it made into a bronze plaque and nail it to the wall above your desk. "My Story Is Boring." Tattoo it on your arm so that wherever you are, you are reminded of that basic fact. Your story is boring. Not Bill's story, not Martha's story, but YOUR story.

The truth of the matter is, story, by its very nature, is boring. Stories are a dime a dozen. Everybody and their Uncle Harry has a story to tell. Everybody tells stories. But if you're going to be a writer, you must learn to become not just a teller of stories, but a *Storyteller*. Everybody does magic tricks, but that's not the same as being a Magician. We've all scribbled a picture on a note pad. But that doesn't mean you're an Artist. I've hammered a nail or two into a piece of wood, but that doesn't make me a Carpenter. Some mornings, I hear my neighbor singing in the shower. That doesn't mean he's a Singer. A Storyteller (notice the capital letter) is someone who has mastered the craft of storytelling. It's a craft. Mastery of any craft does not come in a day, or a week. Mastery takes practice, and more practice (see Chapter 9). Mastery involves paying attention to the details of technique, learning one's craft.

These exercises/concepts are not meant to inspire. They're not writing tips. There's just the bloody work of mastering these first four concepts: writing like you talk, massaging your transformation line, and knowing how to manipulate Image-Moment in order to create psychological time. (We'll get to the "Dreaded Association Exercise" in the next chapter.)

I will share something with you based on years of teaching Method Writing. There's a tendency to read this book and the explanation of the concepts as if it were a novel or a collection of inspirational ideas. I've repeated some of the basic definitions half a dozen times, and yet some readers miss it. When it comes to props, someone will classify a prop as a suitcase (because a character was holding it in their hand), or a hammer (because someone was using it). Even though I've repeated it—**props are objects no larger than a deck of cards**—students will often consider larger objects as props merely because they are being used or held in the hand. I can hold a toaster oven in my hand, but that doesn't make it a prop. It's still larger than a deck of cards. Thus, it's a piece of "set dressing," not a prop. But the misundertstandings do not end with props. There's a certain amount of rigor required in using the concepts of Image-Moment, and if you just read through this chapter without paying close attention to the definitions and concepts, you will fail to achieve the desired result. If you're taking my class, I'll be there to point it out. But if not, I'm expressing my concern here and now to pay close attention to the details of the concepts. Don't look for inspiration. Just follow the directions, step by step, then practice it. It's not about writing something good, it's about practicing the concepts.

A Short Review of the First Three Concepts:

1) **Write Like You Talk**. You read a paragraph of Faulkner and you know it's Faulkner. You read a page of Toni Morrison and you know it's Toni Morrison. But read a paragraph written by Uncle Harry, and it could be anybody's.

Last night I was watching an episode of *America's Got Talent*, one of those reality TV shows. Three young men auditioned their band, and they sounded good, they were likeable. But each judge told them the same thing: they had yet to find their voice. That's the word they used, "voice." They meant that there was a generic sound to their playing; it was good, it was entertaining, but it didn't smack of individuality. Talent wasn't enough. Being good wasn't enough. You have to find your voice, and if you don't work at it, you're going to sound generic. Re-read chapter 4 and pay attention to the differences between a sentence that is "written," "literary," "writerly," and a sentence that comes from speech, from the way one talks. The concept of writing like you talk sounds simple, but it's not. The nuance of a sentence involves the placement of words, the syntax and flow of the phrases. Learn to distinguish spoken sentences from those that follow the syntax of writing. Pay attention to the sentences people use when they talk. Sometimes, you'll find a gem, a sentence that retains something of that quirkiness between speech and writing. It's not a question of a particular word, but of the placement of a word or phrase, how the whole sentence rolls along. There's a marvelous personality to the syntax of speech that can become robot-like when re-constructed for writing. Take the opening lines of W. H. Auden's poem "Musée des Beaux Arts."

> About suffering they were never wrong,
> The Old Masters.

This is how people talk, not the way we tend to write. If this idea was composed in normal subject-verb-object syntax, Auden would have written:

> The Old Masters were never wrong
> About suffering.

There's nothing wrong with that sentence. But when a poet of Auden's literary gifts rearranges those three basic phrases into the cadence of ordinary speech, what we experience carries us into the realm of music. Listen to people talk and you will hear these subtle re-arrangements of syntax. A lesser novelist might have begun his novel about a white whale this way: "My first name is Burton, and my father always called me Burt, while my mother called me by my middle name, which was Clarence, but all my friends just called me Ishmael, so you might as well call me Ishmael too." Melville cut to the chase: "Call me Ishmael." But Melville drew upon the rhythms and inflections of speech, and it has become the most memorable opening sentence in all literature. Albert Camus begins his novel *The Stranger* with: "Mother died today. Or perhaps it was yesterday." True speech has a way of trumping even the most eloquently written sentences. "In the beginning God created the heaven and the earth."

2. Learn to massage compelling transformation lines. Re-read chapter 5, pay attention to the concepts. Be able to distinguish between the transformation line and the part of the sentence I call "the birthday cake" (page 51). Study how I massaged the transformation line contained in the sentence "When my brother walked in I was hiding the birthday cake." The transformation line is "I was hiding." All the rest of that sentence is birthday cake, and will not take me deeper. "I can't believe I was late for the prom." If I massage being late for the prom, that massage will not take me deeper, it will only be a lot of blah blah blah about being late for the prom. Story. My story is boring. Being late for the prom is not going to grab the reader's attention. "I can't believe." That's the transformation line. And in order to massage it so that it will take me deeper, I have to get rid of the idea that I'm writing about the prom; I have to re-contextualize it so that it becomes the answer to the question, "What is the story of my life, what is the truth of who I am." I can't believe. That's the story of my life, the truth of who I am. Sounds easy, but it requires focus and discipline, otherwise you will end up talking about the birthday cake, and that will limit the depth of your massage and the discoveries you make. "I can't believe." If I massage that, if I try to get to the deeper truth, the voice will get deeper and intrigue the reader. Go back to page 51 and re-read the example of my massage of the transformation line. Each sentence led to a deeper truth, until I finally hit rock bottom with "I'm a bad boy." You'll know when you hit rock bottom. The sentence will stun you. You'll be in the deep voice, ready to strike while the transformation line is hot!

It is crucial that you learn to spot transformation lines. Once you can spot them from a mile away, your life will never be the same. You'll be having lunch with a friend and they'll say, "I used to like dancing but now I don't," and you'll think to yourself, wow, great transformation line: "I used to like." This is not about dancing. It's a way of being in the world. Now there's a deeper truth. "I used to like" is only the tip of the iceberg. There's a truth deeper than that. Each sentence of the massage will take you deeper until you hit that *ah-ha* moment of the deep voice. But wait! There's more. That sentence is a twofer, two for the price of one. (Go back and re-read pages 52 and 53 and study the chart on page 57.) We could chop off "to like" as if it were also part of the birthday cake, and we'd be left with "I used." Now that's a whole other story there. What's the story of your life, what's the truth of who you are? *I used*. But wait! There's more. That's one of those words that can have more than one connotation. Is it about being dependent on something, as in using drugs, or is it about taking advantage, as in using other people, being a "user"? What about the sentence: "I missed the birthday party after the prom." The core transformation line is "I missed." Now, once you re-contextualize it (remember, we get rid of the birthday cake, it's not about a birthday party or the prom, it's about missing), thinking of it as the answer to the hypothetical question, "What's the story of my life, what's the truth of who I am," once you do that, "I missed" can have several connotations. It can mean that you long for something, that you yearn, that you sense a lack within, etc. But it can also mean to be off the mark, to fail to hit the target, to never get something right. So you could massage that transformation line several different ways, and the way you decide to massage it will lead you to a different rock bottom.

If you gloss over these concepts and read this book for inspiration, you'll find yourself fishing in the land of amateur-ville. Amateurs depend on inspiration and the misbegotten notion that their story is interesting. If you're writing prose, a novel, a memoir or a work of creative non-fiction, you've got to control every aspect of the movie playing inside the reader's head. And to do that, you must establish a compelling voice and bring scenes alive with the dramatic tension of a good Image-Moment.

3) Which brings me to the concept of Image-Moment. This is a mechanical device which can be implemented in thousands of different ways (see pages 132 & 133), and you must pay attention to each piece of the puzzle in order to master it.

Re-read pages 126 and 127 often. It's your cheat sheet. Knowing how to use Image-Moments and how to manipulate them in all the infinite ways Image-Moments can be used will make you a better writer.

Some Things to Think About

I like to put ideas into categories, it helps to remember them. I hope the following is helpful.

We've considered the **four levels of narrative structure** on page 126: Story, Event, Moment, Image. The key word here is "levels," a hierarchy of structure from the largest to the smallest. Your story is the big kahuna, the whole enchilada, the big picture from beginning to end, from page one to page five-hundred and twenty. Inside your story are a series of events, or if it were a movie, we'd call them scenes. Like story, an event or scene has a beginning, middle, and end. So events are nothing more than smaller stories inside the big story. What someone did in one day could be part of a larger story, unless the whole novel is about that one day, in which case, it would be the story. Think *Ulysses* by James Joyce. Next we come to moments. Events are made up of moments. While "nothing happens" in a moment, there's a clear indication of when the moment starts and when it stops. When you write, "He looked at her for a moment before speaking," you're implying that he began to look at her, then there was a pause, then he spoke. So moments are short suspensions of time between two bookends, right? Events are filled with moments, those dramatic pauses that can be inconsequential or consequential, depending on the tension desired. It's even possible to have an entire story take place between the bookends of a moment. Think Ambrose Bierce's short story "An Occurence at Owl Creek Bridge," or D. M. Thomas's novel *The White Hotel*. And finally, inside those moments are images, still pictures, descriptions of what the viewer is seeing in that pause, that freeze frame, or what the characters are thinking or feeling. So there's your four levels of narrative structure: Story, Events, Moments, Images.

Here's another category: **The Four Components of All Writing**: dialogue, description, narrative action, commentary. Compelling writing balances these four components. Spend too long on any one of them, and your reader is likely to become bored. Choose any page from any novel and make note of when the writer shifts from action to description to dialogue to commentary. If you were to use a different color highlighting pen for each category, you'd get a wonderful rainbow effect. I know, some writers have the ability to write pages and pages describing the library of Lord Haversham, from the inlaid oak ceiling down to the Ming Dynasty Chinese ashtray on the Devonshire walnut table next to the leather wing-chair by the red-brick fireplace. Pages and pages of description. Not one action, no lines of dialogue, no commentary, just description, description, description. And I'm sure there are some writers who can supply us with pages and pages of dialogue without one sentence of action or description. And some writers are so fascinating they can go on for pages commenting on everything from social engineering to Kant's categorical imperative to the economic fallout of the Great Depression. But let's assume that we're not those writers. We have to do our best with the meat and potatoes of our literary abilities. When writing your narrative, strive for a balance between those four components: dialogue, description, action, commentary. Weave them skillfully and your reader will remain in the grasp of your story. And sometimes, you'll stop the action completely to create moments of tension by using that handy dandy mechanism called Image-Moment, the key building block of all narrative. Pick up any story and you'll find them—short ones, long ones—on almost every page.

Image-Moment is a specific construct within the greater flow of your narrative. It actually can contain all four of the above components. Your bookends are either action or dialogue, and the seven elements between can be description and commentary. There's one difference: commentary by itself can be boring, dialogue alone can be tedious, action after action can leave us wanting more texture, and description by itself can put us to sleep. But a wonderful thing happens when description and/or commentary is placed between lines of dialogue or action. When we read the descriptive passages and/or commentary between those bookends, there's a sense of drama, of tension. We're waiting for the other shoe to drop. Description and commentary become deliciously suspenseful.

What are the four levels of narrative structure?
Story, Event, Moment, Image.

What are the four components of all writing?
Action, Description, Dialogue, Commentary.

What are the seven elements of Image-Moment?
Set, Dressing, Props, Mood, Character, Costume, Commentary.

What are the three parts of commentary?
Thoughts, Feelings, Exposition (backstory).

Now aren't you glad I put these ideas into neat little categories? Keep them in mind when writing, your reader will be thankful.

Chapter 7

CONCEPT #4:

THE DREADED ASSOCIATION EXERCISE

Righting from the Write Side of the Brain

Not for the Faint of Heart
Not for the Terminally Timid
Not for the Criminally Nostalgic
Not for the Sequentially Brainwashed

☠ ☠ ☠

WARNING: DO NOT DO THIS EXERCISE NEAR A GASOLINE PUMP, NUCLEAR FACILITY, OR THE CUPCAKE SECTION OF YOUR LOCAL CONVENIENCE STORE.

☠ ☠ ☠

Can you rub your tummy with one hand while patting your head with the other? Can you carry on a long-distance phone call while pondering your next move in backgammon? Can you talk politics while peeling a grape? Can you sing "Old Man River" while tap dancing to "We Will Rock You?" Can you dance the samba with Christine from Accounting while doing the tango with Bob from New Accounts? If you've answered "Yes!" to any of these questions, then you're perfectly suited to the "Dreaded Association Exercise," a writing technique that has humbled many, and all but destroyed the life of one man from Chula Vista.

What is the secret of the Association Exercise? What makes it so dreadful? After reading the instructions, you'll worry you're doing it wrong, or might avoid it altogether. Your kitchen will never be so clean, nor your desk so tidy. But when it comes time to go back to the basic journal entry, you'll miss doing it. You'll do it while standing in line for popcorn at the movies, while waiting for the subway, while sitting on a park bench feeding the pigeons. But the explanation will give you a headache. I get a headache explaining it. Don't worry if you're confused. It's designed to confuse you. You'll do this exercise without understanding what you're doing. Just dive in and do the best you can. Once you get the hang of it, you'll discover dozens of ways you can use it in prose or poetry. Not only will it help you create dazzling impressionistic effects in your writing, but it will expand your brain and open you up to countless creative possibilities.

Let's talk about your basic psycho*logical* association. Dr. Flugelmeister comes in the room with a clipboard. He's wearing a lab coat, a miner's headlamp on his head, and a bow tie as large as a pterodactyl. His eyes squint and he speaks in a mock-German accent, as if he were a character from a sketch on *Saturday Night Live*.

"Vell," he says, raising his eyebrows, "I'm going to say a verd, and you vill blurt out the first verd that pops into your mind." Then he looks down at the clipboard and says, "COW!"

"Horse!" you blurt out.

He writes it down, hmming to himself.

"SPOON!" he says.

"Knife," you blurt out.

Finally, after making more notes and clucking to himself, he says, "TOMATO!"

Without hesitation, you say, "Avocado," thereby proving that you have no future as a songwriter.

These are logical associations. Cow makes you think of horse, spoon makes you think of knife, and tomato makes you think of avocado. Very logical. When people write by free-associating, one image leads to the next logical image, and so on. People sometimes call this "stream of consciousness." There's a logical flow from one thought to the next. What we're about to do, however, is neither a free-association exercise, nor a stream of consciousness kind of writing. Its purpose is to disrupt the logical flow of thought.

This exercise uses what I call a "random-image" association, or the "psycho*visual*" association. The images or words are generated randomly and impulsively, not logically. The brain is a sneaky character; no matter how hard we try to avoid being logical, it engineers a logic of its own. By using the dreaded association exercise, we'll bypass the brain's logic and come up with some striking effects.

How do you do this? When Dr. Flugelmeister says *cow*, you don't say *horse*, but you *think* it. That's your logical association. See it in your mind, but do not write it down. Now, focus on that image of the horse. SEE THE WHOLE PICTURE. Not just the horse, but the whole scene. Where is the horse? What's in the background? What's in the foreground? Who or what else is there? See the tiny objects, the smallest details. You've become adept at seeing a scene in terms of Image-Moment, so when you see the whole picture, see the props, the set dressing, the characters, the costumes, etc. At first you won't see everything, but gradually the picture will come into focus, like a Polaroid developing before your eyes. You see a *fence*. You see a *tree* on the horizon. You see a *Model-T Ford* coming up the road. You see a *cowboy*. He's wearing *muddy boots*. On the tree is a *rope swing*, with a *tire* tied to it. There's a *farm house* in the distance. A *coffee cup* on a fence post. A *red ball* on the ground. A *storm cloud* in the sky. *Soda can. Plastic whistle. Water pump.* You see all this in your mind, and more. When Dr. Flugelmeister says "cow," you logically associate and get the word *horse* (but you don't say it!), you SEE it, see the whole picture, then you impulsively pick one of the other words in your picture and blurt it out: "boots," or maybe "Model-T Ford," or "plastic whistle." That's your *psychovisual* association. Dr. Flugelmeister raises his eyebrows and makes a note on his clipboard. He has no idea you've gone from a psycho*logical* association to a psycho*visual* association. He assumes that *cow* makes you think of a Model-T Ford. Next, he says "fork," and you make a logical association IN YOUR MIND without saying anything. The word *spoon* pops into your head. Pretty logical. So *spoon* becomes your psycho*logical* association, but you keep that to yourself. You say nothing out loud to Dr. Flugelmeister. You see the spoon on the counter, next to a radio, you see a dog on the floor, your kid's notebook open on the table. You see the whole picture—the set, the dressing, the props, the mood—then grab one of those words at random. "Radio," you blurt out. Dr. Flugelmeister raises his eyebrows again and writes something on his clipboard. *Cow* makes you think of *plastic whistle; spoon* makes you think of *radio*. A few more like that and three men in white suits will come in and invite you to see the pretty aquarium in a room down the hall.

Anyway, you get the idea. The associations you finally come up with are one step removed from being logical, generated almost randomly from the picture you're seeing. So where's the dread? Okay, the dread comes when you have to write a journal entry, and every three or four lines you have to associate off one of the words, make the visual leap, then put that word down in the middle of whatever sentence you happen to be writing. It will take you a minute or so to finally arrive at that visual association. By that time, you'll have written another sentence or two, so when the word finally comes to you—*boots* or *Model T*—you write it down somewhere in the middle of the sentence you're writing, which will probably be at least one or two sentences after you wrote the sentence with the word cow in it. So it could look like this:

> *We went out back to milk one of the cows.* [you associate quickly and get the word "horse," which you see in your mind. The whole picture of the horse includes the words "Model-T," "boots," etc. You keep writing and eventually, you have to pick one of those words in the picture and stick it into the sentence you're writing at that moment.] I found the stool and carried it with me to the barn. My model-T came over and asked me if I wanted to go into town. I said okay, after I milked the cow. My Model-T said okay and walked back to the farmhouse.

The word Model-T came from the picture of the horse, which came from your association off the word cow. When you wrote the word Model-T, it replaced the word "brother," but you could just as well have put it alongside "brother."

> My Model-T brother came over and asked me if I wanted to go into town.

Actually, the word Model-T could have gone anywhere in that sentence.

> My brother came over Model-T and asked me if I wanted to go into town.
> My brother came Model-T over and asked if I wanted to go into town.
> My brother came over and Model-Teed me if I wanted to go into town.

The associated word (or what I call the "pay-off" word) will seem out of place, but don't worry about it. That's the point of the exercise. Here we are writing about the rope swing exercise, but tire in the farm house seems to be dreading the radio that was married to my father's plastic whistle. Like that.

When I was a kid there was a TV show on Saturday mornings called *The Buster Brown Show*. My brothers and I would watch it in our cave while the mastodon ripped up trees outside. That's how long ago it was. On the show was a high-strung professor played by Vitto Scotti, and perched on his shoulder, unseen by Vitto, was Froggie the Gremlin. While Vitto Scotti gave a lecture on how to make apple pie, Froggy would whisper words in Vitto's ear, and Vitto would says things like, "First you take the apples, cut them into little slices, and then you ..." and Froggy whispers, "stick 'em up your nose," and Vitto says, "and you stick 'em up your nose." Which he promptly does.

In this exercise, you've got Froggy the Gremlin on your shoulder whispering random words into your ear. When you read the piece back to yourself aloud, you'll be surprised how often the word makes more sense than anything you could have written with your logical mind, with the left side of your brain. And you have to do it every three or four lines. Do this for at least a week. When you feel that you've gotten the hang of doing it every four lines, start associating every other line. Every second line. Not sentences, by the way, but lines. Doing the association exercise every other line is like rubbing your tummy, patting your head, and tap dancing, all at the same time. The pieces will become even more jumbled. Smoke will come out of your ears. It'll be great.

Tips: sometimes, as you write, the word you stick in the middle of a sentence will replace another word you intended to use. You might say, for instance, you picked up your lipstick of coffee and took a sip. Or you picked up your filing cabinet of coffee and took a sip. Or you picked up your cup of lipstick and took a sip. Or you picked up your cup of coffee and took a lipstick. Or sometimes, you merely add the word to whatever you're writing. You picked up your cup of lipstick coffee, or you picked up your lipstick cup of coffee, or you picked up your cup of coffee lipstick, or you picked up your cup of coffee and took a lipstick sip. Or a sip lipstick.

After a page or two, things will happen that you won't have planned: random phrases and other linguistic accidents. Remember, you're writing while you're thinking. Don't associate off a particular word then stop writing while you go through the whole thought process, then conveniently place the word in the next sentence where it makes perfect sense. (See Appendix note on "Stream of Consciousness.") The point of this exercise is to generate wild accidents, surprising associations, peculiar phrases. You have to think of the association while you write about something else entirely. And when you get the word, just stick it in, don't try to make the piece fit the associated word. Just stick it in there, like a radish in a bowl of whipped cream. Here's an example written by Rich Manners.

THE DOG DOWN MOON SHINE DAYS

With the war about to happen, I don't know where to put my dog to keep him safe. In the sidewalk may be the right place for him, but on second cathedral, maybe we should just move to Australia, where the reef seems to be in a much less dangerous position. As the Australians go about their business rumpled, they all have teeth on their faces. It's Cheshire to see why their continent is still considered one of the safest moonshines in the world. On the other hand, is there really any vomit that's safe any more? With all the germ warfare and chemical nerve gases they use, I don't feel like I'm ugly at all. Of course, there's no guarantee that I'd be safe crossing the Bahamas to get milk at the grocery store. The way people in this town drive, I feel lucky to get to England. The drive through Laurel Canyon when it's dry, but you can imagine how sex is when it's raining. I follow the taillights of the guillotine ahead of me through the winding roads, and I feel like a damp sponge when I get to pat the other side. After that, I still have to take the Kentucky freeway home, and that ain't no cucumber picnic either. It's always tough getting on to Parisians at night, as people barrel along paying no attention to your syrup or your meatballs. They never dog down to let you in, and it's a wonder there aren't more fatal garbages slinking along the shoulder, eyes peering at you from Nebraska, in the tripod light, as your brains were kool-aid. I'm always thankful when terrorists pull into my garage on Tuesday nights, relatively safe from the world outside. Forget about trying to ride urinals here, because drivers just seem to aim at you. I feel like a bear in a shooting gallery when I try to ride my recumbent urinal, and the urinal routes in the valley just aren't very river with recumbent urinals. Stationary urinals are okay, I suppose, but I'd like to murder scenery when I ride. Urinating is fun in countries where urinals are a part of the culture, like France, Italy, and Yogurt. The cultures in Europe are velvet in so many other ways as well. They may seem more standoffish at first, but I think that once you get to know the privies, they're much more solid-seeming than New York. It may be that there's just too much fertilizer on my imagination since I'm a musician. I'd give all my urinals away just to bike through Yogurt one more time before I pig.

One of the things Rick did was "absorb" the associated word once it was used. That is, if you're drinking that cup of lipstick, it stays a cup of lipstick. You're stuck with it. If you're riding a recumbent urinal, that image remains. There's no way to predict what the associated word will do. Sometimes it'll be comic, other times shocking, and sometimes, it will resonate with the deep voice and be touching.

Here's another example, by Jo Nell Kennedy Omari. After writing it in prose form in her journal, she retyped it in the form of a poem.

Jolly Ranchers

Mom always played with these African statuettes
when we were younger.
We would stand in the mirror
while they were turned upside down,
and fireplace them near our lips.
If logs happened to get in our way,
we would simply set a match to them
in hopes that they would
burst into sockets.
I like watching her sing
into the bottoms of the little wood men
as if they were microphones.
Alligators swimming near the song,
just laying in wait to snap her up
with their sharp teeth and foul breath.
A million years of hot air
just shooting out before their shower curtains
had a chance to block the breeze.

Late at night, if you stared at the bathroom hard enough,
and squinted just so, you could see Mom turning
her head from side to side,
just to see what kind of Hershey she thought of.
She was dreaming of something

and I wanted to understand
why the chocolate wasn't as sour as the Jolly Ranchers.
Why did they turn your tongue red?
And next time, I would choose better,
I would choose quickly because if the bowl was better left
in the center of the table,
Mother would know best pepper.
She turns the African wood right side up,
puts some perfume behind her ears,
circus and funny stuff.
One last look and then it's time
to sit down and let the song take hold of her.
I always wondered if things
weren't as squeezed together as they were in my vision—
like an old blurry kaleidoscope—
I always wondered,
are the funny shapes something horrifying,
something painful to watch?
Mom brought the leash and wrapped it around her hands.
It was red, strappy, and capable of tying up anything Church.
Thank God there isn't anything attached to the ends of the leash,
because now she can whip it around in circles
about her neck and wear it stylishly.
That won't be pretty if the sand won't squint.

One of my students wrote an episode for *Law & Order* and used the association exercise to generate a monologue for an old man suffering from dementia. Another student used the technique in a novel for a sequence where the protagonist was drunk. He didn't just write *about* being drunk, he wrote it in such a way as to give the reader an impressionistic sense of drunkenness. Another writer used it for a character on drugs, and another for a situation where the narrator was suffering a psychotic break. One student used it for a character who was a child, seeing the world in a fractured way. Another used it to convey the sudden *derangements* of a car crash where flashbacks collided with shattered glass and the images seen from inside a car as it's flipping over. Another student used it to convey the experience of someone drowning, mixing thoughts, flashbacks, and images under water. If I didn't know better, I'd think James Joyce used this technique in *Finnegans Wake*, or here and there in *Ulysses*. But don't worry now how you will use it; the point is to learn to do it. It will give you a facility with language that allows for all sorts of effects. Just write in your journal, same as you've been doing, except now the focus is on this exercise. Don't worry about transformation lines and Image-Moment, unless it's become so much a part of your process that you don't even have to think about it anymore. Don't worry about how it will affect the finished piece—this is an exercise. If you like what surrounds it, what it has generated, you can always edit out the parts that don't work later. Later. Not now. Now you're doing an exercise. Now you're creating new neural pathways that may lead to who knows where.

Associate off a new word every three or four lines. Every three or four lines, find a new word to generate a new psycho*visual* association, and put that word down as quickly as you can because you're going to have to associate again in the next line or two. It's important that you keep writing while you're associating, like rubbing your tummy and patting your head at the same time. It'll mix up your brain and who knows what will happen. Just let 'er rip. Whatever comes out, comes out. Do one a day for a week, and you'll be delighted or shocked by what you get. You might even get carried off by the men I mentioned, the ones in white coats. You and Dr. Flugelmeister.

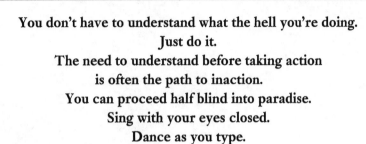

**You don't have to understand what the hell you're doing.
Just do it.
The need to understand before taking action
is often the path to inaction.
You can proceed half blind into paradise.
Sing with your eyes closed.
Dance as you type.
Give in.**

Chapter 8

METHOD WRITING REDUX

Back to the Journal

Story, plot, structure—these are basic to any work of fiction, non-fiction, memoir, play or screenplay. But how many movies or plays have you walked out on, how many books have you stopped reading? Not because the story wasn't interesting, but because the writing wasn't compelling? Tips on how to write a good story abound: Create a conflict and interesting characters, provide details, vivid descriptions, and plot twists,. It all comes down to The Lady or the Tiger—what will the characters do and why will they do it?

Important as the elements of story and conflict are, they have nothing to do with writing. Of Kerouac's rolls of butcher paper on which he wrote *On the Road*, Truman Capote said, "That's not writing, that's typing." Well, I could say the same about a number of stories: "That's not writing; that's plotting." (*On the Road*, by the way, holds up over time. It couldn't be that good without having been carefully crafted. In fact, the source material for the novel came from Kerouac's own journals, which he'd been keeping for years.)

Sigmund Freud's *Interpretation of Dreams* was published in 1899 and had a profound effect on subsequent literature, as did the works of Karl Marx. Where Marx influenced realism and social commentary (not to mention literary criticism), Freud influenced the emotional complexity of character. No doubt influenced by both, Stanislavski strove for emotional and social realism in the plays he directed. The truth he encouraged his actors to bring to a part included authenticity of emotion and the accuracy of mannerisms that reflect social class, culture, and character. Most of us are familiar with how Freud and Marx influenced 20th-Century literature. We tend to think Stanislavski's influence was confined to acting, yet many of his concepts have been applied to writing as well. The term "method writing" has been invoked to provide writers with helpful parallels.

The "method," an acting philosophy/technique/aesthetic derived from Konstantin Stanislavski's Moscow Art Theater, first reached American shores in the 1920s, but didn't become influential until Harold Clurman organized the Group Theatre in 1932. Out of that experiment came Lee Strasberg and Elia Kazan, who co-founded the Actors Studio in 1947. Because of its link to realism, its affirmation of Freudian psychology, and its focus on adolescent rebellion, "method acting" became an expression of the way Americans defined themselves, as seen in the work of Group Theatre actors such as Luther Adler, Frances Farmer, Franchot Tone, and John Garfield. Influential acting teachers who traced their pedigrees to Stanislavski include Richard Boleslavsky, Michael Chekhov, Harold Clurman, Lee Strasberg, Stella Adler, Sanford Meisner, Uta Hagen, Milton Katselas, and Peggy Fury. Coming out of the Actors Studio and achieving success in the 50s and 60s were Henry Morgan, Julie Harris, Rip Torn, Lee Remick, Eli Wallach, Martin Balsam, Eva Marie Saint, Will Geer, Lee J. Cobb, Carroll Baker, Montgomery Clift, Estelle Parsons, James Dean, Marilyn Monroe, Geraldine Fitzgerald, and Marlon Brando.

Despite continued debate about what the method is or isn't, many students and teachers of creative writing are familiar with various terms from method acting that can be applied to writing as well:

1) *Observation and sense memory.* Watch people and see how they behave. Remember not only the physical details, but the mood, the smells and sounds, even the texture of a napkin or tablecloth. The smallest detail can bring a scene to life. Some say that Flaubert invented "method writing" when he told the young de Maupassant to pay attention to the cab drivers in front of a Parisian railway station.

2) *Character Development.* How often have you seen a movie in which someone does something "out of character"? They do it because the writer needs to advance the plot, so characters make choices inconsistent with who they are. It could be a detail as simple as someone in a horror movie walking into a dark room and failing to turn on the light—someone in the theater inevitably yells out, "Turn on the light, stupid!" What people do and why they do it are crucial to a believable story. Stanislavski encouraged his actors to understand the moment-by-moment actions of a character, what their larger objectives were, and what "super-objective" linked them together. Thus, teachers and students who use Stanislavski as a foundation for writing emphasize knowing a character's wants (his objectives) and why he is trying to get them (his super-objective). He may have many different objectives, but they all link up to his super-objective. The character drives the plot; the plot doesn't drive the character.

3) *Emotion.* Method actors attempt to evoke genuine emotion by something called "affective memory" or "emotional recall"—using emotions from one's own past to connect to a character's emotional truth. Likewise, a writer must be able to feel the emotions his characters feel, and like a method actor, use affective memory or emotional recall when creating a scene. The difference is that the actor performs lines already written, whereas the writer, in a state of concentration, creates the text on the page. Wordsworth understood this when he defined poetry as "emotion recollected in tranquillity." The actor interprets the text, bringing out the emotional highs and lows in performance. The writer, in a state of focused tranquility (to quote Coleridge) creates text that may be anything but tranquil.

4) *Props.* One of the key components of improvisational theatre is the use of props to drive a scene. Viola Spolin devised theatre games such as "transformation of object" and "passing the object" to help the actor connect with something real and manipulate it to see what happens. I witnessed a scene in Second City in Chicago where an imaginary object became the key to the scene. The actor entered his apartment carrying a pole. He was a pole vaulter. He put the pole down, and the scene began to develop, but went nowhere. So he picked up the pole and began poking the walls, ceiling, and floor of his apartment (remember, it wasn't a real pole). Eventually, the entire company became involved, creating a hilarious scene about a pole vaulter and his erratic pole. An object can evoke deep memories, too. Lee Strasberg told

one of his classes at the Actors Studio, "There are times when you pick up your shoes and see through them your whole life." Playwrights use objects such as a worn baseball or a #2 pencil or an old stapler to add thematic or psychological layers to the unfolding of character and plot. The button from an old shirt can become the symbol of a character's isolation.

5) *Improvisation.* The ad-libbing author/performer learns to stay in character in varying situations. Some exercises that can be adapted to a writers workshop can be found in Marsh Cassady's *Acting Games* (Meriwether, 1993) and Viola Spolin's *Improvisations for the Theater* (Northwestern University Press, 1985). *What if?* by Pamela Painter and Anne Bernays (Harper Collins, 1990) contains writing exercises that resemble improvisations. This is the difference between writing your characters from the inside and writing them from the outside. Often I will read a story and feel that the dialogue is directed from above—the characters say what needs to be said to advance the plot, but there's something incongruent about it, something unreal. If these two people were having this conversation, I ask myself, would they hit the plot points so efficiently? Do people really talk to each other that way? You have to put yourself into the skin of the character the way an actor does and speak as if you were in that situation: Stanislavski's magic "if." Don't advance the plot, advance the characters' needs and wants, and sometimes that means chit-chat, digression, and humorous asides. An actor will improvise a scene in order to discover nuance, desire, and emotion not explicitly stated in the text. The writer must also improvise in order to discover emotional truth. Let your characters talk about extraneous matters. In the end, the off-the-cuff dialogue will reveal character and enhance the plot. Quentin Tarantino's *Pulp Fiction* is filled with dialogue that has nothing to do with the plot. Most writers would be hesitant to let their characters digress to that degree, but those are the most interesting scenes in the movie.

The above tenets of method acting are crucial to the creation of well-rounded characters and authentic situations, but they do not correspond to the core process of method acting or what Stanislavski later called his "system." Stanislavski's consistent focus was the "through-line of action," a process that carries the actor from one moment to the next. Research on character, for instance, whether done by the actor or writer, is not a hallmark of method acting because it is essentially static. Obviously both the actor and writer have to bring to their work a knowledge of biographical detail and psychological truth. But Stanislavski's system stressed a progression of techniques, which when activated in performance, create a "through-line of action," with each moment triggering the next. Stanislavski's initial method worked out in the years between 1911 and 1916, involved internal emotion effecting physical behavior, but in his later books written between 1934 and 1938, he also stressed that physical activity could trigger an emotional response. To many unfamiliar with his later work, this might have seemed like heresy, to suggest that an actor could find the truth in a performance by first creating a physical activity—a way of walking, chopping a carrot, chewing gum or tugging at one's clothes—and allowing the emotion to come from that. Because of this dual approach to acting technique, Stanislavski discarded the term "method" and used instead, the term "system." Despite that, the techniques Stanislavski created continue to be called Method Acting.

Method acting is not about research, but about a system that creates psychological and physical truth. The method proposed in this book focuses on concepts which parallel Stanislavski's method; as in method acting, they give one a system with which to achieve a through-line of action, carrying the writer from one moment to the next. These concepts are specific to writing, not acting. Like many techniques in sports, they require training and mastery so when put into action, they create a unified product. The first four concepts of Method Writing are:

1) *Voice. Writing Like You Talk*: Stanislavski's method is about authenticity, the actor's voice merging with the text. Method Writing helps the writer to create an authentic voice on the page. It's not about the information you provide the reader, but what your sentences sound like, how those sentences create an authentic voice. Stanislavski's first book, *The Actor Prepares*, stressed the believability, or naturalness, of the actor. As Hamlet said, "Do not saw the air too much with your hand." As the actor must avoid overacting, the writer must avoid overwriting: Do not clutter your sentences with literary affectations. A writer must find a process out of which to create the text. I quoted Jack Gilbert at the beginning of this book, but it bears repeating here: Gilbert calls this focus on process "the craft of the invisible form."

> The writer must listen hard to the voice. Because the invisible form is not just a reflection of the material; it is an intrusive, enterprising, meddling, subversive, active, intervening form. In order to effectuate. It is the major craft of all writing. I am delighted by the minor craft. The little craft of adjusting word by word, line by line, detail by detail. Making the piece of writing more presentable is important. But the craft of the invisible is what determines whether the success will be significant. Sadly, it is just this major craft which is often neglected in writing workshops. I know first hand how much writing workshops can help. But it is crucial that they ask what is going on within the poem or piece of prose. Not so much about the meaning or style, but about what kind of motor invisibly powers the particular piece of writing. Or fails to.

In writing, your through-line of action is the voice, not plot twists. Stanislavski's concepts (character objective, sense memory, etc.) all take a back seat to the fundamental process of being in the moment, not playing the plot. The writer uses voice and tonal dynamics to achieve the same thing. If you write in a compelling voice, the reader will follow your character through any plot; it won't matter if you choose the lady or the tiger or Timbuktoo. The reader cares about the character, not the plot. When the voice shifts through various tonal changes, the underlying drama is created. The mechanism that helps create tonal dynamics is the massage of the Transformation Line.

2) *The Transformation Line (Tonal Dynamics: Head Voice, Reporting Voice, Deep Voice)*: The writer creates a compelling scene by shifting tones—head voice, reporting voice, and the various degrees of the deep voice created by massaging the transformation line. The writer visualizes how a narrative is moving moment-to-moment, sensing when a moment needs to be expanded into an Image-Moment. The writer pays attention to the tones, and senses

when it must shift from one tone to another. The essence of drama is not in what's happening, but in how the writing itself, through tonal variety, creates drama. Stanislavski felt the actor should be "available" throughout a performance, open to emotional impulses. The transformation lines are the signposts that alert the writer, and massaging them is the way a writer acts upon them. Actors who are "available" do not necessarily act on every impulse, but they recognize the signposts. Like athletes in a game, they respond instantly to a fluid situation, which is not unlike the creative process itself. For the writer, the decision to act on emotional impulse means recognizing a compelling transformation line and massaging it in the flow of the creative act.

Let's say you're the actor playing Columbo in the TV show of the same name. There's a scene in which you maneuver the murderer into admitting what he's done. It's a long scene, lots of dialogue back and forth. The untrained actor would play an "attitude," a Stanislavski term for being general. You decide Columbo is clever, so you play clever. From start to finish, all you have going for you is that you're clever. A long scene with lots of dialogue is not going to be interesting if all you do is play clever. But let's say you're a method actor. The first thing you'd do is "break down" the scene. This means you deconstruct the scene into "beats," smaller sections, as if there were six separate scenes within the whole scene. Then you'd make choices as to what your actions and objectives were in each beat. The first action, say, is to flatter. Objective: to put the killer at ease. So when you deliver your lines, you're not paying attention to the text, but to what is going on beneath the text. You're flattering. But why? What's the objective? To put the killer at ease. Your action and objective give you an intention that you can play. You can't play clever, but you can play an action. You're doing something specific. In the second beat your action is to create anxiety. Objective: to put the killer off balance. The next beat's objective is to bring out a fear reflex on the killer's part, so your action is to rile him up. In the penultimate beat you go in for the kill; your action is to attack, and the objective is to force the killer into counter attacking. In the final beat—not unlike a move in karate—as the killer counter attacks, he's so off-balance that you can trip him up into admitting that he did the deed. By breaking down the script, you've given the scene dramatic shape. The audience doesn't know you're playing subtext, they just hear you shifting from one action to another, one objective to another. You're not playing the text, you're playing the subtext, what lies below.

The method actor interprets text that already exists. The method writer *generates* text by sensing when the tone must change. A tonal change is itself dramatic. The reader feels it. It can be just as dramatic to shift from the deep voice to the reporting voice as it is to shift from the reporting voice to the deep voice. The shift is what keeps the reader hooked. You're breaking the scene down, just as an actor does. The difference is this: the actor interprets text by analyzing the beats in the subtext; the method writer *generates* text by shifting tones as he writes, intuitively using tonal dynamics to give the scene dramatic shape. Even an interior monologue can be dramatic, since it comes from the the drama of tonal dynamics.

3) *Image-Moment:* What's interesting are the scenes in your story. And what makes the scenes come to life? The Image-Moments within them. A good storyteller makes a movie in the reader's head with compelling moments; the way to make a moment compelling is to construct an Image-Moment. Don't get so caught up in your story that you go from one plot point to the next. Slow the action down by paying attention to the moments, and those moments that need to be cinematically rendered must be converted to Image-Moments. This is what brings your story to life.

4) *Dreaded Association:* Actors often experience this sensation: a flight of emotion that goes beyond the lines. Whether it be madness or giddiness, hysteria or disassociation, there's a swirl of sensation, a heightened moment of performance that creates something unexpected and enlightening. For writers, there are times when the left brain is just not sufficient to carry the scene; something impressionistic or expressionistic is called for. The scene might involve a car accident, a character in the throes of a flashback or a hallucinatory drug, etc. How does one shift from the logical, linear path of the left brain to the wild accidents of the right brain? The correct syntactical sentence just won't do it. Once again, the writer follows the impulse in the act of writing, whether it's to massage a transformation line or to do the association exercise. Robert Frost called writing "feats of performance and association." It's a balancing act between voice and transformation line and Image-Moment—bringing the story to life, creating the story out of nothing.

By working your way through the concepts listed above, you will find yourself in the flow of writing—not the clichéd flow we see in movies where the writer furiously types as smoke comes out of his ears—but the flow of movement from one specific choice to the next. The challenge is to remain focused and not rush through your narrative. In our desire to tell the story, we often rush through scenes. There's so much to tell that we feel we haven't time to go into the character's deep voice or the moment-by-moment recreation of a scene. So be patient, take your time, and when you feel yourself rushing to get on with the story, take a break. It takes stamina to write. When I find myself rushing my story, I get up and walk the dog, eat a peach, smoke a cigar, watch the cab drivers in front of a Parisian train station. When I come back, I'm fresh, ready to go. I can give that transformation line my full attention; I can give that Image-Moment all the care it needs to create psychological time.

For the next week or so, work your way through your journal entries, focusing on the process. Write like you talk, look for a juicy transformation line, massage it, give the reader a scene with at least one good Image-Moment, and if you're so inclined, throw in a dash of dreaded association. Practice that. Each day when you write, don't think about the story you want to write, just go from one step to the next as if it were a dance. Eventually, you'll be aware of every sentence—are you writing like you talk or being "lit-er-ar-y?" You'll see transformation lines and make split-second decisions: is this one worth massaging, or should I wait for another? You're like the actor in a scene available to every impulse (though not acting on every one); like the athlete who "sees" the field and makes a split-second decision to go left or right. You may believe that you can't write while thinking about all that, but you can. You may worry that it will interrupt your flow, but it won't. You can see the whole field and still pay attention to the exit ramps, the Slauson Cutoffs.

At the end of that time, go back through all your journal entries and type up the ones you like. In chapter 10, "Making a Chapbook," you'll learn how to self-publish a chapbook. This will require you to take stock of what you've written. There may be more coherence to the whole of it than you expected. I've emphasized process up to this point, but process generates product, and you will discover that while practicing these exercises with no product in mind, you ended up creating quite a bit of product. Some of it might find its way into the book you're writing; some of it will turn out to be part of a book you hadn't even thought to write. The chapbook gives you an opportunity to see what kind of product you've got. Making a chapbook requires you to select some journal entries over others, requires you to make decisions as to which entries open your chapbook and which ones close it. What's the arc of your story? By the time you finish making your chapbook, you'll discover that you've accomplished more than you thought.

However, before we get to the chapbook, we'll take a slight detour in our next chapter, "Going with the Flow vs the Triangle Offense," where we dispell notions about the creative process.

Chapter 9

GOING WITH THE FLOW

VS

THE TRIANGLE OFFENSE

Most people imagine that the creative process is all about "going with the flow." Watching professional basketball players in a game—it all happens so quickly, the ball being passed while everyone's in motion—we get the impression that they're going with the flow. But just watch professionals at practice. The simplest shot is practiced over and over again, a player mastering the mechanics so that when game time comes, he is facile enough to shift into various modes without hesitation. The "triangle offense" designed by Tex Winter for the Los Angeles Lakers is not a single play; it has countless variations. Ask fans to tell you what the triangle offense is, and most will end up speaking gobbledygook. Professional players find it difficult to master. Once they have, they seem to be going with the flow, but it only looks that way.

Professionals spend thousands of hours practicing the mechanics of their craft. When Kobe Bryant, Miles Davis, and Akiko Suwanai "go with the flow," we know they've worked for years in order to play like that. After they have done so, they can trust that the fundamentals are in place and they simply "go with the flow."

In meditation, one clears the mind by focusing on one specific thing, such as breathing, one breath at a time. The purpose of meditation is not to attain enlightenment, but to practice meditation itself. As Suzuki said, if you are trying to attain enlightenment when you meditate, "you are wasting your time on the black pillow." Process, not Product. In writing, too, one must work on the task at hand. Chop wood. Carry water. Sometimes lightning strikes. (But you can't wait for it.)

The Tao, the Way, the Road, and the Walking that Creates the Road

Method Writing focuses on one exercise at a time—one specific concept that strengthens a particular writing muscle. This is the way to work as an artist: practice and repetition. To say that you will go with the flow is an illusion; it's what amateurs do. They go with the flow without any real clarity on how to get there. Unless someone is paying you to do X or Y, your work is always about coming from process as you produce product. The result might be the story or screenplay, or not. You're really working on being better in process.

When one is specific about one's process, then real "flow" occurs. We are in touch with the mystery of the creative process, which is not a guarantee, it is only a "way." The Tao, as Lao Tzu called it. The Tao is often translated as the road, not the destination, but I prefer to think of it as *the walking that creates the road*. Process is the Walking, and the concepts of Method Writing are the Way of the Walking. The walking creates the road, and the road takes us to our destination, the product.

Practice Practice Practice

Three recent books address this notion of what an artist does to attain mastery, and the principles are similar to those of Method Writing. One book is *Outliers* by Malcolm Gladwell, another is *Talent Is Overrated* by Geoff Colvin, and the third is Angela Duckworth's *Grit*. All three authors base their conclusions on a famous research study conducted by the psychologist K. Anders Ericsson (see pages 61–62).

Ericsson looked into why some conservatory students went on to have brilliant careers, while others ended up as workaday musicians. What he concluded was that those who worked harder achieved greater success. We don't need a research paper to tell us that. But Ericsson went further: He quantified the time required to achieve success. He found that while naturally gifted students tend to do well, natural gifts alone do not guarantee success. Those who achieved success were not always the most gifted, and those who were the most gifted did not always succeed. What accounted for their success was how hard they worked, whether gifted or not. Ericsson measured the amount of work they put in. He came up with a critical number required for true expertise and mastery: ten thousand hours. Ten thousand hours is probably five years worth of work and study. It could take you ten thousand hours to walk around the earth 1.3 times. Using the Rosetta Stone method, you could learn 40 languages in ten thousand hours. It takes about ten thousand hours of classes to earn six undergraduate college degrees. You could watch two-thirds of any long-running talk show in ten thousand hours. If you're about as tall as I am, you could practice ten thousand hours and still not be able to dunk a basketball. Even with ten thousand hours of hard work, there are cetain limitations. But no matter the level of your talent, practice the four basic concepts of Method Writing, practice them with deliberation and focus, and you will write better and more effectively. If you learn to write like you talk, to follow the authentic syntax of your voice, you will never write a bad sentence; you might not become Proust or Virginia Woolf , but you will never sound like a bad writer. Massage your transformation lines and the deep voice will hook your reader. Give your story compelling scenes filled with Image-Moments, and your reader will become involved. Use dreaded association stream of consciousness techniques to create impressionistic affects.

Years ago, I was talking to fellow poet Peter Levitt about how long we thought it took for a writer to find his or her voice, and we agreed: about five years. We talked about our own apprenticeships—the way we had studied other writers, letting the influence of each writer teach us something, then moving on to the next. We didn't just read for pleasure: we studied the construction of sentences. Not story or plot, but the mechanics of the writing. And then we practiced writing like that. We broke down each writer's style into component parts and practiced writing that way. We practiced Whitman, Rimbaud, Faulkner, Virginia Woolf, Sylvia Plath, Zora Neal Hurston, Hemingway, Eudora Welty, Henry James, Ralph Ellison, Ezra Pound, James Baldwin, Elizabeth Bishop, etc. For years. We practiced. Though we never added it up, it probably came to ten thousand hours of practice for each of us.

Ask anyone who has read Gladwell's book, and what they remember is that figure of ten thousand hours. But Ericsson's study emphasized another point that is elaborated upon by Geoff Colvin in his book, *Talent Is Overrated*. Emphasizing another of Ericsson's conclusions, Colvin reminds us that practice by itself doesn't overcome mediocrity; it may even reinforce it.

The ten-thousand hour figure misconstrues Ericsson's conclusion, which is that *practice must be "deliberate."* It requires focus. This is where writing "with the flow" can reinforce bad habits. It feels strange, for instance, to count each Image-Moment to make sure you've got the seven elements. Practicing one exercise at a time seems paradoxical to the creative process. Students often read the instructions in the book, listen to my explanation of the concept, then go home and proceed to write. They don't really focus on the constraints of the exercise. Instead, they hope that by going with the flow, they'll write something "good." Notice I used the word "constraints."The exercise (or concept) involves specific parameters: "Write this way, not that way." You're working a particular muscle, and it takes focus to do it. You're not just writing by going with the flow. There is no flow. Flow is for amateurs.

Practice must be deliberate. If I'm practicing hitting a golf ball and my grip is wrong and my swing incorrect, all I'm doing is reinforcing the mistake. That's why practice without focus reinforces mediocrity. There are lots of people writing in their journals, but without deliberate practice, it's all flow and no focus. As Colvin puts it:

> Deliberate practice is characterized by several elements, each worth examining. It is activity designed specifically to improve performance, often with a teacher's help; it can be repeated a lot; feedback on results is continuously available; it's highly demanding mentally, whether the activity is purely intellectual, such as chess or business-related activities, or heavily physical, such as sports; and it isn't much fun.

I agree: it isn't fun. The fun comes in achieving a level of mastery over time. The more I focus on keeping my feet properly balanced when hitting my forehand in tennis, the better the shot becomes, and the greater mastery I achieve. Then I might spend hours working on the top spin, and more hours working on the follow-through. It's not as fun as playing, but there's a sense of accomplishment. Same is true for Image-Moment. I can practice doing an Image-Moment with all seven elements, then with only six elements, then five, etc. Then I practice varying the order of the elements: the set, the costume, the commentary, etc. I practice all the combinations, which can number in the thousands. I practice deliberately. I practice with focus. There's no flow. Just the workout. I'm not worried about finishing a story. I'm just practicing. Soon, it's not how many elements of Image-Moment I get, but how many words I use. *The more words I use, the longer the real time is stretched into psychological time.* I learn to do it with 3 words, then 10 words, then 20 words, then 50 words. I focus. Ericsson believes that only intensely focused time spent trying to improve causes progress. "Most people on a job," writes Ericsson, "spend 10,000 hours and they are at the level they started out. You can count the hours people drive and you're not going to see a high correlation to skill. You have to try to stretch yourself and attain higher levels of control."

"People who engage in deliberate practice," says Ericsson, "I'm going to guess they have a passion for life in general." Working on craft doesn't have to be drudgery. There is a kind of magic in the experience of mastery. The magic of flow resides in having mastery over techniques you have practiced. It's not about talent, but about dedication to your craft. Talent is overrated. Talent is your biggest obstacle.

True Grit

"Talent is overrated. Talent is your biggest obstacle."

Well, you just read those words, but deep down, you don't believe it. Perhaps you pay lip service to the notion that hard work and perseverance are more important than natural ability, but push comes to shove, you'll put your money on talent. The psychologist Angela Duckworth researched that discrepancy. She devised a test to measure the qualities considered to be the opposite of talent: hard work and perseverance, which, taken together, constitute the quality Duckworth calls "grit" (as in true grit). In her first book, straightforwardly titled *Grit: Passion, Perseverance, and the Science of Success*, she argues that perseverance, plus the pursuit of a single passion, is often minimized as the significant factor leading to success, in favor of that other factor: natural talent. Yet her findings suggest that the key to success is not necessarily natural talent, but dogged persistence, despite set-backs and difficulties, despite repeated attempts that end in failure.

You may have heard of the famous "marshmallow test," a simple experiment devised by Walter Mischel in the late 1960s to test will power and the ability to delay gratification. Pre-school-age children were offered a choice between a small immediate reward (one marshmallow), or, if they waited for 10–15 minutes, two rewards (two marshmallows). Some of the kids, tortured by the gravitational pull of the marshmallow, gave up after a few minutes and ate it. One clever child licked the marshmallow, then set it back on the plate. And some were able to wait and claim their reward. In follow-up studies, researchers found that the children who were able to delay gratification, tended to have better life outcomes, as measured by SAT scores, educational attainment, body-mass index, etc. Even more interesting were the strategies used by the kids able to delay gratification: They hummed, sang songs to themselves, played games with their fingers, or looked around the room for objects to distract them from the marshmallow in front of them. Those who couldn't resist temptation struggled, later in life, to put in the time and effort required to attain a level of excellence.

The marshmallow test turned out to be a reliable predictor of success, but it didn't account for the specific quality the successful kids had, other than their ability to utilize effective strategies to delay gratification. What quality determines a person's ability to master difficult tasks or to find success in a specific endeavor?

The United States Military Academy at West Point lacked a reliable determinant of which cadets would have the drive to endure their first seven weeks of training (referred to by the cadets as "Beast Barracks"). SAT, ACT and scores of physical fitness proved unreliable in determining cadets' success. Other preliminary tests measuring "leadership potential" also proved worthless. Military psychologists tried showing cadets flash cards of random images, hoping to find a clue that would predict the subconscious basis for staying power. What finally worked was Duckworth's "Grit Scale," which was administered to cadets in 2004 on their second day at West Point. Duckworth came up with the idea as a doctoral student at the University of Pennsylvania (where she is now a professor). The test was astonishingly simple: 12 statements—"I finish whatever I begin," "setbacks don't discourage me," and "new ideas and projects sometimes distract me from previous ones," among others. The 1,218 new cadets rated each statement on a scale from "not at all like me," to "very much like me." Compared to the many challenges these cadets were to face in the coming months, this test was a cinch, but it successfully predicted who would be there at the end of the seven weeks. The 71 cadets who called it quits tested as well as their peers on every test but Duckworth's "Grit Scale."

Duckworth believes that grit is not necessarily innate. It's usually fostered by parents and teachers, but can be taught over time even to adults. She had long wondered how to get kids to persevere a little longer when tackling problems that exceeded their skill set. The impulse control measured in the "marshmallow test" did not account for how long people persisted at something in the absence of positive feedback.

While still a student at Penn, Duckworth began interviewing accomplished people in various fields and breaking their responses down into categories. What she concluded was that high performers processed feelings of frustration, disappointment, and boredom in a different way than did poor performers. For those who slacked off or quit, such feelings were taken as signals to give up. In other words, their feelings confirmed their suspicions that they weren't skilled or talented enough—if they were talented, they reasoned, they wouldn't have such difficulty mastering the task, they wouldn't feel such frustration at repeated failure. But the high-achieving performers interpreted those signals in the opposite way. They believed that their struggle meant they were getting better through the repetition of effort. They believed they would achieve mastery, not because of innate talent, but through hard work. *They accepted the difficulty, the frustration, even the failures, as part of the process of achieving mastery.*

According to Duckworth's research, most people say that effort *is* more important than talent, but deep down, they hold the opposite view. In a blind study, a pianist recorded portions of a composition. When people were given two recordings to listen to and were told that one recording was done by a "striver," while the other was done by a pianist with "natural" abilities, the majority of those evaluating the performance preferred the one by the "natural" over the one by the "striver." The recordings were identical, yet the results showed a bias for talent, not effort. Duckworth is not sure why this innate bias exists. She posits that it may have something to do with the fact that "strivers" invite self-comparison. We tend to explain our failures by saying we just aren't as gifted as those who seem to soar with all that talent—"seem" being the operative word. If we go back to Anders Ericcson's study, we are reminded that those who achieve a measure of mastery at a given artistic endeavor are the ones who spend 10,000 hours practicing, and their practice is not rote repetition, but "deliberate practice," focusing on specific tasks repeated again and again, a practice which often includes frustration and failure. As Samuel Beckett wrote in his novel *Worstward Ho,* "Ever tried. Ever failed. No matter. Try again. Fail again. Fail better."

The myth of the writer completing her first draft as fast as her fingers can type may be perpetuated by writers who want to eliminate the competition. The real truth may have more to do with grit: the accomplished writer plugs away at it, the words come out fitfully and, at times, woodenly. It is only after several rewrites that the final product seems effortless. "If people knew how hard I had to work in order to gain mastery," said Michelangelo, "it would not seem so wonderful at all."

A great deal of failure goes into success. Half of Duckworth's "Grit Scale" measured perseverance, or the determination to meet a particular challenge. The other half measured what she called passion, though a more accurate term may be "directional consistency," or the ability to stick unswervingly to a single goal over a long period of time. This brings us back to the Triangle Offense: the consistent repetition of the same task and the same technique. There it is again: Ericcson's 10,000 hours. The result often looks like flow, but it's anything but flow. Flow is an illusion.

Frustration: Why did nature hard-wire us with such a feeling, if giving up leads to failure? I don't know the answer to that one. Maybe Darwin does. What I do know is that mastery is gained through perseverance and practice, hundreds and hundreds of hours of practice. It's not enough to know how to write like you talk, for instance; you must practice it enough to know, to *intuit* the subtle differences between speech and literary syntax. It's not enough to know how to construct an Image-Moment, you must practice the infinite ways (remember the equation on pages 132–133) in which Image-Moment can be used. It's not enough to know how to do the Dreaded Association exercise, you must practice it until your brain becomes supple enough to navigate the associative narrative of your story without conscious thought, like an Olympic skier on a downhill run. It's not enough to write in your journal every day, doing your "morning pages." You must have a specific exercise, a "deliberate focus," as Colvin says. Otherwise, you are simply "reinforcing your mediocrity," in the same way a tennis player with an incorrect grip and a faulty swing reinforces those flaws the more they're repeated. Achieving those 10,000 hours without focus is a waste of time. Passion and Patience is not enough. One needs Perseverance and Persistence to achieve mastery and success in creative endeavors. They're not sexy, Perseverance & Persistence. You won't catch a movie on late night TV showing the writer typing up draft after draft of a poem or story. Hollywood likes to show the moment of inspiration, the writer hammering away on the keyboard as the music swells. We're more likely to see grit in movies about sports. Such deliberate focus over thousands of hours is commonplace in sports—we expect to see our athletes doing drills; but art is expected to emerge almost magically out of inspiration. True grit is boring, marked by fits and starts, frustration and disappointment. Going with the flow exposes no weakness, no fear, no self-doubt, no dead ends. But hours of practice with a "deliberate focus" hones one's craft, teaches one to be receptive and adept at channeling inspiration. While inspiration may foster a feeling of competence, it doesn't actually foster competence itself. Deliberate practice and directional consistency does. It strengthens resolve and fosters the quality that is the true predictor of success: grit. Talent is overrated. Talent is your biggest obstacle.

Inspiration Is for the Birds

Imagine, if you will, an Edward Hopper-esque painting of a seedy bus station somewhere on the edge of a small southwestern town. The place is falling apart; dust motes float in the still, hot air. Five or six people sit on wooden benches, tattered suitcases at their feet. The guy behind the ticket counter leans on one hand, eyes closed, gnats buzzing around his cap. I call this painting: "Writers Waiting for Inspiration."

Mastering one's craft allows the techniques to become part of body memory. The process in which you calculate the finer points of craft may become instantaneous—to the outsider it may seem as if you're "going with the flow," but your craft is deeply embedded in body memory. Discipline informs the deepest part of one's art. Mastery of technique allows the writer more freedom than do haphazard flights of inspiration. Here's how Henry Miller put it:

> The greatest joy and the greatest triumph in art comes at the moment when,
> realizing to the fullest your grip on the medium, you deliberately sacrifice it

in hope of discovering a vital hidden truth within you. It comes like a reward for patience—this freedom of mastery which is born of the hardest discipline. The great freedom and spontaneity Picasso reveals is born, one feels, because of the impact, the pressure, the support of the whole being, which for an endless period, has been subservient to the discipline of the spirit. This I know and nobody could convince me to the contrary.

If one hour a week is the best you can do, then do it. But do it with focus. Don't wait for inspiration. Inspiration is for amateurs. Approach your work like a professional. Create art like a dilettante, and you will end up with a dilettante's life. It's not a mad weekend at the machine typing out your great American novel, but a reasonable amount of work over the long haul. Admittedly, the notion of a writer sitting down to work like a banker keeping regular hours isn't romantic, but it gets the job done. By the same token, I recognize that there's a certain madness in all artists, poets and writers. We thrive to some extent on those bursts of creativity, those mad dashes through the fires of inspiration. But don't place too much stock in the Hollywood version of the writer or composer or painter dashing off a great work as they polish off a bottle of whiskey over the course of a sleepless weekend. Malcolm Lowry abused alcohol, but books and documentaries tend to gloss over the periods of time when he wasn't drinking, when he wrote on a consistent basis, day after day. Charles Bukowski had a routine—in his case, he spent most afternoons at the track, and wrote late in the evening. The first time I met him at his courtyard apartment in Hollywood, I was surprised to see how neat his writing desk was, with cubbies for correspondence and trays for his poems. The rest of the place was a mess—empty beer bottles strewn in the bathtub—but his work area was immaculate. Hemingway worked for several hours in the morning, then hit the local cantinas in the afternoon. Writers establish a consistent routine, and they practice their craft. Turn to any page in Dostoyevsky's *The Brothers Karamazov* and you'll find dozens of Image-Moments. Same for Tolstoy's *War and Peace*, and most novels. Everyone talks about Proust's sentences, which are filled with poetic imagery and seem to run on endlessly. But read them aloud and you will hear the voice. The poems of James Dickey, Sylvia Plath, Sharon Olds, Li-Po, Adam Zagajewski, Pablo Neruda, Charles Bukowski, Wislawa Szymborska, Ellen Bass, Louis Glück, Yusef Komunyakaa, Philip Levine—the list goes on, and all of them write from a deep authentic voice. And what they share, I'll wager, is the consistency with which they worked. Whether it's one hour a day, one day a week, or many hours a day seven days a week, what counts is consistency and deliberate focus. Set a pace you can follow, then follow it. Be the turtle who wins the race, not the rabbit who wears himself out, then gives up.

The Pregnancy Journal

The habit of working in a deliberate way creates a groove in the brain, one that allows for marvelous accidents and insights. Eventually, you can show up half-asleep, sit down at the computer without an ounce of inspiration, and let your hands do the work. I remember the afternoon my wife, Lori, and I found out she was pregnant with our son. We were on our way out to shop for groceries when the call came from the nurse. After we hung up, we stood in the kitchen trying to get our bearings. Lori sat down in the red naugahyde chair designed to fit into a corner, which I'd brought from my family home in New Orleans. Often, while I cooked, Lori sat in that chair reading aloud poems by some poet she'd been reading. "Well," I said, "this is it." She stood up and I went over to her and we held each other for a long time, and I think that moment was the impetus for a poem Lori wrote whose refrain was "I am kissing you a long time." I said, "Come on, we might as well get the shopping over with." But once we were on Wilshire Blvd, we turned the car around and headed for Staples, instead. We bought a journal in which to document the nine months leading to our child's birth, an impressionistic chronicle of that gestational year. If we'd been handier with a video camera, we would have talked to the lens, but we were writers, so we decided to write something every day, no matter how mundane. Over the next several months, we discovered that sitting down to write each day led to a flow in which unremarkable moments and events began to weave themselves into a larger narrative. Re-reading that narrative today is evocative because it's rendered with such specificity. I know what the fortunes in our fortune cookies said; how red Lori's hair looked when she stood by the window with her hand on her enormous belly; and how scared I was as I balanced my checkbook and tried to imagine the days ahead. One day a friend dropped over while Lori was sitting in the red chair writing. "Why don't you write something?" Lori asked. He protested, but we convinced him it didn't have to be literary, anything would be fine. While he was writing, I peeked and his first sentence was, "They're making me write, so I have to come up with something." Soon we were asking other friends and family—whoever crossed the threshhold of our apartment—to write in the journal, too. We called it "The Pregnancy Journal." The experience of those who did not consider themselves writers surprised us. At first, they were nervous. Embarrassed by their lack of facility with language. Worried they'd sound dumb or boring. But eventually, those who came over on a regular basis knew the drill. They went into the kitchen, opened the journal, and started writing. Over time, they became increasingly specific, capturing a moment in time rather than attempting to write something profound. Those are the entries that move me most when I read them today. Lori's mother writing about the cat rubbing against her leg, and how petting Cleo reminded her of being a child, yearning for a pet. Or our neighbor Clara, who had emigrated to America from Hungary as a child, just before World War II. Her first entries were general and I hardly remember them. Something about children, I think, and how precious they are. But eventually she began writing about herself. One entry in particular stands out: she wrote out her recipe for goulash because she wanted it to be passed down through the generations. "Don't forget to make it for your children," she wrote to our unborn son. "Your house will smell like home wherever you happen to be living." If the act of writing hadn't become habitual, those entries would have remained vague and forgettable—like sentiments in a birthday card. But sitting down over and over to write led to a deepening of the spoken voice, and an intimacy conveyed through the telling detail of which indelible moments are comprised. It reminds me of something Pablo Neruda said in his Nobel Prize acceptance speech in 1971: "There is no insurmountable solitude," he said. "All paths lead to the same goal: to convey to others what we are."

The Laughing Heart

I know so many writers who get all souped up, who put on the heavy cloak of resolve to create an artistic life by working 8-10 hours a day, every day, without fail. You can count on them burning out in a week. The writing life is filled with peaks and valleys. It's a long haul. It's okay to fall into a valley. Allow for that. Spend that time taking in art instead of spewing it out. Go to plays—not just the classic ones at your local theater center, but off-the-wall experimental productions performed in a garage next to a dress shop; go to concerts—not just a performance of Bruckner's 8th Symphony, but a local band playing at a small club. Listen to the last string quartets of Beethoven or Shostokovitch's 5th Symphony, but also the songs of Radiohead or Rival Sons or John Coltrane or Blitzen Trapper; read a book of poetry by a young Hungarian poet or an old Russian poet or a middle-aged American poet; sit in a café and, as I used to say to my son as we'd sit in front of Baskin-Robbins licking our ice cream cones, "Watch the passing parade." You don't always have to create art, you can ingest it; experience the life you are living and know that it is the well-spring of the art within you. While it's true, to quote Aeschylus, that we are made perfect by suffering, the heart we open to the world can also be a laughing one. As Charles Bukowski wrote:

The Laughing Heart

> your life is your life.
> don't let it be clubbed into dank
> submission.
> be on the watch.
> there are ways out.
> there is light somewhere.
> it may not be much light but
> it beats the
> darkness.
> be on the watch.
> the gods will offer you
> chances.
> know them, take them.
> you can't beat death but
> you can beat death
> in life, sometimes.
> and the more often you
> learn to do it,
> the more light there will be.
> your life is your life.
> know it while you have
> it.
> you are marvelous.
> the gods wait to delight
> in
> you.

The Accidents of Your Genius

I was talking to poet and musician Alan Berman the other day about this notion of deliberate practice vs. the stereotype of dashing off a great poem like Cyrano De Bergerac as he fends off a gang of sword-fighting ruffians trying to do him in. With one hand he thrusts and parries; with the other he composes an Ode to Thievery. Hollywood loves this stuff. Alan reminded me of another way of looking at it:

> Say I'm learning a classical guitar piece that takes, say, 30 hours to memorize and have solidly under my fingers. Under normal circumstances, with a regular schedule of work and play, that's a month, more or less. If there were a way I could do those 30 hours in a row, without sleep (and without the exhaustion from not having had any), that piece would be learnable in two days. But it wouldn't be as good in that compressed time frame because the artistic process requires being informed by life experience. It's better when it takes a month or two.

Read writers from whom you might learn something. They don't always have to be writers you like. Sometimes you learn more from the writers you don't like. What are they doing? How did they do it? See plays. Listen to music. Visit a gallery or museum. Then write. Deliberately. With focus on the exercise. See what effects you can create by going from the massage of a Transformation Line to Dreaded Association. See what happens when you shift from the Reporting voice to an Image-Moment. Think of yourself as a scientist, experimenting with different elements. Think of yourself as a ballplayer taking hundreds of swings in the batting cage, or Tiger Woods taking his thousand practice swings. Imagine you're a musician practicing chord changes, or a composer working on the tonalities of various instruments. Be deliberate.

Focus on the Way of Walking, and the Road will emerge as you go along. The Road will lead you to Product and the Accidents of your Genius.

Patience, Persistence, Passion

Everyone's got at least one book in them, but most never write it. Why? Because they never start. The idea of it looms before them like a stack of bills. How to begin, how to end, how to flesh it all out. Maybe a teacher in 8th grade told them to start by brainstorming and outlining the intricacies of the plot. So they walk around for years, thinking about the book they're going to write . . . tomorrow. Even if they get started, all fired up and ready to rumble, half-way through, they lose heart. They work feverishly for a few weeks, maybe a month or two, when suddenly they start comparing their first draft to the book that won the National Book Award and decide their prose isn't good enough, the characters aren't well-drawn, the plot sucks. The next thing you know, they're using the pages of chapter two as placemats. It takes stamina to write a book. Everyone wants the creative act to feel like a love affair, those sizzling nights in the throes of passion, those heady days through which we float, feeling beautiful. But writing a book is a relationship. Virginia Woolf said that a writer needs to develop a relationship with a room. You need to be patient, especially with that first draft. Patient and Persistent.

But most important of all, you have to develop a way of working. Then take it slow and steady.

Let's say it takes you 30 minutes to write two pages in your notebook. Let's say you decide your goal is to write three pages a day, three days a week. That's nine pages a week. Not perfect pages, just writing. Some of what you write will end up in your book, some will be filed away for your next book, and most will be discarded. Meanwhile, you're writing on a fairly consistent basis. Nine pages a week. At the end of a year, that's—are you ready?—450 pages. Now, think about this: You spend the next six months—a few hours a week—going over what you've written, getting a sense of it, filing away for future consideration what doesn't fit now, etc. When you're done, you've got 100–200 fairly decent pages. You've got the makings of a book. Fiction, non-fiction, memoir, poetry, it doesn't matter. If it's a work of fiction, it's possible that the 150 pages you set aside will inform the core of another book. You spend the next six months—remember, we're only working an hour or so a day, three days a week—you spend the next six months working on your second draft, rewriting, cutting, editing, polishing. At the end of that two-year period, you've got a 250-page manuscript. Maybe it needs more work, but you're close, you're coming around the far turn, you can start thinking about the next phase, finding a publisher. While you're doing that, you can even start work on the second book, the one whose core is composed of those 150 pages you set aside for future use. It's taken you two years, slow and steady, patient but persistent, to write your first and second draft. It might take you another year to write your third and to find an agent or publisher. And maybe another year or two before the book finally comes out.

Think about this: Most writers come out with a book every five years on average. Unless you're a writer of genre fiction—detective, romance, adventure, science fiction, suspense, etc., completing a well-written book every four to five years is par for the course. And you can do that working an hour or two a day, three days a week. Work through process, and the product will emerge.

The Great Voice Within You

I know it's easy to get bogged down in the dailiness of life. We keep postponing the time we promised ourselves we'd set aside to write. But it's possible to find that time, if you persevere.

As Mary Oliver says in the final stanzas of her poem "When Death Comes,"

> when it's over, I don't want to wonder
> if I have made of my life something particular, and real.
> I don't want to find myself sighing and frightened,
> or full of argument.
> I don't want to end up simply having visited this world.

Chapter 10

MAKING A CHAPBOOK

It was one of those slushy days. Everyone in class was on edge. Raincoats were thrown on the floor, along with umbrellas and rain caps. Our feet were cold, our clothes damp. There was one more class to go before the last class pot-luck party. Everyone had focused on process for weeks, but maybe it was the rain or annoyance that time was getting on and most people in the class hadn't finished what they'd set out to finish: their first book. A student approached me during the break while I was stirring Splenda into my decaf. One of those confidential teacher-student chit-chats.

"Listen," he said, "I'm really digging all this process stuff, but when do I actually start to write my novel? I've got a ton of ideas."

I looked up and took a sip of coffee. He was holding his journal. When he'd bought it new, it must have been shiny, with its black leather cover and impressive black ribbon, which served as a bookmark. It was expensive leather too, even I could see that, but now it was smudged from opening and closing on cafe tabletops, and the pages were thick from all that ink, words and sentences, like yeast, causing the journal to swell. I took another sip and said, "You've written part of your novel already." I gestured toward his journal. "It's in there."

"You mean these journal entries? This isn't my novel, it's just writing exercises."

"How do you know? Have you gone back and read what you've written? I bet you've got material in there that'll fit into your novel. One of your journal entries might end up being chapter one. Another might close your novel or fit somewhere in chapter five. Just because you generated those pages doing exercises doesn't mean the product you've ended up with can't be used as part of a novel. Cut away the fat, see what you've got. Maybe it's a book of poems. Short stories. Who knows? Check it out."

He opened the journal and began reading. "Hmmm," he said. He turned a page and read some more. I drank half the cup of coffee while he said "hmmmm" a few more times, clucked his tongue, nodded his head. Then he looked up and said, "You're right." Then he went back to his seat and sat on his raincoat.

Process Generates Product

You've come a long way in a short period of time. Step back and take stock. See what you've done. The purpose of the chapbook is to show you that. So far, your writing has been in your journal. You may view that work as merely a workout in process. But all art is generated in this way: *from process,* not *toward product.* The work you do in your journal is a way for you to practice focusing on process and away from product. This must become a habit, internalized through constant repetition. Not an intellectual understanding, but a knowledge of the body. That's what your journal is for. But while you do this, you'll discover that out of process comes product.

In doing the chapbook, you're elevating those journal entries into something akin to product, so you can step back and say, "Look how this piece evolved and became something."

WHAT IS A CHAPBOOK?

Some claim the term "chapbook" comes from the late 19th Century when publishers at yearly conventions distributed the first chapter of an upcoming book for promotional purposes. This small pamphlet was called a "chapbook." According to the *OED*, the word actually derives from:

> the Middle English, a variant of cheap, and carries with it the sense of "to buy and sell or barter."

Before the great vowel shift, the word chap sounded something like *cheap*. A chapman (pronounced *cheapman*) was an itinerant peddler who sold all sorts of household items, farm implements, and pamphlets, usually religious or political tracts, but sometimes verse. These pamphlets came to be called chapbooks (pronounced *cheapbooks*). By Shakespeare's time, it was common for poets to issue their small books of poetry in pamphlet style, or chapbooks.

American and British poets in the 20th Century have commonly issued chapbooks, usually self-published in limited editions. Ezra Pound's first book, *A Lume Spento*, was a self-published chapbook printed in an edition of 100 copies, half of which he threw away in despair off the Academia Bridge where the San Vio meets the Grand Canal in Venice (which is the answer, by the way, to that age-old question, "What do Billy Joe McAlister and Ezra Pound have in common?"). Today, a copy of that chapbook is worth thousands. E.E. Cummings published his first book of poems as a chapbook, as did countless other poets. One of the most famous acts of self-publishing goes back to Whitman, who helped the printer set the type for *Leaves of Grass*, which contained his ground-breaking long poem "Song of Myself." Charles Bukowski's first three books were chapbooks. Some chapbooks are done simply, while others are elaborately produced with graphics and art work, and sometimes splashes of color added by hand.

When you do your chapbook, therefore, you are taking part in a tradition that goes back centuries. As you put your book together, find the common thematic elements and arrange the pieces from first to last in a way that creates a thematic arc. Some of your journal entries will work better as poems. Perhaps your chapbook will include both prose and poetry. It can be anything you want it to be, don't hem yourself in by what you think is proper or correct. Think about the design. Give it an element of uniqueness.

Your title page should have the name of the publisher, the city of publication, and the year, usually at the bottom of the page:

Shadow House Publishers
Tierra del Fuego, 2013

and on your copyright page, you can put an address from which people can order additional copies. Don't forget to put a price on the book, usually on the back cover.

Think of an original name for your publishing company, even if this is the only book you do. My partner Michael Andrews founded Bombshelter Press because he stored his Vandercook motorized printing press in a bombshelter his father had built in the '50s. Some press names are formal, like Random House and Houghton Mifflin. Others are playful or tongue-in-cheek, like Big Mouth Press and The Sheep Meadow Press.

The main objective is to set forth a few of your written pieces in a format that gives them respect. You will find that the whole becomes greater than the sum of the parts, and the book may indicate where you were headed without realizing that you were heading there. One of my students, Leigh Curran, continued to expand her chapbook in subsequent classes, and eventually the book was published as a novel, *Going Forward Sideways*. The story of the protagonist was told in the third person, but throughout the book were sections from the protagonist's journals, which carried the story forward, and gave the reader both a first-person and third-person account. The book got good reviews, and she's working on a second one.

Another student, after putting her chapbook together, realized that it had dramatic potential, and eventually it became a one-woman show, which led to a producer buying the film rights. It was a movie all along, having grown out of a series of journal entries. *Remembrance of Things Past* by Marcel Proust is one of the great novels of the 20th century; its form is essentially that of a series of journal entries. James Joyce used multiple narrative techniques in *Ulysses*, his epic work about a day in the life of Stephen Dedalus and Leopold Bloom. This is definitely not a novel born out of an outline or brain-storming session. Though it has parallels to Homer's *Odyssey*, Shakespeare's *Hamlet*, and other less major references, it has the feel of a great journey taken by an artist willing to wander lost in the wilderness of process. Such a book requires a monumental commitment to process. A project of such scope and originality only comes together through the accretion of thousands of sentences over a period of thousands of days.

A chapbook is an opportunity to look back as you move forward, a chance to glimpse the product emerging from process.

Making Your Chapbook

Some of you already know how to make a booklet using computer programs like ClickBook, or any one of a number of desktop publishing programs or modern word processing software. If you know how to do this, you really don't need much of what follows. I'm teaching you the old fashioned, cut-and-paste method with real glue that sticks to your fingers. If you do this step by step, everything will turn out fine. If you read this through once and begin without taking it by the numbers, you'll make mistakes.

BY THE NUMBERS IN TEN EASY STEPS

1) Type up your journal entries, prose pieces, or poems (give each one a title).

2) Now decide what size your chapbook will be. A folded piece of paper will measure 5½" by 8½"—which is the standard size of most chapbooks, since it's economical. If your chapbook is this size, you have to set your margins accordingly, so that your text measures no more than 4 inches across (which allows for a ¾-inch margin), and no more than 6½ inches tall (which allows for an inch margin top and bottom). You can squeeze in a few more lines, but it'll end up looking crowded. Experiment with font size, but I have found that 10 or 11 point is usually just right. (A lot depends on the font you choose: fonts take up different amounts of vertical space. Times New Roman 9pt, for example, is smaller than, say, Arial 9pt. Play with it a little and see what suits you.)

3) So now your poems and prose pieces are all typed up, formatted for margins, and you're ready to go. That was the hard part. The rest is fun. This is where you get your fingers all gluey.

4) Make a nice, clear work space. The dining room table works fine. The more room, the better. Set all your materials out in front of you: scissors, glue (I recommend rubber cement), a ruler, and a few paper clips. Put on a good CD: Johnny Cash, Sarah Vaughn, Ludo, Adele, Miles Davis, Shostakovich's *Symphony #5*, Bright Eyes, whatever fits your mood. When I do my chapbooks, I like to listen to rock 'n' roll, loud guitar riffs, lots of drumbeats. But when I'm doing the finishing touches, I put on Jane Olivor's version of Don McClean's "Vincent," or Samuel Barber's *Adagio for Strings*. A glass of wine; perhaps a nice cabernet.

5) Determine how many pages your chapbook will be. (Look at a few books to see how the page numbers work). How do you know how many pages of text you have? By counting the number of 5½ by 8½ pages your pieces will take up. So you have to go through them, one at a time and make a tally. Some pieces will take 1 page, others 2 or more pages. When done, total it up. Let's say you come up with 27 pages of text. Now add in the other pages.

> Title page
> Copyright page
> Dedication (optional)
> Foreward or Introduction—2 pages
> Table of Contents
> Blank pages

Where do the blank pages go? Well, if your table of contents takes only one page, you're probably going to have the other side blank, since you don't want to start your book on a left hand side. Same is true for a Dedication page, the other side of it will probably be blank. You have to count those as pages, otherwise, when you figure out how many sheets of paper you're going to need, you're going to come out all wrong. Anyway, counting the above added pages, we come up with 6 pages plus 2 blank pages (one on the back of the contents page, one on the back of the dedication page), for a total of 8 extra pages to be added to the 27 above, making a grand total of 35 pages.

Now, remember this: your final page count has to be a multiple of 4. And you must always round up, not down. So 35 becomes 36 pages. That's how many pages your chapbook will have. And if you fold nine sheets of paper in half, you now have a 36-page, blank mock-up for your 36-page chapbook.

6) Set your blank mock-up on the table with each page folded in half and each one inserted inside the other. Just for the time being, put a paper clip on top at the fold. You should be able to turn each page, like a book, and if you count each page, you should come up with a page count of 36.

7) Now all you have to do is go through it one page at a time, and glue in your pages, starting with the title page, then the copyright page, etc. I recommend that you go through it page by page, without using glue, just laying each piece on the page, just to make sure it all works out before you start gluing. You don't want to get to page 32 and realize that you miscounted. Once you're satisfied that everything works out, turn the music up and start gluing.

8) Now your cover. Get another sheet of paper, fold it in half, and wrap that around your 36-page mock-up. Glue your cover design on the front. Glue your back cover design on the back. If your pages didn't have page numbers on them before, now's a good time to add page

numbers. I suggest that you start your page count with the title page, though you don't actually put a number on the title page. You put 2 on the copyright page, but don't put a page number on the dedication page. But still count it. Your actual text may not begin until page seven or nine. Once that's done, you're done.

9) Take it to a copy place and tell them how many copies you want. Pick out the kind of paper you want your cover printed on, whether card stock, astro-bright paper, or just plain white. You want the book stapled on the spine, or saddle-stitched.

10) Pick up your book. Sit in the car and go through it, page by page. You're on your way.

PATIENT INSISTENCY

Rabbi Akiva ben Joseph (approximately 50–135 AD) was one of the greatest of the Tannaim (scholars of the Mishnah, the earliest written form of the Oral Torah) and founder of rabbinic Judaism. Akiva was not an educated youth and assumed that he could never become learned or accomplish anything. He was a mere servant boy. One day, as he was getting water from the local well, he noticed that the rope attached to the bucket had worn a deep groove in the stone from being pulled up every day. How could the pliable rope wear such a deep groove in the stone, he wondered. He asked one of the village teachers, who told him that while the rope rubbed the stone only a little each day, over time, it was enough to wear away the stone. "Every day," the teacher repeated, "a little bit more stone is eroded away." Then the teacher quoted a line from the book of Job (14:19) as if to make it prophecy: "The waters wear away the stones!" "Hmmmmm," thought the boy, "if that rope can cut through stone, I can learn, I can accomplish anything. All I have to do is a little each day."

Another version of this legend goes this way: Akiva, noticing the stone at a well that had been hollowed out by drippings from the buckets, said to himself, "If these drippings can, by continuous action, penetrate this solid stone, how much more can the persistent work of God penetrate the pliant, fleshy human heart, if that word but be presented with patient insistency." Who among us can cut a groove in a stone overnight? But like the rope, we can wear away a little of the stone each day. Like the water, we can allow the great voice within us to hollow out the stone. Don't lose heart. There will be those with more obvious talent than you who will never make their art, never write that book. And there will be those with far less talent than you who will forge right ahead and write a book and get it published, because they were patiently insistent.

Of course, such comparisons are useless, because it is not about talent anyway. Not only is talent overrated, but it can be your greatest enemy if you rely on it, rather than taking those ten thousand practice swings with deliberate focus. Whether it's the concept of Method Writing, or another approach to your creative process, whether you're in a class or not, just take it one day at a time. Be patient, persistent, and passionate about your work, rubbing against the stone a little at a time.

Write like you talk.

Massage your transformation lines.

Include a few Image-Moments in your scenes.

Throw in a Dreaded Association Exercise every now and again just to shake up the narrative.

All you need write is a few pages a week.

At the end of the year, you'll have written several hundred pages (do the math, five pages a week = 250 pages a year).

Don't lose heart.

You can write your book.

You can find a place in the world for the great voice within you.

Appendix

NOTE ON "STREAM OF CONSCIOUSNESS"

Stream of consciousness is often confused with **interior monologue** and **free association**. Narrative tends to follow a logical thread. A first person narrator may be speaking his thoughts and ideas, narrating a story, but the narrative follows a logical pattern, it's not free association.

> Call me Ishmael. Some years ago—never mind how long precisely—having little or no money in my purse, and nothing particular to interest me on shore, I thought I would sail about a little and see the watery part of the world. It is a way I have of driving off the spleen and regulating the circulation. Whenever I find myself growing grim about the mouth; whenever it is a damp, drizzly November in my soul; whenever I find myself involuntarily pausing before coffin warehouses, and bringing up the rear of every funeral I meet; and especially whenever my hypos get such an upper hand of me, that it requires a strong moral principle to prevent me from deliberately stepping into the street, and methodically knocking people's hats off—then, I account it high time to get to sea as soon as I can. This is my substitute for pistol and ball. With a philosophical flourish, Cato throws himself upon his sword; I quietly take to the ship.
>
> —Herman Melville, *Moby Dick*

Free association is another matter. Rather than telling a story from point A to point B, the author seems to ramble from one thought to another.

> Woof! Woof woof! *Woof! Woof!*
> Barking in the night. Barking, barking. I shriek but no one answers. I scream but there's not even an echo.
> "Which do you want—the East of Xerxes or the East of Christ?"
> Alone—with eczema of the brain.
> Alone at last. How marvelous! Only it is not what I expected it to be. If only I were alone with God!
> *Woof! Woof woof!*
>
> —Henry Miller, *Nexus*

A writer like Gertrude Stein takes free association to more extreme limits, creating sentences that not only have no linear narrative story, but seem to slide from one image to another without connections.

> Nickel, what is nickel, it is originally rid of a cover. The change in that is that red weakens an hour. The change has come. There is no search. But there is, there is that hope and that interpretation and sometime, surely any is unwelcome, sometime there is breath and there will be a sinecure and charming very charming is that clean and cleansing. Certainly glittering is handsome and convincing.
>
> —Gertrude Stein, *Tender Buttons*

It's possible to combine free association with interior monologue.

.... and it's midafternoon and I find myself standing at a phone booth on a corner somewhere downtown, I don't know where, but I'm sweaty and a pounding migraine thumps dully in my head and I'm experiencing a major-league anxiety attack, searching my pockets for Valium, Xanax, a leftover Halcion, anything, and all I find are three faded Nuprin in a Gucci pillbox, so I pop all three into my mouth and swallow them down with a Diet Pepsi and I couldn't tell you where it came from if my life depended on it. I've forgotten who I had lunch with earlier and, even more important, *where*. Was it Robert Ailes at Beats? Or was it Todd Hendricks at Ursula's, the new Philip Duncan Holmes bistro in Tribeca? Or was it Ricky Worrall and were we at December's? Or would it have been Kevin Weber at Contra in Noho? Did I order the partridge sandwich on brioche with green tomatoes, or a big plate of endive with clam sauce? "Oh, god, I can't remember," I moan.

—Bret Easton Ellis, *American Psycho*

Journal writing is a kind of free association, going from one thought to another without apparent connection.

I have to go to the bank today. Father always went to the bank on Friday. When Friday comes, I think of it as the beginning of the weekend. Who wants to do business on the weekend? I liked those long weekends in the summer when I was a boy. The paper came late today, and when I went out to get it, the only thing at my doorstep was a dead mouse, a present the cat left me. Anyway, I probably should get started on the garage. There are so many projects to do around the house. Oh, and I have to call Julie. She promised to help me bake a cake.

This is not stream of consciousness, nor is it interior monologue. The narrator is *speaking* to us, out loud, as it were, associating freely. But interior monologue gives us a character's *thought* process. We're inside her head, privy to random thoughts and associations. It can be first person or third person, but there's the sense that we've invaded her mind, that we're privy to her inner thoughts. They're not necessarily *talking* to us. They're *thinking*, the thoughts could be random and a bit jumbled, and we get to overhear it. The following paragraph shifts from omniscient author to third-person interior monologue.

Mrs. Dalloway said she would buy the flowers herself.

For Lucy had her work cut out for her. The doors would be taken off their hinges; Rumpelmayer's men were coming. And then, thought Clarissa Dalloway, what a morning—fresh as if issued to children on a beach.

What a lark! What a plunge! For so it had always seemed to her, when, with a little squeak of the hinges, which she could hear now, she had burst open the French windows and plunged at Bourton into the open air. How fresh, how calm, stiller than this of course, the air was in the early morning; like the flap of a wave; the kiss of a wave; chill and sharp yet (for a girl of eighteen as she then was) solemn, feeling as she did, standing there at the open window, that something awful was about to happen; looking at the flowers, at the trees with the smoke winding off them and the rooks rising, falling; standing and looking until Peter Walsh said, "Musing among the vegetables?"—was that it?—"I prefer men to cauliflowers"—was that it?

—Virginia Woolf, *Mrs. Dalloway*

Woolf slides in and out of omniscient voice and close voice. When in third-person close, it's Clarissa Dalloway's thoughts we're hearing, her interior monologue. (It's not only Clarissa's voice we hear, we find ourselves in the heads of a few other characters in the novel, as well).

When we use the technique of stream of consciousness, however, we're no longer being told *about* the moment, we're *experiencing* it. The author purposefully creates a mash-up of words and phrases as if to mimic the experience of *consciousness* itself. Grammar, syntax, logic, and the norms of speech are thrown to the winds—the sentences, phrases, the words themselves, like objects caught in a tornado, fly off in a linguistic cloud. It is the *experience* of consciousness itself that the author is trying to convey. We're not just hearing someone speaking to themselves (which would be interior monologue), we're experiencing all sorts of thoughts and free associations, impressions, images, perceptions, memory and feelings—jumbled together without regard for logic or narrative; grammar and syntax collide in random patterns. That's what it's like to be inside someone's mind. We're no longer in the Kansas of straightforward narrative, we're in the Oz of consciousness. The effect can be dis-orienting, even difficult to read, but one must give in to the experience and not expect it to be comprehensible in the manner of a typical narrative. It's abstract, expressionistic, cubist—take your pick.

The technique in its more primitive form was pioneered by Dorothy Richardson in *Pilgrimage*, a sequence of 13 semi-autobiographical novels—the first, *Painted Roofs*, published in 1915, is considered the first complete stream of consciousness novel to be published in English. The last novel in the sequence, *March Moonlight*, was published in 1967, ten years after her death in a nursing home at the age of 84. Most of us, however, would point to James Joyce as its foremost originator in *A Portrait of the Artist as a Young Man* (1916) and *Ulysses* (1922). The stream of consciousness technique was modified by Virginia Woolf in *Mrs. Dalloway* (1925), and further modified by William Faulkner in *The Sound and the Fury* (1929), and carried to an extreme of linguistic deconstruction in Joyce's *Finnegans Wake* (1939). The term itself was coined by William James in his *Principles of Psychology* (1890), in which he attempted to describe the flow of inner experience. When applied to literature, the term refers to thoughts and feelings which "flow" through the mind of the character, often with no apparent logic. To create the effect, the writer presents a seemingly random mingling of thoughts, feelings, images, sense impressions, etc., all of which seem to happen at the same time—a big, fat jumble of words that evoke subjective experience. Sentence fragments interloop with other sentence fragments, connected by even more random images and associations. If you handed in an essay written in stream of consciousness, your tenth grade teacher would think you'd gone mad—a teacher-parent conference with the school psychologist would not be far off.

The classic work of fiction that uses the technique of "stream of consciousness" is *Ulysses,* a novel by the Irish author James Joyce. It was first serialised in parts in the American journal *The Little Review* from March 1918 to December 1920, and then published in its entirety by Sylvia Beach on February 2, 1922, in Paris. One of the most important works of Modernist literature, it has been called a demonstration and summation of the entire movement. Before Joyce, no writer of fiction had so foregrounded the process of thinking. Reading stream of consciousness is like listening to the radio while someone is talking to you, while thinking your own thoughts as the mind makes note of passing images, while God (the author) talks in your head. In *Ulysses*, Joyce uses both interior monologue and stream of consciousness, but the two narrative strategies are often confused.

Ulysses chronicles the passage of Leopold Bloom through Dublin during an ordinary day, June 16, 1904 (the day of Joyce's first date with his future wife, Nora Barnacle). The title alludes to Odysseus (Latinized into Ulysses), the hero of Homer's *Odyssey*, and establishes a series of parallels between characters and events in Homer's poem and Joyce's novel (e.g., the correspondence of Leopold Bloom to Odysseus, Molly Bloom to Penelope, and Stephen Dedalus to Telemachus, Odysseus's son). Joyce fans worldwide now celebrate June 16 as Bloomsday. Since its publication, the book has attracted controversy and scrutiny, ranging from early obscenity trials to protracted textual "Joyce Wars." *Ulysses's* stream-of-consciousness technique, careful structuring, and experimental prose—full of puns, parodies, and allusions—as well as its rich characterisations and broad humor, made the book a highly regarded novel (if not the most highly regarded) in the Modernist pantheon. In 1998, the Modern Library ranked *Ulysses* first on its list of the 100 best English-language novels of the 20th century. Some lists ranked Ulysses second to Marcel Proust's *Remembrance of Things Past*, with William Faulkner's *The Sound and the Fury* coming in third. The first and second sections of Faulkner's book are also characterized by stream of consciousness.

Perhaps the most well-known epidsode of *Ulysses* is Molly Bloom's soliloquy, consisting of eight sentences—fifty pages of unpunctuated prose, except for the period marking the end of the book and another period after the fourth sentence, making it the longest "sentence" in English literature, 4,391 words (surpassed in 2001 by Jonathan Coe's *The Rotters' Club*). Strictly speaking, Molly's soliloquy is interior monologue, not stream of consciousness.

In the course of the monologue, Molly accepts Leopold into her bed, frets about his health, and then reminisces about their first meeting when she knew she was in love with him. The final words of Molly's reverie, and the very last words of the book, are:

> . . . . so there you are they might as well try to stop the sun from rising tomorrow the sun shines for you he said the day after we were lying among the rhodedendrons on Howth head in the grey tweed suit and his straw hat the day I got him to propose to me yes first I gave him the bit of seedcake out of my mouth and it was leapyear like now yes 16 years ago my God after that long kiss I near lost my breath yes he said in his life and the sun shines for you today yes that was why I liked him because I saw he understood or felt what a woman is and I knew I could always get round him and I gave him all the pleasure I could leading him on till he asked me to say yes and I wouldnt answer first only looked out over the sea and the sky I was thinking of so many things he didn't know of Mulvey and Mr Stanhope and Hester and father and old captain Groves and the sailors playing all birds fly and I say stoop and washing up dishes they called it on the pier and the sentry in front of the governors house with the thing round his white helmet poor devil half roasted and the Spanish girls laughing in their shawls and their tall combs and the auctions in the morning the Greeks and the jews and the Arabs and the devil knows who else from all the ends of Europe and Duke street and the fowl

market all clucking outside Larby Sharons and the poor donkeys slipping half asleep and the vague fellows in the cloaks asleep in the shade on the steps and the big wheels of the carts of the bulls and the old castle thousands of years old yes and those handsome Moors all in white and turbans like kings asking you to sit down in their little bit of a shop and Ronda with the old windows of the posadas glancing eyes a lattice hid for her lover to kiss the iron and the wineshops half open at night and the castanets and the night we missed the boat at Algeciras the watchman going about serene with his lamp and O that awful deepdown torrent O and the sea the sea crimson sometimes like fire and the glorious sunsets and the figtrees in the Alameda gardens yes and all the queer little streets and pink and blue and yellow houses and the rosegardens and the jessamine and geraniums and cactuses and Gibraltar as a girl where I was a Flower of the mountain yes when I put the rose in my hair like the Andalusian girls used or shall I wear a red yes and how he kissed me under the Moorish wall and I thought well as well him as another and then I asked him with my eyes to ask again yes and then he asked me would I yes to say yes my mountain flower and first I put my arms around him yes and drew him down to me so he could feel my breasts all perfume yes and his heart was going like mad and yes I said yes I will Yes.

Stream of consciousness goes beyond interior monologue. In Molly's soliloquy, we overhear her thoughts, not the larger flow of consciousness. In the case of a third person narrator, we also experience the omniscient authorial voice, along with the "stream" of "consciousness" that floods the mind. The section below, also from *Ulysses*, is from episode 11, "The Sirens," and takes place in the bar/pub of the Ormand Hotel. The scene opens with the two barmaids, red-haired Miss Douce and blond Miss Kennedy, or bronze and gold, as Joyce calls them. In the course of the chapter, we also encounter the bartender (referred to as boots), Pat the waiter, and various characters in the novel, including the main three: Leopold Bloom, the Irish Jew, approaching the bar as he thinks about his lusty and beautiful wife Molly, who is having an affair with Blazes Boylan. We hear of Stephen Dedalus, who will eventually meet up with Bloom and have an adventure that night in the red-light district of Dublin. Blazes Boylan is supposed to be hooking up with Molly at 4 P.M., and Bloom knows this, painfully tolerating this affair. Stephen's uncle Simon Dedalus enters the bar and sings various songs. Bloom thinks about the letter he wrote to a mysterious Martha, a woman he has begun a correspondance with, though no affair has yet ensued. Blazes finally leaves for his tryst with Molly, and Bloom dejectedly leaves also, encountering the third siren, a familiar prostitute whom he avoids by pretending to look in a shop window. The cider has made Bloom gassy, and the episode ends with the sounds of Bloom farting as he stands by the shopwindow. To make matters even more complicated, the narrative voice shifts from first person to third person. What Joyce is giving us is the experience of consciousness, not an objective, third person narrator presenting the scene in a linear, orderly fashion. Below is a small portion of that episode in the novel.

> Bronze by gold, Miss Douce's head by Miss Kennedy's head, over the crossblind of the Ormond bar heard the viceregal hoofs go by, ringing steel.
> —Is that her? asked Miss Kennedy.
> Miss Douce said yes, sitting with his ex, pearl grey and *eau de Nil.*

Miss Kennedy sauntered sadly from bright light, twirling a loose hair behind an ear. Sauntering sadly, gold no more, she twisted twined a hair. Sadly she twined in sauntering gold hair behind a curving ear.

Bloomwho went by Moulang's pipes, bearing in his breast the sweets of sin, by Wine's antiques in memory of bearing sweet sinful words, by Carroll's dusky battered plate, for Raoul.

The boots to them, them in the bar, them barmaids came. For them unheeding him he banged on the counter his tray of chattering china. And

—There's your teas, he said.

She poured in a teacup tea, then back in the teapot tea. They cowered under their reef of counter, waiting on footstools, crates upturned, waiting for their teas to draw. They pawed their blouses, both of black satin, two and nine a yard, waiting for their teas to draw, and two and seven.

Yes, bronze from anear, by gold from afar, heard steel from anear, hoofs ring from afar, and heard steelhoofs ringhoof ringsteel.

Bloowhose dark eye read Aaron Figatner's name. Why do I always think Figather? Gathering figs I think. And Prosper Lore's huguenot name. By Bassi's blessed virgins Bloom's dark eyes went by. Bluerobed, white under, come to me. God they believe she is: or goddess. Those today. I could not see. That fellow spoke. A student. After with Dedalus' son. He might be Mulligan. All comely virgins. That brings those rakes of fellows in: her white.

By went his eyes. The sweets of sin. Sweet are the sweets.

Of sin.

In a giggling peal young goldbronze voices blended, Douce with Kennedy your other eye. They threw young heads back, bronze gigglegold, to let freefly their laughter, screaming, your other, signals to each other, high piercing notes.

Ah, panting, sighing. Sighing, ah, fordone their mirth died down.

—Oh greasy eyes! Imagine being married to a man like that, she cried. With his bit of beard!

Married to Bloom, to greaseaseabloom.

By Cantwell's offices roved Greaseabloom, by Ceppi's virgins, bright of their oils. Nannetti's father hawked those things about, wheedling at doors as I. Religion pays. Must seem him about Keyes's par. Eat first. I want. Not yet. At four, she said. Time every passing. Clockhands turning. On. Where eat? The Clarence, Dolphin. On. For Raoul. Eat. If I net five guineas with those ads. The violet silk petticoats. Not yet. The sweets of sin.

Flushed less, still less, goldenly paled.

Into their bar strolled Mr Dedalus. Chips, picking chips off one of his rocky thumbnails. Chips. He strolled.

With grace of alacrity towards the mirror gilt Cantrell and Cochrane's she turned herself. With grace she tapped a measure of gold whiskey from her crystal keg. Forth from the skirt of his coat Mr Dedalus brought pouch and pipe. Alacrity she served. He blew through the flue two husky fifenotes.

In came Lenehan. Round him peered Lenehan. Mr Bloom reached Essex bridge. Yes, Mr. Bloom crossed bridge of Yessex. To Martha I must write. Buy paper. Daly's. Girl there civil. Bloom. Old Bloom. Blue Bloom is on the rye.

Two sheets cream vellum paper on reserve two envelopes when I was in Wisdom Hely's wise Bloom in Daly's Henry Flower bought. Are you not happy in your home? Flower to console me and a pin cuts lo. Means something, language of flow. Was it a daisy? Innocence that is. Respectable girl meets after mass. Tanks awfully muchly. Wise Bloom eyed on the door a poster, a swaying mermaid smoking mid nice waves. Smoke mermaids, coolest whiff of all. Hair streaming: lovelorn. For some man. For Raoul. He eyed and saw afar on Essex bridge a gay hat riding on a jauntingcar. It is. Third time. Coincidence.

Boylan, eyed, eyed. Tossed to fat lips his chalice, drankoff his tiny chalice, sucking the last fat violet syrupy drops. He spellbound eyes went after her gliding head as it went down the bar by mirrors, gilded arch for giner ale, hock and claret glasses shimmering, a spiky shell, where it concerted, mirrored, bronze with sunnier bronze.

Yes, bronze from anearby.

In liver gravy Bloom mashed mashed potatoes. Love and war someone is. Ben Dollard's famous. Night he ran round to us to borrow a dress suit for that concert. Trousers tight as a drum on him. Musical porkers. Molly did laugh when he went out. Threw herself back across the bed, screaming, kicking. With all his belongings on show. O, saints above. I'm drenched! O, the women in the front row! O, I never laughed so many! Well, of course, that's what gives him the base bareltone. For instance eunuchs. Wonder who's playing. Nice touch. Must be Cowley. Musical. Knows whatever note you play. Bad breath he has, poor chap. Stopped.

Bloom ate liv as said before.

Piano again.

Which air is that? asked Leopold Bloom.

All is lost now.

Bloom bent leopold ear, turning a fringe of doyley down under the vase. Order. Yes, I remember. Lovely air. In sleep she went to him. Innocence is the moon. She hold her back. Brave, don't know their danger. Call name. Touch water. Jingle jaunty. Too late. She longed to go. That's why. Woman. As easy stop the sea. Yes: all is lost.

—A beautiful air, said Bloom lost Leopold. I know it well. Never in all this life. Bloom askance over liverless saw. Face of the all is lost. Jokes old stale now. Wagging his ear. Napkinring in his eye. Now begging letters he sends his son with. Crosseyed Walter sir I did sir. Wouldn't trouble only I was expecting some money. Apologise.

Piano again.

Sorrow from me seemed to depart.

Through the hush of air a voice sang to them, low, not rain, not leaves in murmur, like no voice of strings of reeds or whatdoyoucallthem dulcimers, touching their still ears with words, still hearts of their each remembered lives. Good, good to hear: sorrow from them each seemed to from both depart when first they heard. When first they saw, mercy of beauty, heard from a person wouldn't expecet it in the least, her first merciful lovfesoft oftloved word.

The level of fragmentation depends on how turbulent the stream the writer wants to portray, how chaotic the situation is at that moment in the narrative. Sometimes it's pretty tame and easy to follow, like a babbling brook; at other times , the reader does his best to ride the rapids of words to the bottom of the waterfall.

> The billy flood rose or an elk charged him or the sultrup worldweight from the excelsissimost empyrean (bolt, in sum) earthspake or the Dannamen gallous banged pan the bliddy duran. A scribicide then and there is led off under old's code with some fine covered by six marks or ninepins in metalmen for the sake of his labour's dross while it will be only now and again in our rear o'er era, as an upshoot of military and civil engagements, that a gynecure was let on to the scuffold for taking that same fine sum covertly by meddlement with the drawers of his neighbor's safe.

> —James Joyce, *Finnegans Wake*, p. 14

Joyce has created a musical passage based on word play and double entendre. Stream of consciousness can also capture a moment impressionistically. Below is a paragraph from a story I wrote using the stream-of-conscious technique to heighten the experience of being underwater with one's thoughts.

> I stood there in my bathing suit, staring down at the water below. Clear blue through and through to the white sandy bottom. Then the leap, the flying out beyond the rocks and rush of air sunlight summer days backyard tea time water swooping the fancier tune of father dancing with mother and mother dancing with me and underwater car door banging my head no tea-time no summer time rain gushed gutters thunderstorm no dancing for mother no dancing for father on the floor bottles of sand booze tide rip tide swoosh into the realm of the beer booze tune-time tea-time fishes pulling me further toward the boat toward sunlight sandy bottom back days and there they are on the boat waving to me cheering swimming toward them tea time tune-time home.

There are moments like that in life, where we experience a flood of sensations, of disparate thoughts. If we were to write it down one thought at a time in linear sentences, the reader would get the *facts* of the experience, but not the *feel* of the experience.

Joyce claimed that he got the idea from French novelist Edouard Dujardin, whose novel *Les Lauriers Sont Coupés* (The Laurel Trees Are Cut Down) was published in English as *We'll to the Woods No More* in 1887, but Dujardin's experiment was tame compared to what Joyce did with it. Dujardin (and French critic Valery Larbaud) coined the term *monologue intérieur* to describe the stream of consciousness technique as it was used by another novelist, Paul Bourget. Some critics have divided the technique into categories: direct interior monologue, indirect interior monologue (both of which present a linear thought pattern), and stream of consciousness, which attempts to recreate the continuous flow of sense perception, thought, feeling, and memory in the human mind. The literary convention called "stream of consciousness" represents a blending of mental processes in fictional characters, usually in an unpunctuated or disjointed form, violating the norms of grammar, syntax, and logic. Molly Bloom's monologue at the end of *Ulysses* is more an interior monologue than stream of consciousness. In effect, she's not *thinking* so much as she's *speaking* aloud her thoughts. Marcel Proust's novel *Remembrance of Things Past* is *about* stream of consciousness, especially the connection between sense impressions and memory, but it does not actually use interior monologue or stream of consciousness. The French philosopher Henri Bergson contributed to the dialogue on its usage, as did Freud in his *Interpretation of Dreams* (1899), and Shiv K. Kumar in *Bergson and the Stream of Consciousness Novel*. Some of these ideas were hashed out by the Russian Futurists. D. H. Lawrence, writing about Joyce, Woolf, and Richardson, said that reading some of their passages was like being trapped inside a wool mattress that was slowly being shaken up; before long, you turned into wool, too, "along with the rest of the wooliness."

If the narrator were to present her perceptions in a coherent fashion, going from one perception to another, I would call this "path" of consciousness, rather than stream of consciousness. Stream of consciousness presents a holographic experience that cannot be linguistically deconstructed. One could have a conversation, for instance, while other thoughts drift through the mind: We see a woman on a bench stick a paper clip into a ball of cheese. We listen and nod, all the while thinking *I'm tired* or *my lips are dry* or *my underwear is too tight*. The writer gives the reader an experience of that state of mind by using the convention of stream of consciousness, in which the conversation, the images of the paper clip and cheese, as well as the interior thoughts are jumbled together "along with the rest of the wooliness."

If you'd like to explore some books by authors who use the technique of stream of consciousness in varying forms, James Joyce's *Ulysses* is the classic text, but it can be difficult. Nevertheless, it's worth the effort. I also recommend Virginia Woolf's *To the Lighthouse*. The first two sections of Faulkner's *The Sound and the Fury* puts us into Benjy's mind, an interior monologue that confuses events in time and space with no clear boundary between. Unlike the episode in *Ulysses* in the Ormand Bar, Faulkner maintains a straightforward interior monologue, no "stream of consciousness." But the interior monologue itself is a "stream" in which the narrator seems to have no fixed point of reference. Benjy is 33 years old but has the mental age of a child less than three years old, making no distinction between something that happened when he was six with something that happened when he was 16 with what is happening to him in the present. He hears the men who are playing golf call for a "caddie," which he then confuses in his mind with his sister, Candace, who went by the name of Caddy. Going through the fence that lines the golf course reminds him of other times he went through the fence, and his mind jumps from scenes when he was told to put his hands in his pockets when he was six to similar scenes when he was older. So while the flow of the narrative is all interior monologue, it has the effect of stream of consciousness since the events in time and space are jumbled and confused.

> Through the fence, between the curling flower spaces, I could see them hitting. They were coming toward where the flag was and I went along the fence. Luster was hunting in the grass by the flower tree. They took the flag out, and they were hitting. Then they put the flag back and they went to the table, and he hit and the other hit. Then they went on, and I went along the fence. Luster came away from the flower tree and we went along the fence and they stopped and we stopped and I looked through the fence while Luster was hunting in the grass.

"Here, Caddie," He hit. They went away across the pasture. I held to the fence and watched them going away.

"Listen at you, now." Luster said. "Aint you something, thirty-three years old, going on that way. After I done went all the way to town to buy you that cake. Hush up that moaning. Aint you going to help me find that quarter so I can go to the show tonight?"

We went along the fence and came to the garden fence, where our shadows were. My shadow was higher than Luster's on the fence. We came to the broken place and went through it.

"Wait a minute." Luster said. "You snagged on that nail again. Cant you never crawl through here without snagging on that nail."

Caddy uncaught me and we crawled through. Uncle Maury said to not let anybody see us, so we better stoop over, Caddy said. Stoop over, Benjy. Like this, see. We stooped over and crossed the garden, where the flowers rasped and rattled against us. The ground was hard. We climbed the fence, where the pigs were grunting and snuffing. I expect they're sorry because one of them got killed today, Caddy said. The ground was hard, churned and knotted.

Keep your hands in your pockets, Caddy said. Or they'll get froze. You don't want your hands froze on Christmas, do you.

"It's too cold out there." Versh said. "You don't want to go out doors."

"What is it now." Mother said.

"He want to go out doors." Versh said.

"Let him go." Uncle Maury said.

"It's too cold." Mother said. "He'd better stay in. Benjamin. Stop that, now."

We went out doors. The sun was cold and bright.

"Where you heading for." Versh said. "You dont think you going to town, does you." We went through the rattling leaves. The gate was cold. "You better keep them hands in your pockets." Versh said. "You get them froze onto the gate, then what you do. Whyn't you wait for them in the house." He put my hands into my pockets. I could hear him rattling in the leaves. I could smell the cold. The gate was cold.

Caddy was walking. Then she was running, her book-satchel swinging and jouncing behind her.

"Hello, Benjy." Caddy said. She opened the gate and came in and stooped down. Caddy smelled like leaves. "Did you come to meet me." she said. "Did you come to meet Caddy. What did you let him get his hands so cold for, Versh."

"I told him to keep them in his pockets." Versh said. "Holding onto that ahun gate."

"Did you come to meet Caddy." she said, rubbing my hands. "What is it. What are you trying to tell Caddy." Caddy smelled like trees like when she says we were asleep.

What are you moaning about, Luster said. You can watch them again when we get to the branch. Here. Here's you a jimson weed. He gave me the flower. We went through the fence, into the lot.

When referring to the writing we do in our journals, going from one thought to another until we hit upon a coherent linear story, many use the term "stream" of consciousness, but I prefer to call it "path" of consciousness, or "interior monologue." Even the term "stream" has come under some reconsideration by neuroscientists who liken the activity of the brain and consciousness as more like a rhythmic pulse, rather than the steady flow of a stream. The follwing article by Gregory Hickok, a professor of cognitive science at the University of California, Irvine, and the author of *The Myth of Mirror Neurons: The Real Neuroscience of Communication and Cognition*, offers some interesting insights into recent neurological data.

It's Not a 'Stream' of Consciousness

In 1890, the American psychologist William James famously likened our conscious experience to the flow of a stream. "A 'river' or a 'stream' are the metaphors by which it is most naturally described," he wrote. "In talking of it hereafter, let's call it the stream of thought, consciousness, or subjective life." While there is no disputing the aptness of this metaphor in capturing our subjective experience of the world, recent research has shown that the "stream" of consciousness is, in fact, an illusion. We actually perceive the world in rhythmic pulses rather than as a continuous flow. Some of the first hints of this new understanding came as early as the 1920s, when physiologists discovered brain waves: rhythmic electrical currents measurable on the surface of the scalp by means of electroencephalography. Subsequent research cataloged a spectrum of such rhythms (alpha waves, delta waves and so on) that correlated with various mental states, such as calm alertness and deep sleep.

Researchers also found that the properties of these rhythms varied with perceptual or cognitive events. The phase and amplitude of your brain waves, for example, might change if you saw or heard something, or if you increased your concentration on something, or if you shifted your attention. But those early discoveries themselves did not change scientific thinking about the stream-like nature of conscious perception. Instead, brain waves were largely viewed as a tool for indexing mental experience, much like the waves that a ship generates in the water can be used to index the ship's size and motion (e.g., the bigger the waves, the bigger the ship).

Recently, however, scientists have flipped this thinking on its head. We are exploring the possibility that brain rhythms are not merely a reflection of mental activity but a cause of it, helping shape perception, movement, memory and even consciousness itself. What this means is that the brain samples the world in rhythmic pulses, perhaps even discrete time chunks, much like the individual frames of a movie. From the brain's perspective, experience is not continuous but quantized.

Another clue that led to this discovery was the so-called wagon-wheel illusion, in which the spokes on a wheel are sometimes perceived to reverse the direction of their rotation. This illusion is easy to induce with a strobe light if the rotation of the wheel is such that each strobe flash captures the spoke location slightly behind the location captured on the previous flash, leading to the perception of reverse motion. The illusion results from "sampling" the scene in discrete frames or time chunks. The telling fact, for perceptual scientists, is that this illusion can also occur during normal observation of a rotating wheel, in full daylight. This suggests that the brain itself, even in the absence of a strobe light, is sampling the world in discrete chunks.

Scientists have uncovered still more clues. It turns out, for example, that our ability to detect a subtle event, like a slight change in a visual scene, oscillates over time, cycling between better and worse perceptual sensitivity several times a second. Research shows that these rhythms correlate with electrical rhythms of the brain. If that's hard to picture, here's an analogy: Imagine trying to see an animal through a thick, swirling fog that varies in density as it drifts. The distinctness of the animal's form will oscillate with the density of the fog, alternating between periods of relative clarity and opaqueness. According to recent experiments, this is how our perceptual systems sample the world—but rather than fog, it's brain waves that drive the oscillations. This is not to say that the brain dances to its own beat, dragging perception along for the ride. In fact, it seems to work the other way around: Rhythms in the environment, such as those in music or speech, can draw neural oscillations into their tempo, effectively synchronizing the brain's rhythms with those of the world around us.

Consider a study that I conducted with my colleagues, forthcoming in the journal *Psychological Science.* We presented listeners with a three-beat-per-second rhythm (a pulsing "whoosh" sound) for only a few seconds and then asked the listeners to try to detect a faint tone immediately afterward. The tone was presented at a range of delays between zero and 1.4 seconds after the rhythm ended. Not only did we find that the ability to detect the tone varied over time by up to 25 percent—that's a lot—but it did so precisely in sync with the previously heard three-beat-per-second rhythm. Why would the brain do this? One theory is that it's the brain's way of focusing attention. Picture a noisy cafe filled with voices, clanging dishes and background music. As you attend to one particular acoustic stream—say, your lunch mate's voice—your brain synchronizes its rhythm to the rhythm of the voice and enhances the perceptibility of that stream, while suppressing other streams, which have their own, different rhythms. (More broadly, this kind of synchronization has been proposed as a mechanism for communication between neural networks within the brain.)

All of this points to the need for a new metaphor. We should talk of the "rhythm" of thought, of perception, of consciousness. Conceptualizing our mental experience this way is not only more accurate, but it also situates our mind within the broader context of the daily, monthly and yearly rhythms that dominate our lives.

Whether we conceptualize consciousness as an evenly flowing "stream" or as a "rhythmic pulse," the fact remains that the written convention used by many writers will essentially stay the same: a jumble of impressionistic images, dialogue, and thoughts that attempt to convey that sense of "consciousness" rather than the linear thought process classified as "interior monologue." So next time someone refers to writing in a journal as "stream of consciousness," you can suggest that they use the term "interior monologue," in which they're just writing down their thoughts in a sequential fashion, which is what is done in 99% of all prose. When the author wishes to convey that sense of consciousness that is all encompassing, including what one sees and hears and thinks simultaneously, especially when consciousness is distorted by drugs, traumatic moments, or psychotic episodes, then the writing is not simply the "thought process" but the process of consciousness itself, and to convey that, we would use the techniques pioneered by writers like James Joyce.

Here's a partial list of some other important books, some of which use stream of consciousness, others that hew closer to free association and/or interior monologue. But they'll give you a sense of how writing can extend beyond the parameters of straightforward linear narrative.

Salman Rushdie: *Midnight Children*
Hubert Selby, Jr.: *Last Exit to Brooklyn*
Shashi Deshpande, *That Long Silence*
Samuel Beckett's trilogy: *Malloy, Malone Dies*, and *The Unnameable*
Roberto Bolaño: *By Night in Chile*
William Burroughs: *Naked Lunch*
Julio Cortazar: *Hopscotch*
Dave Eggers: *A Heartbreaking Work of Staggering Genius*
James Ellroy: *White Jazz*
Anita Desai, *Cry, the Peacock*
James Joyce: *Portrait of the Artist as a Young Man*
Dimitris Lyaco: *Z213:Exit*
Henry Miller: *Black Spring*
Gasper Noe: *Enter the Void*
Thomas Pynchon: *Gravity's Rainbow*
Leslie Marmon Silko: *Ceremony*
Mieko Kanai: *The Word Book*
Dalton Trumbo: *Johnny Got His Gun*
Jean Rys: *Wide Sargasso Sea*
Clarice Lispector: any one of her books
Virginia Woolf: *Mrs. Dalloway, To the Lighthouse, The Waves*
William Faulkner: *Absalom, Absalom*
Toni Morrison: *Beloved*
Eimear McBride: *A Girl Is a Half-formed Thing, The Lesser Bohemians*
Jose Saramago: *Blindness*
Mark Haddon: *The Red House*
Jack Kerouac: *Lonesome Traveller*

THE ART OF GENIUS:
EIGHT WAYS TO THINK
LIKE EINSTEIN *or Shakespeare*

Michael Michalko

How do geniuses come up with ideas? What links the thinking style that produced *Mona Lisa* with the one that spawned the theory of relativity? What can we learn from the thinking strategies of the Galileos, Edisons, and Mozarts of history?

For years, scholars have tried to understand genius by analyzing statistics. In 1904, Havelock Ellis noted that most geniuses were fathered by men older than 30, had mothers younger than 25, and were usually sickly children. Other researchers reported that many were celibate (Descartes), fatherless (Dickens), or motherless (Darwin). In the end, the data illuminated nothing.

Academics also tried to measure the links between intelligence and genius, but found that some run-of-the-mill physicists had IQs much higher than Nobel Prize-winner and genius Richard Feynman, whose IQ was a respectable 122. Genius is not about scoring 1600 on your SATs, mastering 14 languages at the age of 7, or even being especially smart. As psychologist Joy P. Guilford and others have demonstrated, creativity is not the same as intelligence.

Most people of average intelligence can figure out the expected conventional response to a given problem. For example, when asked "What is one-half of 13?" most of us immediately answer six and one-half. That's because we tend to think *reproductively*. When confronted with a problem, we sift through what we've been taught and what has worked for us in the past, select the most promising approach, and work within a clearly defined direction toward a solution.

Geniuses, on the other hand, think *productively*. They ask "How many different ways can I look at this problem?" and "How many ways can I solve it?" A productive thinker, for example, would find a number of ways to "halve 13":

6.5

1 | 3 = 1 and 3

THIR TEEN = 4

XI | II = 11 and 2

XIII = 8

The mark of genius is the willingness to explore *all* the alternatives, not just the most likely solution. Asked to describe the difference between himself and an average person, Albert Einstein explained that the average person faced with the problem of finding a needle in a haystack would stop when he or she located a needle. But Einstein would tear through the entire haystack looking for all possible needles.

Reproductive thinking fosters rigidity. This is why we so often fail when we're confronted with a new problem that appears on the surface to be similar to others we've solved, but is, in fact, significantly different in its deep structure. Interpreting such a problem through the prism of past experience will inevitably lead you astray. If you think the way you've always thought, you'll get what you've always gotten.

For centuries, the Swiss dominated the watch industry. But in 1968, when a U.S. inventor unveiled a battery-powered watch with no bearings or mainspring at the World Watch Congress, every Swiss watch manufacturer rejected it because it didn't fit their limited paradigm. Meanwhile, Seiko, a Japanese electronics company, took one look at the invention and proceeded to change the future of the world watch market.

Biologists have long known that a gene pool lacking in variation will sooner or later be unable to adapt to changing circumstances. In time, the genetically encoded wisdom will convert to foolishness, with consequences fatal to the species. Similarly, we all have a rich repertoire of ideas and concepts based on past experiences that enable us to survive and prosper. But without any provision for variation, they become stagnant and ineffectual.

By studying the notebooks, correspondence, and conversations of some of the world's great thinkers in science, art, and industry, scholars have identified eight thinking strategies that enable geniuses to generate original ideas:

1 Geniuses look at problems from all angles.

Einstein's theory of relativity is, in essence, a description of the interaction between different perspectives. Sigmund Freud's analytical methods were designed to find details that didn't fit traditional paradigms in order to come up with a completely new point of view. To solve a problem creatively, you must abandon the first approach that comes to mind, which usually stems from past experience, and reconceptualize the problem. Thus geniuses do not merely solve existing problems; they identify new ones.

2 Geniuses make their thought visible.

Once geniuses have a certain minimal verbal facility, they develop visual and spatial abilities that allow them to display information in new ways. The explosion of creativity in the Renaissance was intimately tied to the development of graphic illustration during that period, notably the scientific diagrams of Leonardo da Vinci and Galileo Galilei. Galileo revolutionized science by making his thought graphically visible while his contemporaries used more conventional means. Similarly, Einstein thought in terms of spatial forms, rather than along purely mathematical or verbal lines. In fact, he believed that words and numbers, as they are written or spoken, did not play a significant role in his thinking process.

3 Geniuses produce.

Thomas Edison held 1,093 patents, still the record. He guaranteed a high level of productivity by giving himself idea quotas: one minor invention every 10 days and a major invention every six months. Johann Sebastian Bach wrote a cantata every week, even when he was sick or exhausted. Wolfgang Mozart produced more than 600 pieces of music. In a study of 2,036 scientists, Dean Keith Simonton of the University of California at Davis found that the most respected scientists *produced more "bad" works than their less successful peers.*

4 Geniuses make novel combinations.

Like playful children with buckets of building blocks, geniuses constantly combine and recombine ideas, images, and thoughts. Einstein didn't invent the concepts of energy, mass, or speed of light; he simply combined them in a novel way. The laws of heredity were developed by Gregor Mendel, who combined mathematics and biology to create a new science of genetics.

5 Geniuses force relationships.

Their facility to connect the unconnected enables geniuses to see things others miss. Da Vinci noticed the similarity between the sound of a bell and a stone hitting water—and concluded that sound travels in waves. Organic chemist F. A. Kekule intuited the shape of the ring-like benzene molecule by dreaming of a snake biting its tail. When Samuel Morse was trying to figure out how to produce a telegraphic signal strong enough to transmit coast to coast, he observed teams of horses being exchanged at a relay station. His solution? Give the traveling signal periodic boosts of power.

6 Geniuses think in opposites.

Geniuses, according to physicist David Bohm, are able to think differently because they can tolerate ambivalence between two incompatible subjects. Another physicist, Niels Bohr, argued that if you hold opposites together in your mind, you will suspend your normal thinking process and allow an intelligence beyond rational thought to create a new form. Example: Bohr's ability to imagine light as both a particle and a wave led to his conception of the principle of complementarity. [Jack's note: Bohr is also famous for responding to an equation by one of his peers, who complained that the equation made no sense and was just plain crazy, by saying, "Well, it's crazy, but maybe it's not crazy enough."]

7 Geniuses think metaphorically.

Aristotle believed that the ability to perceive resemblances between two separate areas of existence—to think metaphorically, in other words—is a special gift. Alexander Graham Bell compared the inner workings of the ear to a stout piece of membrane moving steel—and, in the process, conceptualized the telephone. Einstein made some of his most stunning discoveries by drawing analogies between abstract principles and everyday occurrences, such as rowing a boat or standing on a platform watching a train pass by.

8 Geniuses prepare themselves for chance.

Whenever we attempt to do something and fail, we end up doing something else. That's the first principle of *creative accident*. We may ask ourselves why we have failed to do what we intended, which is a reasonable question. But the creative accident leads to the question: What have we done? Answering that one in a novel, unexpected way is the essential creative act. It is not luck, but creative insight of the highest order.

Alexander Fleming was not the first physician studying deadly bacteria to notice that mold formed on an exposed culture. A less gifted physician would have dismissed this seemingly irrelevant event, but Fleming thought it was "interesting" and wondered if it had potential. It did: penicillin. One day, when Edison was pondering how to make a carbon filament, he found himself mindlessly twisting a piece of putty in his fingers. He looked down at this hands and found the answer to his problem: Twist the carbon like rope.

This may be the most important lesson of all: When you find something interesting, drop everything and go with it. Too many talented people fail to make significant leaps of imagination because they've become fixated on their preconceived plan. But not the truly great minds. They don't wait for gifts of chance; they make them happen.

ON MICHAEL MICHALKO'S
"THE ART OF GENIUS"

The subtitle of Michalko's article is "Eight Ways to Think Like Einstein," but I added the words "or Shakespeare," because I believe creative thinking is the same, whether it's scientific or artistic. As a matter of fact, the author saw fit to title the essay "The Art of Genius," recognizing that genius is not just a measure of intelligence, but a way of thinking, of processing experience; in short, an art. Whether or not we are endowed with an intelligence quotient that qualifies us as geniuses, we can learn to respond as geniuses do. According to the article, Nobel laureate Richard Feynman's I.Q. was below genius, but he thought productively, not reproductively. Of the eight ways to think like a genius, I've commented on three of them and indicated how they can be applied to writing.

1) Geniuses make their thought visible. For writers, that means writing before they have an idea. Don't wait for inspiration. Write *from* process, not *toward* product.

3) Geniuses produce. That means they write. They develop a discipline that is not dependent upon inspiration. I ask you to write 2+ pages a day as a way of getting you to produce, whether you feel like it or not, whether you have something to say or not. Like most geniuses, you'll "produce more 'bad' works than your less successful peers."

8) Geniuses prepare themselves for chance—what I call the magic accident, or the accidents of genius. When you write from process, you're letting the piece come to you, which means lowering the walls of expectation and opening the doors of perception. But one cannot do that without a point of focus rooted in process. If someone tells you not to think of elephants, you're going to think of elephants. The only way not to think of elephants is to focus on something else. Thus, by focusing on "writing like you talk," by massaging your "transformation line" to deepen your voice, and by creating a provocative "Image-Moment," you put yourself in a position for accidents to happen—the creative accidents of your genius. Thus, despite the "bad" stuff you'll inevitably produce, there will be creative accidents you could never have anticipated. To quote the article: "This may be the most important lesson of all: Too many talented people fail to make significant leaps of imagination because they've become fixated on their preconceived plan. But not truly great minds. They don't wait for gifts of chance, they make them happen." Well, I don't think you can *make* them happen, but you can get rid of the walls that keep them out. It is a reliance on talent that prevents creative accidents from happening. Talent will guarantee good. Genius allows for the great. By focusing on process, you'll side-step your talent, and the opportunities for your genius to respond become greater. We're not just learning to write better, we're learning to write more creatively.

But there's a catch here. Everyone thinks taking chances means writing from inspiration. When you're inspired you supposedly take risks. The opposite is true. When we're inspired, which is infrequent at best, there's a part of us (the talent part) that doesn't want to screw up the moment, so inwardly, we take no chances. We let talent take over. The crucial point I'm making is you must develop a set of habits that allows for accidents, a way of working that facilitates risk taking. That means you will follow impulses to a dead end sometimes, but who cares! Who cares if you crash more often than not? It's the magic accident you're after. Follow your impulses. Train yourself to follow an impulse in your writing, because the mind follows the body. Fling your body out into the space of chance, and the mind will follow and take credit for whatever riches you find there.

FIRST PERSON VS. THIRD PERSON

After class one evening a student approached me, concerned about her writing. "All I've been doing," she said, "is writing about myself. When do we get to develop a character in third person?"

I understood her concern. Writers want to explore new worlds in their writing. Like an actor who wants to play a character removed from himself, you change the pitch of your voice, the way you walk, and maybe like Robert De Niro in *Raging Bull* or Renée Zellweger in *Bridget Jones' Diary*, you gain weight.

Many writers feel uncomfortable writing in first person. They hear their eighth grade English teacher telling them not to use "I" so much. But when we write about ourselves—whether we call it poetry, fiction, non-fiction, creative non-fiction, memoir—it's always a construct. We select details, interpret events, present ourselves (. . . I mean the narrator) as more or less noble than we really are. There's always a certain amount of artifice. In my family, we often sat around the kitchen table with friends and recounted the story of how my dad got drunk on a plane once without my mother knowing how he did it. Like many alcoholics, my father was ingenious. He inserted a straw in a flask which he tucked into the left inside pocket of his jacket. All he had to do to take a sip was lower his head. My mother never saw him take a drink the whole flight, but when they got to New York, he was pretty drunk.

"When we got on the plane," my mother exclaimed, "he was sober, and when we got off, he was drunk!" That story was embellished with each re-telling. The first time he was tipsy. The second time he was drunk. The third time he was sloshed. And what about the flask of whiskey? Eventually it became a pint of Jack Daniels. We knew what the truth was, but the story was funnier (or sadder, depending on how you look at it) the more it was embellished. It became part of family lore. Writers embellish. We construct. At some point, trying to separate "what really happened" from what was added later is like trying to unscramble an egg.

Reliable Narrators vs. Unreliable Narrators

We assume that a third-person narrator is telling us the truth. Why wouldn't she? She is supposed to be the objective observer. Third-person narrators are, by definition, reliable. On the other hand, first-person narrators are by definition unreliable. Memory is faulty, events are subject to interpretation. We tend to trust what the narrator tells us, but sometimes the "author"—or what Harold Bloom calls the "implied author" and what James Wood calls the "designated authorial scout"—has ways of letting us know that the first person narrator is unreliable—what he or she says must be taken with a grain of salt. The implied author gives us hints that all is not what it seems. One can know more about the narrator than the narrator knows about himself. There are countless examples, but a good one is Holden Caulfield, the eponymous catcher in the rye. Holden tells his own story, but it doesn't take long to realize that he's on the verge of a nervous breakdown; he is prone to exaggeration and distortion of events. Huckleberry Finn tells his own story, too, but Huck mistakes con men for benign eccentrics; we know the truth before Huck does, giving those scenes on the raft an ironic—often hilarious—aspect. In *The Great Gatsby*, Nick Carraway is our first-person narrator and though it seems it's Gatsby's story we're hearing, it's really Nick's, his innocence lost in the ways of love. His envy and yearning color his interpretation of events. The author, F. Scott Fitzgerald, tips us off to Nick's bias and we learn to read between the lines. Nick is an example of an unreliable narrator who is still "reliable" in the sense that his state of mind is stable though his perceptions are colored by his emotions, like everyone else's. We trust the author to alert us to irony or distortion. We know the first-person narrator is unreliable, but the "implied author" makes sure we know that. And not only are we able to separate the grains of salt, we feel a certain superiority in being able to do so.

An "unreliable unreliable" narrator is rare in fiction. Dostoyevsky's *Notes from Underground* offers us a narrator who is probably crazy, and a recent TV series, *Life on Mars*, features a narrator who cannot be sure if he has traveled back in time or if he is in a coma dreaming an alternate reality. We, the viewer, can't be sure what is real either, not until the series is over. The same is true for another character in a short-lived TV series, *Awake*, in which the protagonist is living two alternate realities, falling asleep into one, in which his wife survived a car accident while his son didn't, then waking into another the next morning, in which his son survived the car accident but his wife didn't. Maybe both are dreams, and the life he'll wake into will be different from either dream. Or maybe he's dead and, like the protagonist in Ambrose Bierce's short story "An Occurrence at Owl Creek Bridge," the entire narrative is occurring in his mind in the instant before he dies. With an unreliable unreliable narrator, we're not in Kansas anymore, and whether or not we return is entirely in the hands of the "author," who is pulling the strings.

Third-Person Omniscient vs. Third-Person Close

The "author" tips us off to the narrator's bias through vocal inflection and choice of words, and through other characters' reactions to the narrator. The writer must know the subtle variations of how a character speaks. The problem is compounded when you tell a story in third person. Third person is more difficult than it seems. It may appear as if a god-like observer simply tells what happened. Tolstoy gets away with it much of the time, but most late-19th and 20th century third-person narration is not as omniscient as that. The dominant mode of third person storytelling is now done in what is called "close third person." In his book *How Fiction Works*, James Wood uses the term "free indirect style." Some writers refer to this as "going into character." What this means is that the third-person, omniscient style slides in and out of the character's voice, language, and point of view. Some sentences are omniscient, using the author's own stylistic flourishes, but gradually the tone changes, and before we know it we're hearing the character's (not the author's) voice. In the section quoted from *Ulysses* illustrating stream of consciousness, Joyce shifts from first person narrator to close third person to omniscient third. To make this work, one must have mastered the nuance of voice, of writing in the first person. Below is something I wrote to illustrate this shift from close third to omniscient third.

> Humphrey Mumford sat in the cold bundled like a hedgehog. The park bench nearly froze his bottom. He wrapped both hands around his body. From a distance, he looked like a man in a straitjacket. He shivered mightily, but it did no good. He had to face Mr. Wickerstaffer about that raise. "If I don't get up there soon," he thought, "I'm gonna freeze my ass off." But asking for a raise from Wickerstaffer was a tricky

proposition. Others before him—smooth talkers and con artists—had tried it. You'd think a worker with the gift of the gab could weasel the old man out of a few pennies more a week, but no, talk as they might, it was all mulch to the prickhead who cared not a sot for his workers; all he cared for was his overstuffed chair by the fire in his stinkin' office, an office so big you'd think he was lord of the manor. Keep calm, thought Humphrey, a hot head on a cold day won't bring the mutton home. He looked out at the skaters in the park: a child of maybe ten waltzing in perfect circles as her mother applauded; a pair of lovers sharing a scarf; a man bundled like Humphrey, struggling to stand. Pity the poor bugger. He oughta fall and get it over with. Humphrey waited. When the man finally fell—a ship sinking under the weight of its freight—Humphrey got up and walked toward the steel and glass office building that rose into the gray sky like a monolith proclaiming the determination of despotism over the mere mortals below.

The first few sentences in the above paragraph are in the author's omniscient voice, then he quotes Humphrey directly—"I'm gonna freeze my ass off." The next two sentences are back in the omniscient voice. Then with *you'd think a worker with the gift of the gab*, it slides into close third person, using Humphrey's language and tone, not the removed voice of the author. The omniscient author doesn't tell us directly that these are Humphrey's thoughts or language. The author assumes the reader will get it. In another sentence, he uses indirect with a quotation: Keep calm, thought Humphrey. The sentences which follow are in third person omniscient again, using description characteristic of the author's style. But with *pity the poor bugger, he oughta fall*, that's Humphrey's language; no direct or indirect quoting, the author just slides into it. The last few sentences shift back to third person omniscient, heightened by the melodramatic touches for humor's sake. This is not Humphrey's voice, nor is it the author simply writing like he talks, it's the narrator. The heightened language clues us in to the exaggeration of tone for comic effect.

"Standard" vs. "Formal" Register or Tone

Throughout that paragraph there are subtle shifts from third-person omniscient to various levels of close third person. In order to do that, the writer must know how to write like one talks. Besides being able to shift from omniscient to close, a writer must also be able to shift from straight-forward narrative, free association, direct and indirect interior monologue, and stream of consciousness (see note on stream of consciousness in the appendix). A third skill involves the ability to shift language and tone, as noted above. Good writers avail themselves of these shifts in "register," that is, dictional changes from various kinds of speech: very low (sometimes called gutter language); low (which involves slang or colloquial speech); standard (correct normal usage); formal or high (grammar and syntax you'd find in written essays and formal speeches, or how the "upper class/aristocracy" would speak); and inverted formal (where a character, usually from the lower class, purposefully speaks ungrammatically, thinking it's high class—Eliza Doolittle in her cockney accent trying to sound high class by inverting proper grammatical constructions, assuming that if it sounds wrong, it must be correct). Most genre fiction is written in conventional register with little variation in tone or diction. But writers with a distinct style often subvert the conventions of register, shifting from grand to the vernacular, from mock-heroic to gutter diction. In order to capture the sense of a human voice, a good writer will slip in words or phrases that disarm the reader and provide a sense of irony and humor. Friends, after watching a football game, can repair to the backyard to puff on black-market Havanas. You would not expect to see the word "repair" in that kind of sentence. It is a word used in formal register, while the rest of the sentence has a standard or even colloquial feel. You wouldn't expect guys watching football to "repair" anywhere. "Repair" belongs in this kind of sentence: *After dinner, the men removed their dinner jackets, donned their smoking jackets, and repaired to the library where they smoked cigars and discussed the affairs of Parliament.* In the first example, "repair" lends an air of forced aristocracy, a comic, mock-heroic tone, alerting the reader to the fact that the guys in their jeans and tennis shoes were affecting the manners of upper class gentlemen, lounging in the backyard with their cigars as if ensconced in wing chairs in front of the fire. With one word deftly placed, the writer tells us more about how the characters behaved than any number of descriptive sentences in standard diction. We see how they sauntered out of the house, the way they sat, the pose of the outstretched hand as they puffed on their cigars, the pretense of it all.

Take the average person, someone who hasn't been trained as an actor, put them in a dramatic scene, and they will stiffen up, losing all sense of natural body language and rhythms of speech. One also finds this in writers who strive to write "well" by removing the nuance of everyday speech, of tone and register from their style, by staying within a narrow range of voice and diction. Writing like one talks involves the exuberance of personality, the mixing of formal and standard register, of perfect syntax and "gutter" vocabulary, and the ability to capture linguistic variation depending on the situation and characters in a scene. In third person narrative, it becomes even more complex: A writer must be able to shift from various points of view, as well as from straight narrative to interior monologue to stream of consciousness. Until you have mastered the ability to write like you talk in first person, however, I would rather you operate heavy machinery on valium than attempt third-person narrative.

I tell my students that I teach backwards, meaning I teach the most advanced concepts first. Level One of Method Writing is the most advanced of all the levels, and of the first four concepts, the first one, writing like you talk, is the most advanced of all. It may seem easy, but the ability to detect when your sentences shift from spoken syntax to formal literary syntax is crucial. Once you have developed an ear for that, you will be better able to control shifts from standard register to formal register, from reliable to unreliable, from unreliable to unreliable unreliable! You will be like a samurai warrior, dicing up sentences, setting the page afire.

COUNSELING ARTISTS: THE TWELVE CHALLENGES OF AN ARTIST

Eric Maisel, Ph.D.

Therapists can help artists they counsel by becoming more aware of the special challenges that artists face. The following twelve areas—the twelve challenges of the artist—are of tremendous importance to actors, musicians, writers and singers, painters and printmakers, dancers and graphic artists, filmmakers and stand-up comics, as well as all creative and performing artists. They are also of critical importance to the mates and families of artists.

1. The challenge to maintain independence or at least a sense of independence.

The artist is not usually able to earn a living by doing art. However, as iconoclastic or individualistic she may be, it is nevertheless likely that she will find herself dependent upon a mate's income or on a parental allowance for support, or will find herself engaged in menial "day" work which barely pays the rent. Therapists should remember that this state of affairs is the rule, not the exception, and that this perennial lack of independence tends to breed "authority" and "control" issues—a desire, for instance, to act out and bite the hand that feeds—as well as a concomitant erosion of self-esteem.

2. The challenge to maintain emotional balance.

Contemporary studies indicate that artists suffer from mood disorders in disproportionately great numbers. Mania and depression mark many an artist's life, and bipolar disorder has recently been dubbed "the artist's disease." The cyclical up and down nature of the artist's work life—an intense, creative effort followed by a fallow period, lack of work, rejection or criticism of work—itself mimics the behavioral look of a bipolar disorder, thereby contributing to the artist's mood swings.

3. The challenge to maintain a balance between isolation and human contact.

The artist often spends the greater part of his life working in isolation. For every hour he plays publicly, the musician may practice hundreds of hours in an empty room; for every hour the writer spends autographing books in public, he may spend thousands of hours alone at his desk. The artist sets his own hours and struggles to achieve a balance between working too long and not working so much that nothing remains of life. Balance is exceedingly difficult to achieve. Most artists suffer either from a sense of shame at working too little or from loneliness that plagues the passionate, compulsive, hardworking artist.

4. **The challenge to do business effectively; to be one's own supporter and promoter.**

The artist must spend a significant amount of time doing business. If she is a painter she must send slides of her paintings and contact galleries, enter competitions and find markets for her work. If she is a writer of short stories, she must research markets and send stories in correct format; and then send them out again upon rejection. If she is an actress, she must audition for available shows, travel when necessary, make connections, and find effective representation. This is not the work the artist loves nor does well. This is also an area where counselors can be especially helpful by role-playing an agent interview or rehearsing for gallery interviews. The directive counselor will support the artist by

Wanting to achieve excellence, comparing oneself to Picasso, Dostoyevsky, Casals, or Nijinsky, fearing that the first stroke on the canvas will be a mistake or the first note out of one's mouth will be flat, dreading the humiliation of public failure—these are aspects of the artist's life that can torture.

offering the reality check that doing business is definitely part of doing art.

5. **The challenge to remain focused; to work regularly and break effectively through blocks.**

It tends to be very difficult for the artist to maintain creative focus. The writer may sour on the novel that he's worked on for a year without even realizing that the project has soured. All he realizes is that he can't get it finished. Or, the painter may discover that his commercial prints sell well but his paintings do not sell at all. Or, the musician may learn that the more provocative his band's music becomes, the fewer gigs the band gets. Artists are frequently plagued by terrible doubts about the direction a given work has taken or the direction their artistic careers have taken.

6. **The challenge to compete and to handle criticism and rejection.**

It was not simply a quirk of circumstance that the two greatest novelists of their time—Dostoyevsky and Tolstoy—avoided one another. It was not simply a quirk of circumstance that Picasso and Matisse avoided one another. Artists are in fierce, and often unconscious, competition with one another.

By the same token, many artists dispute the idea that they are in competition for gallery space or for choice roles, for the attention of the public or for the attention of the media. They argue that the good luck of another artist doesn't disturb them. But, frequently this generosity of spirit is a rationalization, and the pain, anger, and sadness they are really feeling is often not far from the surface.

The artist must also learn to handle criticism and rejection. Everyone will freely criticize the artist's work and may attack with casual cruelty or with barbed subjectivity. Most of her writing will be rejected, most of the parts she wants she will not get, most gallery owners will refuse her a show. If an editor likes her novel because it is commercial, a friend will criticize it because it is commercial. The artist does not even find her own self-criticism easy to handle. At times she may believe that she can't sing, draw, paint or write. These issues are very alive for the artist—so alive, for instance, that Renoir, at the height of his career, suddenly concluded that he couldn't draw and took off for Italy to study drawing anew.

These various challenges often come together for the artist as performance anxiety. The writer and the painter are no more immune to performance anxiety than the singer and actor. Wanting to achieve excellence, comparing oneself to Picasso, Dostoyevsky, Casals, or Nijinsky, fearing that the first stroke on the canvas will be a mistake or the first note out of one's mouth will be flat, dreading the humiliation of public failure—these are aspects of the artist's life that can torture.

7. *The challenge to accept one's finite talent.*
The artist begins with very large dreams. But each age produces only a few great artists. It may take the young novelist two full decades of steady work to realize that he doesn't have *Crime and Punishment* in him. It may take the young musician as long a time to realize that she has no real career as a soloist. Even excellent artists reach a plateau above which they cannot climb, repeating themselves in their work until they are sick of the sameness of their products. The matter of finite talent has already been factored into the equation by every other sort of worker—the therapist, for instance, is generally aware of his or her limitations, and many are never able to make peace with falling short of their dreams. For every Mozart, there are hundreds of despairing Salieris.

8. *The challenge to maintain relationships.*
The issue is of particular importance to family therapists. In addition to the other reasons that cause the artist to experience relationship difficulties (for instance, he grew up in a dysfunctional family), he may also experience relationship difficulties that are directly related to the fact that he is pursuing a career in art and possesses the identity of artist. Some of these common artist-specific interpersonal difficulties include the following:

a. When the artist is spending time with his mate, he may not feel like an artist. Since the artist is "always" working, he may have trouble making sense of leisure time—especially if he hasn't been working as hard or as well as he would have wished. His mate may complain that he is preoccupied, distanced, and hardly present even when they do spend time together.

b. The artist's mate is also an important member of the artist's audience. A casual, negative remark about a painting, story, or performance may have severe, long-lasting consequences in the relationship.

c. The artist may lack rudimentary communication skills. Classical musicians, for instance, often turn over a large portion of their adolescence to practicing and miss normal socializing. Teaching basic communication skills to artists is a valuable therapeutic strategy.

d. Artists, for a variety of reasons, maintain careful distance from other people. Naturally, this makes intimacy difficult. The artist who acquires the habit of insulating herself from criticism and rejection, who is loathe to share the secret she is falling short of her goals, may well have difficulties in letting down her guard even with her mate.

e. As indicated previously, the artist is often dependent upon his mate's income. Many angry discussions may revolve around the question of when the artist will give up his art in order to help pay the bills. The less the mate is satisfied with her job or with the relationship, or as financial pressures arise, the more likely it is that the artist's lack of income will become the focal point of heated arguments.

f. The artist may manifest displaced aggression against his mate or children. The artist, powerless to prevent his publishers from remaindering his latest novel, powerless to demand attention from the media for his short-lived first show, angry at his agent for dropping him, angry at the conductor for criticizing his playing, furious that a less talented actor got the part he really wanted, ends up with much rage to burn. This rage may be displaced in abuse of the artist's mate or children.

9. **The challenge to find community or make peace with a lack of community.**

The artist, although frequently a loner, dreams, nevertheless, of creating community or belonging to a community, or belonging to the sort of society epitomized by Paris in the Twenties, Greenwich Village in the Forties, or Berlin in the Seventies. The number of artists who have lived in Paris or still plan to live in Paris are legion. One evening I discovered that every member of the support group I was leading fell into one of these categories. Usually the artist does not succeed in finding community, in Paris or elsewhere. Unlike the Balinese musician, who is an integral part of the community and has that community available to him, the Western artist tends to fail on both counts: either joining with his society at large or joining together with other artists to form a meaningful alternative community.

10. **The challenge to avoid self-destructive behaviors.**

The artist is often a drug and alcohol abuser. The challenge for the jazz musician, the rock musician, the painter, the writer, the actor, the creative artist stirred by his work and his dream—is to maintain mood equilibrium without resorting to mood-altering drugs. The social environment of the artist makes this challenge double difficult.

Drug and alcohol abuse are not the only self-destructive or compulsively driven behaviors that artists typically manifest. Sexual promiscuity is another. Self-sabotaging behaviors in the workplace—oversleeping for an interview with an agent, acting compulsively rude at a party of wealthy patrons—are also extremely common.

11. **The challenge to handle disillusionment.**

The writer, dancer, painter or actor at forty often realizes that she has little to show for all the love and effort put into her art. She realizes that she could possibly be in the middle of a lucrative and satisfying career in another field, rather than in the middle of a marginal career.

The reality that art is hard also breeds disillusionment. It is difficult to play an instrument beautifully, to write elegantly, to draw well or paint with fresh ideas. There is no way for the artist to rest on her laurels without repeating herself in unsatisfying ways; at the same time the energy and resolve needed to remain creative and fruitful can diminish with the years.

The artist often longs to find another life, to get out of art, but the experience of contemplating that possibility—of shedding so important a piece of identity—is an experience akin to drowning. Therapists can count on the artist resisting her own suggestion to leave art. If the therapist supports her in that decision, the therapist can also count on strong transferential issues arising.

12. *The challenge to integrate personality.*

The character or personality traits that help the artist make art are not necessarily qualities that allow the artist to live well. The reverse case is equally true: the more healthy the artist lives, the less prepared he may be to do art.

The skepticism that helps the artist reject old ideas and create new ideas may emerge as cynicism and irony in the artist's personal relationships. The artist's non-conformity, which is often a manifestation of his unwillingness to accept the tired, mundane, or sterile aspects of society, can prevent the artist from "acting normally" when such normality is in his best interests. His ability to concentrate and his introspective stance, qualities crucial to the making of art, may at the same time remove him from the company of others, even those he loves. In these and many other ways the artist may find himself in real intrapsychic conflict.

This, then, is a brief overview of the twelve challenges of the artist. I hope, at a later date, to flesh out the ideas presented here with case material, and to provide therapists with useful intervention techniques and information on resources available to artists. By addressing these issues, therapists will experience a real deepening of the therapeutic process with artist clients.

Eric Maisel, Ph.D., is a licensed MFCC and maintains therapy practices in San Francisco and Concord, CA. He is a faculty member of St. Mary's College where he teaches personal and professional assessment. He has recently completed a book, Van Gogh's Blues, *and is presently working on another called* Staying Sane in the Arts: A Ten-Step Program.

AN OVERVIEW OF THE EIGHT LEVELS OF

METHOD WRITING

Level 1: THE FIRST FOUR CONCEPTS: Writing from the Deep Voice, the Craft of the Invisible Form

When asked about my "advanced" classes, I tell people that the most advanced class I teach is the beginning class. Even advanced students struggle with the first four concepts. These concepts are not "rules" to be memorized. They require practice and patience, and cannot be mastered in two weeks. Eventually, however, they will help you to write deeper, truer, and with greater detail.

1) **Write like you talk**. What about all those stylistic flourishes by writers such as Saul Bellow, Virginia Woolf, Marcel Proust, William Faulkner, and Toni Morrison? Such style is grounded in the nuances of speech. One's own voice informs the writer's ability to manipulate tone, whether in first person, omniscient third person, close third person, or any number of subtle variations thereof. (See appendix on first person vs. third person.) There are three basic tones: the head voice, the reporting voice, and the deep voice. We can find the deep voice by massaging the transformation line.

2) **Massaging the Transformation Line**. I'm not sure which is harder, learning to identify a good transformation line, or massaging it. Certainly, the ability to see it in the flow of writing is crucial. Most transformation lines are not obvious and are usually found within a sentence that does not express a deep feeling. Once you separate the transformation line from the "birthday cake" part of the sentence, you can massage it to a deeper truth.

3) **Image-Moment**. The four levels of narrative structure are: *story*, *event*, *moment*, and *image*. The first two are basically the same. Writers tell a story by recounting the events within that story. This involves the proverbial "telling" instead of "showing." Moment and image show the story. But undeveloped moments lack dramatic impact, and images can be static description. By combining image and moment through a technique called Image-Moment, you control the basic building block of all narrative, thereby creating vivid scenes within the story.

4) **The Dreaded Association Exercise**. Alright, it was originally called the Association Exercise, but students came to class dreading it so much that I added the word "dreaded" to the title. Eventually, however, students came to love it. It clicks into the right brain experience, and can be used to render impressionistic or expressionistic experiences: flashbacks, hallucinatory moments, scenes heightened by disruptive action like car wrecks and explosions, or disassociative interior monologues by characters suffering from mental breakdowns or Alzheimer's, as well as a child's point of view. When noted physicist Paul Dirac showed Neils Bohr, the father of quantum physics, an equation he'd been working on, they were both astounded by the results, which seemed to defy much of what they knew from Newtonian physics. "It's crazy," said Bohr, shaking his head, "but maybe it's not crazy enough." Bohr realized that one can't always follow a linear path to describe how nature works. The Dreaded Association exercise would have pleased Neils Bohr, and Albert Einstein, too, who said that "the highest physics always evolves into poetry."

This book covers Level One: The First Four Concepts. The other levels of Method Writing, covered in *Advanced Method Writing*, will further develop the voice's ability to achieve tonal dynamics.

Level 2: The Four Voices

In the first level, you find your own basic voice and learn to shift from reporting voice to analyzing voice to deep voice to achieve a particular tonal effect. The second level covers the four other voices. These tones, styles, literary rhythms—call them what you will—are basic constructs that characterize all writing. One could comb through Western literature and find that there are only four such voices. I call them: **Straight Talk, Lost World, To Be Read & Sung** and **Absence of Field**. These voices are not how one talks; they are characterized by a heightened use of language and stylistic effects. The ability to shift from one voice to another is the essence of tonal dynamics, which lies at the heart of Method Writing.

Level 3: Teeth & Mouth and Surrealism

These two concepts are not new voices. Teeth & Mouth and Surrealism are aspects of any of the voices. The first will give muscle to your sentences, a visceral power the reader feels in the gut; the second is aimed at the mind and gives a "twilight zone" element to your writing. Teeth & Mouth can be used in varying degrees or intensities, but I break it down into first base, second base, and third base, where first base is hardly noticeable, second base assaults the reader, and third base goes over the top to create outlandish imagery and sounds. I break Surrealism into two parts. The first is purely imaginative, that collision of images and ideas that strike us as, well, surreal. The second creates psychological impact. You'll have fun doing this level. It's kind of like going back to second grade and building bizarre structures out of blocks.

Level 4: Disquieting Muses

This level deals with a series of energy states based on female archetypes. All the exercises you've worked on so far will come into play here. Do not confuse the energy states used in this exercise with the muses found in Greek mythology. When I came up with this concept, I used a poem by Sylvia Plath titled "Disquieting Muses" as an example, and the name came from there. The seven female archetypes correspond to energy found in the body: child, virgin, mother, siren (or seductress or whore), huntress, crone (or hag or witch), and Medusa. Combined with the voices you've already learned, these energy states will increase your command of tonal dynamics. When we work on this exercise in class, we try to guess which muse the writer was using. It's a fun game, but mostly we're guessing because there's no way to know for sure what someone else's mother or child or huntress sounds like.

Level 5: Big Dice and Dice-No-Dice

Each number on the dice corresponds to the various exercises studied so far. Throw the dice every four lines, and shift voices as the dice commands. Except instead of six, there are 21 possible combinations. How is that possible? Because there are seven muses, so if the number for muses comes up, you have to throw the dice again to see which one of the seven muses you do. Same holds true for Teeth & Mouth, which has first base, second base, and third base. By shifting voices or tones every four lines, you'll dazzle the reader with tonal dynamics—echoes of Whitman and Sylvia Plath, William Faulkner and Henry James, Virginia Woolf and J.D. Salinger. Imagine sitting in a cafe or coffee shop, throwing the dice every four lines and writing as you go. This exercise teaches flexibility, forcing you to practice reaching for the new tools you've acquired until you become facile with each. Eventually, you'll instinctively shift from one voice to another as easily as an actor shifts from one energy level to another.

Level 6: Wild, Dark, and Passionate

My shorthand reference to this exercise is DWP, but the order in which we do the exercises is Passionate, Wild, then Dark. I save "Dark" for last in case you don't come back. A few of my students have not yet come back from "Dark." We're still looking for them. One was spotted on a mountain top in the Himalayas. Another was seen in a waterfront bar writing a seventh volume to Proust's *Remembrance of Things Past*.

Level 7: Short Poems: A Zen Approach to the Creative Process

After the intensity of the first six levels, this is a breath of fresh air, a zen approach to the creative process. In improvisational theatre there are two ways to approach a scene: "giving space" and "taking space." The short poem exercise gives you the yin and yang of both energies.

Level 8 and Beyond: Freelancing the Concepts or "Simon Says"

In these exercises one chooses a particular poet or writer to exemplify the concepts studied above, but in specific ways and combinations. A poet like Frank O'Hara, for instance, combines Straight Talk, Teeth & Mouth and Deep Voice. Hamlet's soliloquys, each with a unique focus and emotional structure, give one a different sort of workout altogether. Following the stylistic and emotional structure in Rilke's *Duino Elegies* thrusts one more deeply into one's own work. These fundamental concepts are apparent in writers as diverse as Hemingway, Faulkner, Toni Morrison, Proust, Kafka, Jane Bowles, Saul Bellow, Jack Gilbert, Waslawa Szymborska, Walt Whitman, Grace Paley, Samuel Beckett, Virginia Woolf, etc. Modeling the tonal dynamics of these writers consolidates the concepts you've studied, and shows you how effective they can be.

One can do the same with painters and composers. Chopin's *Preludes* (there are 27) makes for a wonderful 8 week series, as does the work of Miles Davis, Anton Bruckner, Connor Oberst, John Coltrane, etc. One can model the dynamics and techniques of painters like Picasso, Marlene Dumas, Van Gogh, Lucien Freud, Kandinsky, Louise Bourgeoise, Alicia Rahon, etc.

Good writing is good writing. No amount of structural unity will turn bad writing into compelling writing. Method Writing deals with the dynamics of voice to create character, and it is character that ultimately determines plot.

> VOICE CREATES CHARACTER
> CHARACTER CREATES PLOT

Biography

JACK GRAPES is an award-winning playwright, poet, actor, and teacher. He's received Fellowships in Writing from the National Endowment for the Arts, and several Artist-in-Residence Grants from the California Arts Council. He is the author of numerous books of poetry, including *Trees, Coffee, and the Eyes of Deer* and *Breaking Down the Surface of the World*. A spoken-word CD, titled *Pretend*, was issued by *Poetry East*. He is also author of a chapbook of poems and paintings entitled *and the running form, naked, Blake*. His *Lucky Finds* is a boxed set of 50 cards that extend and parody the dynamic artistic productions of high-modernist poets such as Ezra Pound and Charles Olson. In the *L.A. Weekly's* "Literary Guide to Los Angeles," his work was characterized as "operating somewhere in the middle ground between pop culture and philosophy." Writing in *Poetry Flash*, John Oliver Simon said, "When I talk to Mexican poets, I find myself thumbing my dog-eared copies of Jack Grapes's books to show what North American poetry can do at this moment." Reviewing Jack's book *Lucky Finds* Matthew Specktor wrote in *Poetry Flash* (Fall, 2004), "Grapes covers a tremendous amount of ground in his poems—abstract and figurative, personal and philosophical, literary and historical—and he does it with wit and flair. To his immense credit, these moves do not seem half-digested; seem, rather, the product of an original, omnivorous sensibility."

In 1989 he began editing and publishing *ONTHEBUS*, a literary journal hailed by *Esquire* as "one of the top 20 journals in the country." The *Los Angeles Times* wrote: "The sheer unfettered and unpredictable range of poetry in *ONTHEBUS* is refreshing in an era of coteries, categories, and other curtailments of art's free spirit. In this willingness to bend, test, even offend literary tastes, *ONTHEBUS* is riskier and more challenging to the reader than most reviews today."

Jack's first play, co-written with Allan Yasnyi, *How Much Can a Grecian Urn?* was a zany musical romp combining Damon Runyon with classical Greek drama. He also co-wrote with Bill Cakmis and starred in *Circle of Will*, a "bizarre metaphysical comedy" about the lost years of Will Shakespeare, which ran for several years in Los Angeles and won theater critic awards for Best Comedy and Best Performance. The play was recently revived in Hollywood and ran for several months.

Over the last 30 years, he has taught thousands of poets and writers in privately held classes, as well as poetry in over 100 Los Angeles schools. Jack was the Los Angeles Coordinator for California Poets-in-the-Schools, served on its board of directors, and was also a board member for PEN Center USA West. In 1988 he founded the Los Angeles Poets & Writers Collective, which sponsors readings, publications, classes, seminars, and workshops. Forthcoming books are: *Advanced Method Writing*, the next five levels; *The Tender Agonies of Charles Bukowski*, a critical study; *How to Read Like a Writer*, a non-fiction work; and *Etherized upon a Table*, which examines the history of modern "poetries" from Homer to the present. His most recent books of poetry are *The Naked Eye: New and Selected Poems, 1987–2012*, *Poems So Far So Far So Good So Far to Go.*, *All the Sad Angels*, and *Wide Road to the Edge of the World*.

More praise for Jack Grapes' Method Writing approach . . .

"I understand now why you call your beginning class in The First Four Concepts the most advanced class of all. I was going over my Method Writing book, and finally something about 'story—event—Image-Moment' clicked in a way it never had before. I realized why a manuscript I've been working on for years was not working. And all I had to do was implement what you were teaching in the beginning class, the basic concepts of Method Writing. I haven't stopped writing since."

Therese Gilardi

"In the interest of getting out and about and creating a life for myself down here in San Diego, I went to the Solana Beach library this week and asked the very nice librarian about writing groups, writing teachers, etc. I told her I'd been attending classes in L.A., and I missed my teacher and the writing community. She asked me questions. Is it a professor? What school did you go to? How does he teach? And, Jack, your method is impossible to describe. I knew that to try to describe something like the "transformation line" and the "dreaded association exercise" was going to overwhelm her. I did the best I could. At one point I almost laughed out loud. Your approach to writing and the creative process is just impossible to describe to someone who is thinking of something more conventional. I've been chuckling all week at the near impossibility of describing you or your teaching methods. Keep being indescribable. That's what makes you you. And I'm ever so grateful I had the opportunity for as long as I did to learn from you."

Victoria Melekian

"There isn't a moment in my current writing life that isn't infused with what I've learned and done in your class. The concepts and exercises of Method Writing have been nothing short of liberating. Given the choice of: A—regurgitating random thoughts onto page after page in the off-chance of stumbling into insight vs. B—imbuing every sentence (no matter how outside one's own box it might feel at the time) with a heightened sense of purpose, I vote B. The exercises have both salvaged some of my old, comatose stories, and provided surprising, sometimes fully fleshed material for new ones."

Jill Glass

"The core concepts of Method Writing have been life-altering, and that's not an exaggeration. Through all my many years of art school in LA and NYC, yours is one of the most relevant classes I have ever taken. I still channel it. Thank you for that!"

Nancy Nimoy

"Your Method Writing course unlocked me enough to write my application to Harvard and earn two Masters' degrees. Much gratitude for your vision, skill, and dedication, and for the amazing genius of your Method Writing program."
  Alison LaMonde

"I want you to know that you've already helped me to open up a door into my writing that was closed, locked, bolted, and welded shut for the last thirty years. No small accomplishment in just two weeks of your Method Writing class."
  Bryan Unger

"I want to thank you for the vast new worlds you have given me through this class and through this process of creativity called Method Writing. Trying to say just how much richer my writing life has become in the past few weeks—words simply escape me. You have truly changed my way of writing, of thinking about words, and I know my writing and my approach to it have changed incomparably. You've changed my life, that's probably enough."
  Barbara Sax

"Thank you for an incredible experience. I've taken many writing workshops in my life, but I've learned techniques from you and gained confidence in ways I never dreamed possible."
  Kathryn Stern

"Thanks to the training I got from you I now am working on books 2 and 3 (hope to get 2 done in two more weeks, then onto the big one) . . . all thanks to you! I never would have thought I had it in me—writing books, that is—until you allowed the real writer in me to emerge from her chrysalis."
  Patti Britton

"I still remember all the exercises from your Method Writing class and how much they've taught me as a writer. They were the "truest" writing instruction I ever had, and I went on to a creative writing program in college and then a creative writing MFA in grad school, and yet your concepts and the way you explain them were what shaped me the most. They changed my life when I was 16, and they continue to do so."
  Alexandra Kostoulas

"I just gave a speech at the Ajijic (Mexico) Society of Artists and once again devoted much of the speech to you and your methods: your incredible ability to change lives by plummeting your students into their authentic deep voices. I know you have heard this message many times, but needed to tell you again how profoundly you have affected my life . . . and hundreds of others who have been influenced by Method Writing. I continue to pass on the lessons I've learned from you, both through art and writing."
  Judy Dykstra-Brown

CPSIA information can be obtained
at www.ICGtesting.com
Printed in the USA
LVHW021143240321
682308LV00004B/168